國貿研究小組 著

國貿實務

國貿業務技術士丙級 ▶ 術科專用 第7版

五南圖書出版公司 印行

序　言

　　勞委會（2014 年升格為勞動部）於 2007 年 8 月開辦國貿業務技術士技能檢定，對國貿相關科系的學生及有心從事國貿業務工作的社會人士，都是一項能夠自我檢視國貿專業知識的絕佳機會，為了幫助有志此項檢定的應考生在準備檢定時有所參考，本書特別依據勞動部勞動力發展署所公布的國貿業務技術士技能檢定規範（詳見附錄五）及國貿業務丙級技能檢定術科測試參考資料內容編輯而成，共計涵蓋基礎貿易英文、貿易流程、出口價格核算、商業信用狀分析及貿易單據製作五大單元，其特色為：

1. 詳實的內容解析及統合整理：每一單元並非只有簡單的重點提示，而是詳實的內容解析及統合整理，即使為初學應考生，亦能透過自學方式，達到絕佳的學習效果。

2. 勞動部勞動力發展署術科測試範例精解：每一單元對於勞動部勞動力發展署所公布的術科測試範例皆有詳細的解答，讓應考生瞭解技能檢定所測試的題型。

3. 五套完整的模擬練習題目：每一單元皆附有五題仿真模擬練習題目，可讓應考生透過不斷反覆操作練習，熟悉題目的所有可能變化或陷阱。

　　本書雖以勞動部勞動力發展署所公布國貿業務技術士技能檢定規範為依據，更就相關國貿課程中實務操作為編製重點，祈使成為授課教師的輔助教材，讓學生在課堂上便能熟悉國貿業務技能檢定內容，以達到最佳的學習方式及效果。

　　本書編輯群涵蓋多位技專院校老師，雖皆有多年授課經驗，但國貿實務所涉層面不僅廣泛，更因政府法令及國際環境而時有變動，編者們畢竟學驗有限，若有任何疏漏之處，尚祈讀者們不吝指正。

📖 國貿業務技術士丙級技能檢定測驗術科相關資訊

測驗時間	120 分鐘
測驗方式	採筆試非測驗題方式，以人工閱卷
題型	選擇題、填充題
計分方式	滿分為 100 分，每一小題 1 或 2 分
合格標準	60（含）分以上
測驗題來源	保密卷，但題型以所公布測試參考資料為準

目　錄

基礎貿易英文

第一章

第一節　基礎貿易英文內容解析

▶貿易英文的書信格式

㈠信端（Heading）

信端即信頭，一般包括發信人的公司行號、地址和寫信日期。一些正式信函的信端還包括發信人或單位的電話號碼、傳真和郵遞區號等。信端的目的是使收信人一看便知道書信來自何處，何時發出，以便於覆信和查閱。

發信人的地址，其書寫方式由小單位到大單位的順序排列。即先寫樓層，次寫號碼，再依巷弄、街道、城市、國家之順序書寫。具體次序是：第一行寫門牌號碼和街名；第二行寫區名、市（縣）名、省（州、邦）名，因寄往國外，故還要寫上國家的名稱；在市（縣）名後面可加上郵遞區號，其後可寫上電話號碼，最後一行寫發信日期。

WONDERFUL TRADING CO., LTD.

4F, No.120, Alley 5, Lane 81, Sec. 1, Chongqing S. Rd

Zhongzheng District, Taipei City 100, Taiwan (R.O.C.)

Tel: 886-2-2358-xxxx

Fax: 886-2-2358-xxxx

Date: June 25, 2018

關於發信日期的寫法，應注意以下幾點：

1. 年分應完全寫出，不能簡寫。

2. 月分要用英文名稱，不要用數字代替。

3. 月分名稱多用公認的縮寫式。但 May、June 及 July，因為較短，不可縮寫。

4. 寫日期時，可用基數詞 1、2、3、4、5、……、28、29、30、31 等，也可用序數詞 lst、2nd、3rd、4th、5th、……、28th、29th、30th、31st 等。但最好用基數詞，簡單明瞭。

故日期可有下列幾種寫法：

(1) Oct. 20, 20—

(2) 10 May, 20—

(3) 3rd June, 20—

(4) Jan. 16th, 20—

其中以第一種方式最為通用。

(二)信內地址（Inside Address, Introductory Address）

信內地址即收信人的公司行號和地址，寫在信紙的左上角，從信紙的左邊頂格開始寫，低於發信人地址和發信日期一、二行。其次序是先寫收信人公司行號，然後寫地址。例如：

WELL TRADING CO., LTD.（公司行號）
131-10 Maple Avenue Flushing,（門牌及街道名）
New York 11355（城市、州省名及郵遞區號）
USA（國名）

(三)稱呼（Salutation）

對收信人的稱呼應自成一行，寫在低於信內地址一、二行的地方，從信紙的左邊頂格開始寫，每個詞的開頭字母要大寫，至於末尾處的符號，英國人用逗號，但美國和加拿大英語則多用冒號。稱呼用語可視發信人與收信人的關係而定。應注意事項有以下幾點：

1. 對沒有頭銜的男性，一般稱呼 Mr.。Mr.用在姓氏之前或姓氏和名字之前，不可只用在名字之前。例如：正確的稱呼應該是 Mr.White 或 Mr. John White，不可是 Mr. John。若稱呼多個男性，則在姓名前用 Mr.的複數形式 Messrs.。對一般以人名為名稱的公司和企業常用這種稱呼。例如：Messrs. Black and Brothers 布萊克兄弟公司。

2.對女性一般稱呼 Mrs.、Madam 或 Miss。Mrs.用在已婚女子的丈夫的姓氏之前，或姓氏和名字之前，一般不用在名字前。Madam 此詞可以單獨使用或加在丈夫的姓名之前。對以女子名字為名稱的公司、企業，可用 Mesdames 稱呼。Miss 多用於未婚女子，此詞可縮寫為 Ms.，用於姓氏之前或姓氏和名字之前，一般不用於名字之前。

3.對收信人的稱呼，也可用頭銜或職位的名稱，不分性別。例如：Professor（縮寫為 Prof.），Doctor（縮寫為 Dr.），General（縮寫為 Gen.）。這些稱呼都放在姓氏之前或姓氏和名字之前，如 Prof.（John）White 等。

4.對外函件中對收信人的稱呼，可用 Gentlemen（而不是 Gentleman），Dear Sir(s)和 My dear Sir(s)等。Gentlemen 之前不能加 Dear，後面也不能帶姓名。用 Sir(s)時，前面常用 Dear 一詞，但也可單獨用 Sir(s)。若收信人是婦女，則無論已婚或未婚，都可單獨使用 Madam 或其複數 Mesdames。

5.收信人稱呼整理如下：

(1)先生（男人）Mr.

(2)夫人（已婚）Mrs.

(3)小姐（未婚）Miss

(4)夫人、小姐統稱 Ms.

(5)夫婦兩人 Mr. and Mrs.

(6)兩位或兩位以上男子 Messrs

(7)兩位或兩位以上女子（已婚）Mesdames

(8)兩位或兩位以上小姐（未婚）Misses

㈣信的正文（Body of the Letter）

信的正文每段第一行應往右縮進約四、五個字母。在寫事務性信件時，正文一般開門見山，內容簡單明瞭，條理清楚。在寫私人信件時，信寫好之後，若有什麼遺漏，可用 P. S.表示補敘。

㈤結束語（Complimentary Close）

結束語是發信人表示自己對收信人的一種謙稱，只占一行，低於正文一、二行，從信紙的中間或偏右的地方開始寫。第一個詞的開頭字母要大寫，末尾用逗號。結束語視發信人與收信人的關係而定。例如寫給機關、團體或不相識的人的信，一般用：Yours (very) truly, Yours (very) faithfully, Yours (very) sincerely 等等。

在歐洲一些國家，多把 Yours 放在 sincerely 等詞的前面；在美國和加拿大等國，則多把 yours 放在 Sincerely 等詞之後。Yours 一詞有時也可省略。

㈥簽名（Signature）

信末的簽名一般低於結束語一、二行，從信紙中間偏右的地方開始寫。若寫信人是女性，與收信人又不相識，則一般在署名前用括弧註上 Miss, Mrs.或 Ms.，以便對方回信時，知道如何稱呼。有的還有署名後，寫上自己的職稱、職務或頭銜。

㈦附件（Enclosure）

信件若有附件，應在左下角註明 Encl.或 Enc.。若附件不只一個，則應寫出 2（或 3，4，5 等）Encls.。例如：Enc: Packing List。

㈧再啟（Postscript，縮寫為 P. S.）

再啟部分用於補敘正文中遺漏的話，一般應儘量少用，正式的函件中更應避免使用。

㈨常用的起首語

1. Thank you for your letter dated Dec. 22.
2. Many thanks for your letter of Sept. 5.
3. A thousand thanks for your kind letter of June 5.
4. Your kind letter of Nov. 22th arrived this morning.
5. Your letter which arrived this morning gave me great comfort.
6. In reply to your letter dated July 4, I want to say...
7. Thank you very much for your letter of Aug. 2.
8. What a treat to receive your kind letter of May 5th!

㈩常用的結束語

1. Awaiting your good news.
2. Looking forward to your early reply.
3. Hoping to hear from you soon.

4. We await your good news.

5. I hope to hear from you very soon.

6. We look forward to your reply at your earliest convenience.

7. Please let us know if you want more information.

8. Your early reply will be highly appreciated.

■ 第一單元　開發信

　　開發信是發給從未有過業務往來，而希望與其建立業務聯繫的潛在顧客。業務關係的建立是交易開始和發展的基礎，貿易公司要保持或擴大業務，就需要廣泛的業務關係。在對外貿易領域裡的一個重要工作就是建立業務關係，沒有顧客，就沒有交易。與潛在顧客建立業務聯繫，無論是對剛成立的新公司，還是對希望擴大業務範圍及成交額的老公司，都是一個極其重要的經營措施。發信人透過某種管道獲知所期望建立業務關係的公司名稱和地址以後，就可以開始向有關方面發函或寄送通函，這類業務信件就是開發信。一般說來，這類信函首先要告知收信人他的公司名稱是如何被知悉的；然後告知對方一些關於發信人所經營的業務範圍。發信人應簡明扼要地寫明他想推銷何種商品或希望購買何種商品。收到任何這類信函之後，必須有禮貌地及時給予完整的答覆，以便樹立信譽和給來函者留下良好的印象。

　　開發信包含了四個要點：

- ·第一要點：發信人資訊來源或自我介紹。
- ·第二要點：公司的經營背景及範圍，發信人是經營什麼產品的，對什麼產品感興趣。
- ·第三要點：發信人的打算。
- ·第四要點：結尾語。

開發信常見語句：

㈠透過……管道獲悉對方的資料常見語句

1. Your name and address have been given by... .
　　我方透過……得知貴公司的大名及地址。

2. ...gave us your name and address.
　　……給予我方貴公司的大名及地址。

3. We got（或 have got）your name and address from... .

我方透過……得知貴公司的大名及地址。

4. We learned（或 have learned）your name and address from... .

我方透過……知悉貴公司的大名及地址。

5. We obtained（或 have obtained）your name and address from... .

我方透過……獲悉貴公司的大名及地址。

6. We heared（或 have heared）your name and address from... .

我方透過……獲悉貴公司的大名及地址。

7. Through……we have learned your name and address.

我方透過……獲悉貴公司的大名及地址。

(二)經營業務常用語句

1. We handle the export business of ... .

本公司經營……的出口業務。

2. We deal in ... .

本公司經營……。

3. We are engaged in the exportation of ... .

本公司經營……的出口。

4. We trade in ... .

本公司經營……。

5. We are in the... business(line).

本公司經營……。

6. ... are our line.

　……是本公司經營的產品。

7. ... are our main exports.

　……是本公司的主要出口產品。

㈢建立業務關係常用語句

1. 與某某建立業務關係，一般用法：

We wish to establish business relations with... .

We wish to enter into business activities with... .

We wish to do business with... .

We wish to do business relations with... .

We wish to do trade with... .

We wish to build up business relations with... .

We wish to make business contact with ... .

我方希望能與……建立業務關係。

2. 與誰建立業務關係用 with，如：

We would like to establish business relations with you. (your company、 your firm、 your corporation, prospective dealers)。

我方希望能與貴公司（你們、潛在顧客等）建立業務關係。

3. 建立什麼樣的業務關係：

We are anxious to establish direct （直接的）business relations with you.

We are anxious to establish pleasant （愉快的）business relations with you.

We are anxious to establish friendly（友好的）business relations with you.

We are anxious to establish good （良好的）business relations with you.

We are anxious to establish mutually beneficial （互利的）business relations with you.

4. 在什麼基礎上建立業務關係 on the basis of...，如：

We are willing to enter into business relations with your firm on the basis of equality, mutual benefit and exchanging what one has for what one needs.

我方願在平等互利、互通有無的基礎上與貴公司建立業務關係。

促進業務聯繫：to promote business relations.

加強業務聯繫：to strengthen (enhance) business relations.

㈣自我推薦常用語句

1. Let us introduce ourselves as a leading trading firm in... (name of place).

   請容我方自我介紹，我們是……（地方）首屈一指的貿易公司。

   * a leading trading firm：主要的貿易公司

2. Our company has been in this line of business for many years and enjoys high international prestige.

   本公司經營這項業務已多年，並享有很高的國際信譽。

   * prestige：聲望、信譽

3. Our products are of very good quality and our firm is always regarded by our customers as the most reliable one.

   我方的產品質量一流，且我方的客戶一直把本公司視為最可信賴的公司。

   * good quality：好品質

   * reliable：信賴的

4. We are desirous of extending our connections in your country.

   我方擬拓展本公司在貴國的業務。

   * are desirous of：渴望、希望

5. We have been having a good sale of ... (name of commodity) and are desirous of expanding our market to your country.

   我方的……（商品）一直很暢銷，而我方想要在貴國擴展本公司的經營市場。

   * a good sale (good sales)：暢銷、銷售佳（sell well：暢銷）

   * expanding our market：擴展本公司市場

6. We have the pleasure of introducing ourselves to you as one of the most reputable exporters.

我方有這個榮幸向貴公司介紹本公司是一家信譽優良的出口商。

* have the pleasure of：榮幸

* introducing ourselves to you as...：謹向貴公司介紹本公司為……

* reputable：信譽優良的

7. We shall be much obliged if you will give us a list of some reliable business houses in ... (name of place).

如果貴公司能提供我方一些在……（地方）具有可靠信譽的公司名單，我方將感激不盡。

* be much obliged：感激不盡

8. We would appreciate it if you could kindly introduce us in your publication as follows.

如果貴公司能在您的出版品上刊登我方以下說明，我方將感激不盡。

* publication：出版品、刊物

* as follows：如次、如下

9. We specialize in this line of business.

我方專門經營此項業務。

* specialize in...：專門經營

* line of business：經營項目、經營種類

10. We have been engaged in this business for the past 20 years.

我方從事此項業務已經有超過 20 年的經驗。

11. Because of our past years experience, we are well qualified to take care of your interests.

因為過去數年的經驗，我方有極佳的勝任能力為貴公司提供服務。

* well qualified：具有極佳資格

　＊ take care of：照顧、處理

12. Our company is well-established and reliable.

　本公司有口皆碑且信用可靠。

　＊ well-established：地位穩固的、有口皆碑的

　＊ long-established：創辦已久的、歷史悠久的

13. We have close business relations with the domestic private enterprises.

　我方與國內私人企業有非常密切的商務關係。

14. We have four manufacturing plants in different countries: China, Japan, Spain and Philippine.

　我方在不同的國家共有四個製造工廠：中國大陸、日本、西班牙及菲律賓。

15. We have full confidence that we will meet all your requirements.

　我方有信心可以滿足貴公司的所有需求。

　＊ meet all your requirements：滿足貴公司的所有需求

16. We have been dealing in this line of business for 50 years.

　我方經營本行業務已超過 50 年了。

　＊ dealing in：經營

　＊ line of business：經營項目

㈤推銷產品常用語句

1. Your name has been given by... and we like to inquire whether you are interested in these lines.

　我方從……獲悉貴公司的名稱，不知貴公司對這一系列的產品是否有興趣。

　*in these lines：在這一類產品項目、在這一系列的產品項目

2. We are pleased to inform you that we have just marketed our newly-developed... (name of commodity).

　我方新研製的……（商品）已推出上市，特此奉告。

* are pleased to：樂意的

* market：n. 市場；v. 上市

* newly-developed...：新研製的 ……、新研發的 ……

3. We are pleased to get in touch with you for the supply of... (name of commodity).

我方盼望能成為貴公司的……（商品）供應商。

* get in touch with...：與……聯繫、接觸

* the supply of...：供應

4. You will be interested to hear that we have just marketed our new product.

我方的新產品剛剛推出上市，相信貴公司樂於知道。

* be interested to ＋ v.：對……感興趣

5. You will be interested in our new product...(name of commodity).

貴公司對我方新出品的……（商品）將會感興趣。

* be interested in ＋ n.：對……感興趣

㈥附寄資料供對方參考常用語句

1. You will find enclosed with this letter a sample of new...(name of commodity).

隨函附上我方新出品的……（商品）樣品，請查收。

* You will find enclosed：檢附……、隨函附上……

2. Enclosed please find catalogue for your reference.

隨函附上產品目錄，敬供貴公司參考。

* Enclosed please find：檢附……、隨函附上……（舊式用法）

* for your reference：供貴公司參考

3. We have pleasure in enclosing our price list No....

我方很樂意地附上第xx號價目表。

4. Our latest catalogue, price list and sample are attached for your reference.

附上我方最新的產品目錄、價目表及樣品，敬供貴公司參考。

* are attached：被附上

㈦樣品、產品目錄常用語句

1. We are sending you some free samples.

我方寄給貴公司一些免費樣品。

* free samples：免費樣品

2. As requested in your letter dated October 12, we sent you the samples by air parcel on October 20.

回覆貴公司在 10 月 12 日的要求，我方在 10 月 20 日用空運包裹寄給貴公司樣品。

* As requested in your letter...：依照貴公司來函要求

3. We enclosed a copy of our latest catalogue, as regards your letter of November 8.

回覆貴公司 11 月 8 日的來函，隨函附上我方最新的產品目錄。

* as regards your letter...：關於貴公司來函

4. Four samples per each item were sent today via UPS Express.

我方已於今天將每款各四個樣品以 UPS 快遞寄出。

5. Please give us your specific inquiries upon examination of the above as we presume they will be received favorably in your market.

在檢視過以上的樣品後，請告知貴公司的特別需求，相信必能符合貴國市場的需求。

6. We are sure that these samples will meet your requirement.

我方確信此樣品會符合貴公司的需求。

* meet your requirement：符合貴公司的需求

7. Enclosed is our new catalogue.

附件是我方新的產品目錄。

8. I have received your full set catalogue. I am very interested in your products.

我方已收到貴公司所提供的整套目錄。我方對貴公司的產品非常感興趣。

9. Thank you for the samples, which you sent to us on Sept.10.

謝謝貴公司9月10日寄給我方的樣品。

10. We have received your catalogues, samples and price lists.

我方已收到貴公司的產品目錄、樣品和價格表。

11. Please let us know if our offer does not contain what you want in order to send you further samples.

假使我方的報價未包含貴公司想知道的資訊，煩請告知以便寄樣品給貴公司。

* in order to：為了……目的

12. Please let me know ahead the amount if payment is required for the samples.

若樣品要收費，煩請事先告知。

（八）期待對方盡速回函常用語句

1. We are looking forward to receiving your early reply.

我方期待能盡早接到貴公司的回函。

* are looking forward to ＋ n.：期待、期望

2. Your early reply would be highly appreciated.

貴公司早日回函，我方將感激不盡。

3. We are waiting for your reply.

敬待貴公司的回音。

4. We look forward to hearing from you soon.

我方期待能盡快接獲回音。

5. We await your earliest reply.

敬待貴公司盡早的回函。

6. Please let us have your early reply.

敬請盡速回音。

■第二單元　詢價信

　　詢價信的發送與接受是為了獲得有關商品、服務和資訊。信函要求應直截了當，清楚準確，用最簡練的語言表達要求，不必過分講究措辭來吸引對方的注意。總之，詢價信要做到簡單、具體、明確、有禮，並且合理。由於詢價信意味著可能的貿易機會，因此詢價信應直接寄給公司，以免被拖延。同時，對詢價信的答覆應迅速，注意語氣要客氣，內容要全面。詢價信實際上是開發信對建立業務關係信函的答覆。詢價，係指買方為了洽購某種商品，向對方發出的有關該項商品的詢問。

　　詢價信大致可以分成兩類。一類是普通詢價（General Enquiry），指對賣方所經營的商品做出要求總體瞭解的詢問，一般主要是要求對方寄送產品目錄、價格表、樣品，或要求對方報價等。另一類是特殊詢價，或說具體詢價（Specific Enquiry），指對某項特殊商品的具體交易條件進行瞭解，一般指對規格、價格、付款條件、交貨條件等的詢問。

　　詢價信包含四個要點：
　　・第一要點：感謝對方的來信，並說明所要求對方報價的商品品名及貨號。
　　・第二要點：發信人的要求。
　　・第三要點：訂購條件。
　　・第四要點：結束語。

　　詢價信常見語句：

　　㈠詢價單字

　　inquire＝enquire：v.詢價
　　inquiry＝enquiry：n.詢價、詢價信

㈡詢價常用語句

1. We would like to make an inquiry.

我方想要詢價。

　* would like to：想要

　* make an inquiry：詢價

2. We would like to know the price exclusive of tax of your...(name of commodity).

我方想要知道貴公司的 ……（商品）不含稅的價格。

　* exclusive of...：除……之外，exclusive of tax 不含稅

3. A client of mine enquiries for 100 cases...(name of commodity).

我方的一個客戶詢價 100 箱 ……（商品）。

　* client：客戶

4. We are desirous of your lowest quotations for...(name of commodity).

我方想要貴公司……（商品）的最低報價。

　* are desirous of：渴望、希望

5. I'm buying for chain stores in Australia. They are interested in...(name of commodity). I'd like to make an inquiry.

我方為澳洲的連鎖店採購商品，他們對……（商品）非常感興趣。我方想詢價。

　* chain stores：連鎖商店

6. Please send us your best CIF quotation for...(name of commodity) .

請報給我方……（商品）最優惠的 CIF 價格。

7. When quoting, please state terms of payment and time of delivery.

貴公司報價時，請註明付款條件和交貨時間。

　* terms of payment：付款條件

　* time of delivery：交貨時間

8. The above inquiry was forwarded to you on January 15, but we haven't received your reply until now. Your early offer will be highly appreciated.

上述詢價已於 1 月 15 日寄給貴公司，可是我方到現在還沒收到貴公司答覆，請早日報價，不勝感激。

　　* was forwarded to... : 寄給……

9. We have many enquiries for the under-mentioned goods.

我方收到許多下述貨品的詢價信。

　　* under-mentioned : 下述所提及的

10. Will you please send us a copy of catalogue, with details of the prices and terms of payment?

請寄給我方一份產品目錄，並註明價格和付款條件。

11. Please quote us your best offer for the above inquiry based on FOB Taiwan as well as CIF New York.

請提供上述產品報價，以 FOB 臺灣和 CIF 紐約為報價條件。

㈢索取商品資料常用語句

1. We are interested in your new product... (name of commodity) and shall be pleased to have a catalogue and price list.

我方對貴公司的新產品……（商品）甚感興趣，希望能寄來貴公司的產品目錄及價目表。

2. We have seen your advertisement in The New York Times and should be glad to have your price lists and details of your terms.

我方從紐約時報上看到貴公司的廣告，但願能收到產品的價目表及詳細資料。

　　* advertisement : 廣告

3. We hear that you have put... (name of commodity) on the market and should be glad to have full details.

獲知貴公司有……（商品）已上市，希望能賜寄完整的詳細資料。

* put...on the market：上市

* full details：詳細資料

4. We should appreciate full particulars of your newly-developed product.

如蒙賜寄貴公司新產品的詳細資料，我方將深表感激。

* particulars：n.詳情、細節

5. We should be obliged if you would send us patterns (or samples) and price lists of your... (name of commodity)

如蒙賜寄有關……（商品）的型錄（樣品）和價目表，我方將甚為感激。

6. Thank you in advance for any information you can give us.

對於貴公司所提供的資料，我方在此先表謝忱。

* in advance：事先、預先

7. Please let us have your information as to the price and quality of the goods.

敬請提供產品價格及品質資料。

* as to ＋事物、as for ＋人：至於、關於

8. Please kindly send us your latest catalogue and price list for our study.

敬請賜寄貴公司最新的產品目錄及價目表供我方研究。

* for our study：供我方研究

㈣期待對方盡速回函常用語句

1. We solicit your close cooperation with us in this matter.

我方懇請貴公司對於此一事件能給予密切的協助和合作。

* We solicit...：關於此事懇請惠予……

2. Your courtesy will be appreciated, and we earnestly await your reply.

貴公司的協助，我方感激不盡，並敬待回音。

* Your courtesy will be appreciated：如承惠辦，不勝感激

* await：敬待、敬候

3. Please call me any time if you have any questions.

如果貴公司有任何問題，歡迎隨時打電話給我方。

4. We are looking forward to your reply.

我方期待貴公司的回覆。

5. We are looking forward to your immediate answer.

我方期待貴公司的立即答覆。

6. Looking forward to entering into a business relationship with you.

期待與貴公司建立合作關係。

7. We look forward to the pleasure of hearing from you.

我方期待貴公司的回音。

8. If there is anything remaining unclear, you are always the most welcome to contact us.

如果有任何不清楚的地方，歡迎隨時與我方聯絡。

* remaining：繼續、依然（不變）

9. Thank you for your cooperation.

感謝貴公司的合作。

▌第三單元　報價信

報價是指交易的一方提出有關交易的主要條件。報價如從不同的角度分類：按形式，可以分為口頭報價、書面報價；按報價人不同，可以分為賣方報價（售貨報價）與買方報價（購貨報價）；按法律約束力不同，可以分為穩固報價（有法律約束力的報價）與非穩固報價（無法律約束力的報價）。按照國際貿易慣例，一方所發報價（要約）在有效期限內對方無條件接受（承諾），契約即告成立。所以，報價，特別是穩固報價，是一件十分嚴肅的商業行為，具有重大的法律後果，必須謹慎對待。

報價信包含三個要點：

- 第一要點：感謝對方的來信，並指出所要報價的商品品名及貨號。
- 第二要點：詳細說明主要的交易條件，如規格、數量、包裝、價格、交貨期間及付款條件等。
- 第三要點：期望進一步的合作。

報價信常用語句：

㈠報價單字

1. quote v.報價、quotation n. 報價、報價信

(1) quote 某人 a price for 某商品：

Please quote us your lowest price for ... (name of commodity).

請向我方報……（商品）最低價。

(2) quote 某人 a price：

Please quote us your lowest price.

請給我方最低報價。

(3) quote a price：

Please quote your lowest price.

請報最低價。

2. offer v. & n. 報價

offer 作報價解釋時，既可作名詞用，也可作動詞用。

(1) offer 作名詞用時，常與動詞 make, send, give 等連用，後接介詞 for 或 on 或 of，接 for 最普通，接 on 較少見。如提及對方已報某商品的價或某數量的價時，則用 of。

① Please make (send, give) us an offer for（或 on）...(name of commodity).

請向我方報…（商品）價。

② Your offer of ...(name of commodity) is too high.

貴公司所報……（商品）價格太高了。

(2) offer 作動詞時，可以不及物。如：

We will offer as soon as possible.

我方將盡早報價。

也可以及物。作及物動詞用時，受詞（賓語）可以是人，可以是物，也可以有雙受詞（雙賓語）。

① We hope to be able to offer you next week.

我方希望能於下週某一天向貴公司報價。

② We can offer various kinds of ...(name of commodity).

我方能報各式各樣的……（商品）價。

③ We can offer you ...(name of commodity) at attractive prices.

我方能以具有吸引力的價格向貴公司報價……（商品）。

嚴格講，quote/quotation 與 offer 不同，quote/quotation 是報價，指某一商品的單價；offer 是報單價外，還包括數量、交貨期間、付款方式等等。另外，offer 比較固定，賣方價格報出後，一般不能輕易變動；而 quote/quotation 則不同，賣方報價後，不受約束，可以根據情況略加調整。儘管有區別，但各國商人則往往把這兩個詞混用，這一點要特別注意。

㈡報價常用語句

1. Thank you for your enquiry. Please tell us the quantity you require so that we can work out the offers.

感謝貴公司詢價。請告訴我方貴公司所需數量以便我方報價。

* so that：為了……、便於……

* work out：計算（金額、費用等）

2. We welcome your enquiry of July 30 and thank you for your interest in our products.

很高興收到貴公司 7 月 30 日的詢價，並感謝貴公司對我方產品的興趣。

3. We would like to make an offer about ...(name of commodity).

我方很樂意對……（商品）提報價。

*make an offer：報價

4. I take great pleasure in receiving your enquiry dated May 10, on the...(name of commodity).

我方很高興收到貴公司 5 月 10 日有關……（商品）的詢價。

* take great pleasure in：十分高興

5. We have received your enquiry and will give you a quotation for 100 dozens of ... (name of commodity) as soon as possible.

我方已收到貴公司的詢價，將盡快提供貴公司 100 打的……（商品）的報價。

* give you a quotation：對貴公司報價

* as soon as possible：盡快

6. Any increase or decrease in the freight after the date of sale shall be for the buyer's account.

銷售日後運費如有上漲或下跌，均由買方負擔。

* for the buyer's account：由買方負擔

7. We enclosed a copy of our price list.

隨函附上一份我方的價格表。

8. All prices are subject to change without notice.

所有的報價隨時會更動，恕不另行通知。

* subject to：可能（會）的……

* without notice：不另行通知

9. This quotation is subject to your reply reaching here on or before January 20.

此報價以在 1 月 20 日或之前收到貴公司的答覆才有效。

* subject to：以……為條件

10. As the prices quoted are exceptionally low and likely to rise, we would advise you to accept the offer without delay.

由於所報價格特別低，並可能漲價，建議貴公司立即接受此報價。

* likely：可能的

* accept：接受

* without delay：不要遲延

11. Please find the attached information and our best offer for our products.

請參考附件資料和我方所提供最優惠的產品價格。

12. We hope you will be satisfied with our samples and quotations.

我方希望貴公司能對我方的樣品和報價感到滿意！

* be satisfied with：滿意

13. This is a combined offer on all or none basis.

此為聯合報價，必須全部接受才有效。

* a combined offer：聯合報價；兩個商品以上的報價，必須全部接受才有效。

14. The quotation is subject to prior sale.

這個報價有權先售。

* subject to：以……為條件

* prior ：在先的、在前的

15. We understand that you are interested in...(name of commodity) and are offering you by our cable of...

獲悉貴公司對……（商品）感興趣，我方於……月……日電報報價如下……

16. We understand that there is a good demand for... (name of commodity) in your market, and take this opportunity of enclosing our Quotation No....for your consideration.

我方瞭解到貴方市場對……（商品）需求強勁，借此良機，附上我方第……號報價單，供貴公司考慮。

* a good demand：需求強勁

* take this opportunity：利用機會

* for your consideration：供貴公司考慮

17. We are enclosing our Quotation No. ... on ...(name of commodity) for your consideration, and hope to receive your trial order in the near future.

隨函附上我方……（商品）第……號報價單，供貴公司考慮，希望近期能收到貴公司試訂單。

* trial order：試訂單
* in the near future：近期

18. We have pleasure in offering you the goods listed on the attached offer sheet No. ...,
    and hope that they will be of interest to you.

   很高興提供所附的第……號報價單所列貨物，希望貴公司有興趣。

   *list：n.目錄、清單；v.把……列入目錄（清單）
   * offer sheet：報價單
   *... be of interest to you：貴公司對……有興趣

19. We have pleasure in recommending to you ... (name of commodity) and enclose Quotation No. ...for your reference.

   榮幸地向貴公司推薦……（商品），隨函附上第……號報價單，供貴公司參考。

   * recommending：推薦

20. Further to our letter of ... we now offer you without engagement, our various items as follows：

   續我方……月……日函，現報不具約束力的各種貨物價格如下：

   * without engagement：不具約束力
   * various：各種、各式各樣

21. We are pleased to inform you that there are 50 tons of ...(name of commodity) now available for export.

   欣告現有 50 噸……（商品）可供出口。

   * available：有現貨的

(三)交貨常用語句

1. Please inform us of the shipping date.

請通知我方裝船的日期。

2. Please ship the enclosed order immediately.

請立即安排所附訂單的出貨事宜。

3. Please tell us when our order will be shipped.

請告知我方的訂單何時會裝船。

4. Please also indicate the delivery time in your quotation sheet.

請在報價單中註明交貨時間。

5. We are pleased to inform you that your order has been shipped.

我方在此通知貴公司，您的訂單已經運送出貨了。

6. As the goods you ordered are now in stock, we will ship them without fail immediately.

因為貴公司訂購的商品尚有存貨，我方將立即安排出貨。

* in stock：現貨、存貨

* without fail：一定、必定

7. Your order for 600 doz...(name of commodity) will be shipped at the end of this month. You should receive them early next month.

貴公司的 600 打……（商品）的訂單會在這個月底裝船出貨。貴公司應該會在下個月初收到這批貨。

8. We are pleased to place the following orders with you if you give an guarantee shipment from Taipei to Seattle by November 10.

若貴公司能保證在 11 月 10 日前將貨物由臺北運至西雅圖，則我方樂於向貴公司訂購下列貨物。

* place the following orders with ...：向……訂購下列貨物

* give an guarantee：給予保證

9. The shipment date is approaching. It would be advisable for you to open the L/C covering your order No. 2986 so as to enable us to effect shipment within the stipulated time limit.

船期即將來臨，建議貴公司開立訂單編號 2986 的信用狀，以便我方在規定的時間內裝船。

* approaching：接近、臨近
* open the L/C：開發信用狀
* covering：有關
* so as to：便於……
* stipulated：規定的

10. Please do your best to ship our goods by S. S. "Hope".

請儘量以「希望」號輪船裝運我方貨物。

* do your best：盡力
* S. S.：steamship 輪船

11. It is due to arrive at Hong Kong on September 30, and confirm by return that goods will be ready in time.

預計於 9 月 30 日抵香港。請函覆確認，貨物將按時備妥。

* is due to：預定的（預定到達的時間……）
* be ready：預備好
* in time：準時

12. Something unexpected compels us to seek your cooperation by advancing shipment of the goods under S/C No. 6789 from October to July.

意外的情況迫使我方尋求貴公司配合，請將第 6789 號售貨確認書裡貨物裝運期間由 10 月分提前到 7 月分。

* compels：迫使

13. The shipping documents are to be delivered to you against payment only.

貨運單據將於付款後交至貴公司。

㈣出貨、包裝常用語句

1. Let us have your instructions for packing and dispatch.

   請告知包裝及裝運指示。

   * dispatch：裝運

2. These are fragile.

   這些是易碎品。

3. Could you use cartons?

   貴公司能不能用紙箱？

4. Could you use wooden cases instead?

   貴公司能不能改用木箱？

5. I am afraid the cartons are not strong enough.

   我方擔心裝貨的紙箱不夠結實。

6. We suggest that you strengthen the cartons with double straps.

   我方建議用兩條包裝帶固定紙箱。

7. This kind of packing costs more.

   這種包裝費用更貴。

8. This kind of packing is much cheaper.

   這種包裝比較便宜。

9. I would appreciate it very much if you could deliver the goods by this Friday.

   如果貴公司能在這個星期五之前出貨，我方將不勝感激。

10. It will be around December when a new stock is supplied.

    大概要到 12 月分左右始有新貨供應。

11. I will let you know as soon as the new supply is available.

當有新貨時，我方會盡快通知貴公司。

12. In spite of our effort, we find it impossible to secure space for the shipment owing to the shortage of shipping space.

雖然我方已盡最大努力，卻因為船位不足而無法保證交貨期。

* In spite of：雖然、儘管

* secure：獲得

* space for the shipment、shipping space：船位、船艙

* owing to：由於

* shortage：不足、缺乏

13. We find both quality and prices of your products satisfactory and enclosed the order for prompt supply.

我方對貴公司產品的質量和價格均感滿意，隨函附上訂單，請供應現貨。

14. I'm sorry to say that your delivery is a week behind schedule.

很抱歉，貴公司的交貨時間比計畫日程晚了一個星期。

15. As the market is sluggish, please postpone the shipment of the order No. 123 goods to August.

由於市場疲軟，請將我方訂單編號 123 延遲至 8 月分出貨。

* sluggish：蕭條的、遲緩的

㈤付款常用語句

1. Attached is an invoice.

隨函附上發票。

2. We request your immediate payment.

我方要求貴公司立即付款。

3. You should pay an invoice for USD500.

根據發票，貴公司應該付款 500 美元。

4. We won't accept payment in cash on delivery, but may consider payment in cash with order.

我方不接受貨到付款，但可以考慮訂貨付現。

* cash on delivery：簡稱 COD，貨到付款

* cash with order：簡稱 CWO，訂貨付現

5. We insist on payment in cash on delivery without allowing any discount.

我方堅持貨到付現，不打任何折扣。

* insist on：堅持

6. You should make payment against our documentary draft upon presentation.

貴公司應憑我方的跟單匯票於見票時付款。

* documentary draft：跟單匯票

* presentation：提示

7. The amount concerned was forwarded to your account of the ... Bank by telegraphic transfer today.

上述的金額已於今日電匯至貴公司……銀行的帳號。

* telegraphic transfer：簡稱 T/T，電匯

8. We insist on payment by irrevocable sight L/C.

我方堅持憑不可撤銷即期信用狀付款。

* irrevocable：不可撤銷

9. Payment shall be made CWO by means of T/T or M/T.

訂貨付現費用應以電匯或信匯的方式支付。

* by means of：用……方式

10. Our terms of payment are by irrevocable L/C payable by sight draft against presentation of shipping documents.

我方的付款條件為不可撤銷信用狀，憑運送單據見票付款。

11. Please extend the L/C to July 20.

請將信用狀的有效期限延至 7 月 20 日。

12. We will not accept L/C 45 days. Please change it to L/C at sight.

我方無法接受見票 45 天後付款的信用狀，請將之修改為即期信用狀。

㈥答覆詢價常用語句

1. Referring to your letter dated...which you inquired for...(name of commodity) have pleasure in cabling you an offer as follows:

關於貴公司……日對……（商品）詢價信，現電報報價如下：

* Referring to：關於

2. In answer to your inquiry for...(name of commodity), we offer you ...(quantity).

關於貴公司所詢……（商品），現可供……（數量）。

* In answer to：回覆

3. As requested, we are offering you the following subject to our final confirmation:

根據要求，我方就如下貨物向貴公司報價，以我方最後確認為準：

* As requested：依要求

* subject to：以……為條件

* final confirmation：最後確認

4. We thank you for your inquiry of Nov. 29, and can offer you...(name of commodity) . This offer will remain open until the receipt of your fax by return.

感謝貴公司 11 月 29 日詢價，現報……（商品），此報價有效期到收到貴方傳真為止。

* the receipt of：收到

5. We thank you for your letter asking for our new catalogue. It is being dispatched to you under separate cover and we hope that you will find many items in it which interest you.

感謝貴公司來函索取我方新的產品目錄，目錄已另函寄上，希望貴公司可以發現感興趣的項目。

* asking for：要求
* under separate cover：另函寄上

6. Further to our letter of ... we have now heard from our works that it is possible to supply...(name of commodity).

續我方……月……日函，我方從工廠獲悉有可能提供……（商品）。

7. In reply to your letter of ...we confirm our fax of today reading:

茲覆貴公司……來函，我方確認今日電傳，電文如下……

* In reply to：回覆

㈦寄送預期發票常用語句

1. We thank you for your inquiry of...(name of commodity) and have pleasure in enclosing our Proforma Invoice No. .... As soon as you have handed in your application for import license, please send us a copy for reference.

感激貴公司的……月……日詢價。現附上我方預期發票第……號。一俟貴公司提交輸入許可證申請書，請即寄我方複件一份，以供參考。

* As soon as：一……就……
* handed in；：提交
* import license：簡稱 I/P，輸入許可證

2. Enclosed please find our Proforma Invoice No. ... for...

附上我方……預期發票第……號，請查收。

3. We are pleased to send you our Proforma Invoice No. ...in triplicate as requested.

按要求，茲寄上我方預期發票第……號，一式三份。

4. We have been informed by ... that you are thinking of purchasing...(name of commodity) and have pleasure in enclosing our Proforma Invoice in duplicate.

我方從……獲悉貴公司正在考慮購買……（商品），現附上我方預期發票，一式兩份。

(八)寄送價目表常用語句

1. Many thanks for your letter of.... We enclosed our Catalogue No. ...and we have quoted our best terms in the attached price lists. We believe that our...(name of commodity) will meet your requirements.

非常感激貴公司……月……日來函，附上我方第……號產品目錄，價目表中我方已報出最好交易條件，相信我們的……（商品）能滿足貴公司要求。

2. We have pleasure in attaching our current price lists for your reference and, as we are able to offer prompt delivery, we look forward to receiving your cable order in the near future.

我方很高興附上現行價目表供貴公司參考。我方可即期交貨，盼不久能收到貴公司電報訂單。

3. At the suggestion of ... we have much pleasure in sending you under separate cover our price lists which we hope might possibly be of interest to you.

鑑於……的建議，今另函寄上我方價目表，望能使貴公司感興趣。

4. We enclose our latest price list No. ... on ...(name of commodity), for which there is regular demand on your market.

隨函寄上我方……（商品）的最新價目表第……號，貴方市場對此有經常性的需求。

* regular demand：經常性的需求

(九)無法供應常用語句

1. We very much regret that we are unable to supply what you require just now.

我方無法提供貴公司現在所需貨物，深感歉意！

2. While we appreciate what you stated in your letter of..., we regret that it is impossible for us to supply...(name of commodity) for the time being.

謝謝貴公司……月……日來函中所述，很抱歉，現在無法向貴公司提供……（商品）。

* for the time being：現在

3. We regret that we are unable to supply you with the small quantity you require.

我方歉難供應貴公司所要求的小批數量。

4. We have taken notes of your requirements for...(name of commodity) but regret being unable to supply at present. We will certainly fax you an offer as soon as there is stock available.

我方已記下貴公司對……（商品）的要求，目前歉難供貨。一有現貨可供，我方將立即傳真報價。

* take notes：做筆記

* at present：目前

㈩期待對方盡速回函常用語句

1. We are confident to give our customers the fullest satisfaction.

我方有信心能提供我們的客戶最大的滿意。

* confident：有自信的

2. We hope to be of service to you and look forward to your comments.

我方希望能對貴公司有所幫助，也敬待貴公司的指教（意見）。

* be of service to you：對貴公司有所助益

3. We are ready to be at your service and await your order.

感謝有這個榮幸為貴公司服務，並敬待貴公司的訂單。

* at your service：願為貴公司服務、聽候貴公司的吩咐

4. Please call me any time if you have any questions.

如果貴公司有任何問題，歡迎隨時打電話給我方。

5. We are looking forward to your reply.

　我方期待貴公司的回覆。

6. We are looking forward to your immediate answer.

　我方期待貴公司的立即答覆。

7. We should appreciate hearing from you immediately.

　能立即知道貴公司的消息，我方將不勝感激。

8. Looking forward to entering into a business relationship with you.

　期待與貴公司建立合作關係。

9. We look forward to the pleasure of hearing from you.

　我方期待貴公司的回音。

10. If there is anything remaining unclear, you are always the most welcome to contact us.

　如果有任何不清楚的地方，歡迎隨時與我方聯絡。

11. Thank you for your cooperation.

　感謝貴公司的合作。

12. If you need any informations, please contact us or visit our website.

　如果貴公司有任何問題，歡迎與我方聯絡或瀏覽我方的網站。

13. If you have any questions, please do not hesitate to let me know.

　若有任何問題，請立即與我方聯絡。

　＊ hesitate：猶豫、遲疑

▶ 第四單元　催款信

　　站在賣方的立場，最重視也最關心的是可否順利收款。國際貿易上多屬交貨後付款，賣方於交貨後請求買方付款，如未獲買方覆函或買方逾期未付款時，賣方應發出催款信。催款信其語句雖可略帶堅定，但仍應婉轉有禮，避免傷了和氣，對方來個相應不理，以致對簿公堂。

催款信包含兩個要點：

- 第一要點：催促付款，如告知對方貨已裝運請如期付款、貨款已逾期未付等。
- 第二要點：請對方盡速付款。

催款信常用語句：

㈠賣方要求買方付款常用語句

1. The following items totaling USD4,000 are still open on your account.
   貴公司的欠款總計為 4,000 美元。

2. It is now several weeks since we sent you our first invoice and we have not yet received your payment.
   我方的第一份發票已經寄出有好幾週了，但尚未收到貴公司的任何款項。

3. I'm wondering about your plans for paying your account which, as you know, is now 40 days overdue.
   我方想瞭解一下貴公司的付款計畫，如所知，貴公司的款項已逾期 40 天了。
   * overdue：逾期的、過期未付的……

4. We must now ask you to settle this account within the next few days.
   請貴公司務必在這幾日內結清這筆款項。
   * settle this account：結清款項

5. May we remind you that your payment has been overdue since June 20.
   提醒貴公司的貨款自 6 月 20 日起已過期了。

6. We are enclosing an invoice covering goods supplied to your order No.123 of...(name of commodity). We shall be glad to receiving your check by return.
   附上貴公司訂單 123 號……（商品）的發票一張，請寄上支票。

7. An early remittance will be appreciated.

請盡早匯款，不勝感激。

* remittance：匯款

8. We trust you will settle the reminder by paying in monthly installments.

我方確信貴公司會按月繳清分期付款。

* settle the reminder：結清餘款

9. We enclose a statement for the period ending on the July 31. We would appreciate a prompt settlement of this account.

隨函附上 7 月 31 日為止的結算表，我方將非常感謝貴公司能迅速結清帳款。

10. We would like to remind you that in your letter of the June 22 you promised to repay before the end of June.

我方想提醒貴公司，在貴公司 6 月 22 日的來函中已允諾在 6 月底前付清欠款。

* remind：提醒

11. We think you may not have received the statement of account we sent you on August 25 showing the balance of USD 50,000 you owe.

我方猜想貴公司可能未收到我們 8 月 25 日發出的 50,000 美元欠款的帳單。

* statement of account：帳單

* balance：尾款、餘款

* owe：欠

12. You have not responded in any way to our recent letters about your past due account.

貴公司對我方最近有關逾期欠款的信函一直沒有任何回覆。

13. We remind you once more of your open account that is now 60 days beyond our terms.

我方再次提醒貴公司的款項已逾期 60 多天了。

* once more：再次、再度

14. Your account is still unpaid in spite of our continual reminders asking for payment or an explanation for your delay.

儘管我方多次的催款信要求貴公司付款或解釋遲延付款的理由，但貴公司卻一直置之不理。

* in spite of：儘管、雖然

* reminders：催款信

* asking for：要求

15. We urgently request that you immediately pay your outstanding balance of USD 10,000.

我方迫切地要請貴公司立即付清 10,000 美元的尾款。

* urgently：迫切地

* outstanding：未清償的

* balance：尾款、餘款

(二)警告收信人不得拖延付款常用語句

1. You must realize that we cannot afford to carry this debt on our books any longer.

貴公司必須瞭解我方無法再提供此項債務的援助。

* afford：提供

* carry：資助、援助

* not any longer：不再

2. Any further delay in paying your balance due cannot be accepted.

我方不能接受貴公司再一次的延遲支付餘款。

* balance：餘款、尾款

* due：欠債

3. You can no longer delay payment if you wish to keep business relations with us.

貴公司如欲維持與我方之業務關係，請不能再延遲付款。

* no longer：不再

* keep business relations：維持業務關係

4. Our next step is to take legal action to collect the money due us.

我方下一步驟將會採取法律行動以收回欠款。

* take legal action：採取法律行動

* due us：欠我方

5. This is unpleasant for both of us and is damaging to your credit-rating.

這對我們雙方都不愉快，並且也將損及貴公司的信用評價。

* credit-rating：信用評價

㈢明確最後付款期限／要求立即付款常用語句

1. We must now insist that you send your payment within the next five days.

我方堅持貴公司必須在未來的五天內付款。

2. Unless I receive your remittance within the next three days, our attorney will be instructed to start proceedings to recover the debt.

除非在未來的三天內收到貴公司的匯款，否則我方將指示律師提出訴訟以收回債務。

* remittance：匯款

* attorney：律師

* be instructed to：被指示

* start proceedings：提出訴訟

3. If we do not receive remittance within five days from the above date, we will have no choice but to pursue other collection procedures.

如果在上述日期後的五天內仍未收到貴公司的匯款，我方將別無選擇的採取其他催款程序。

*pursue：進行

*procedures：程序

4. After April 30, we will have no choice but to cancel your credit and turn your account over to a collection agency.

4月30日後，我方將別無選擇的撤銷貴公司的信用並將欠帳轉給催款代理人。

* turn over：把……移交給

㈣結束語常用語句

1. We look forward to your prompt payment.

我方期待貴公司能馬上付款。

2. Your immediate response is necessary.

貴公司有必要立即回覆。

3. Whether or not we take legal action is now your decision.

我方是否採取法律行動視貴公司現在的決定。

* Whether or not：是否

* take legal action：採取法律行動

4. Please make every effort to ensure that we are not forced to take this drastic action.

請貴公司努力以確保我方不會被迫採取激烈的行動。

* make every effort：努力

* are forced to：被迫

* take this drastic action：採取激烈的行動

5. We must hear from you at once to avoid further action.

我方必須立即知悉貴公司的回覆，以避免採取進一步的行動。

6. Looking forward to your prompt action on this matter.

期待貴公司對於此事採取迅速的措施。

7. Thank you for your kind reply on above request.

感謝貴公司對上述要求的善意回覆。

▶第五單元　索賠信

國際貿易上常見的索賠有貿易索賠、運輸索賠及保險索賠。其中以貿易索賠最多也最複雜，屬於賣方責任而引起買方索賠的主要有：賣方所交貨物的品質、數量、包裝和契約不符，賣方未按期交貨，賣方其他違反契約或法定義務的行為。屬於買方責任而引起賣方索賠的有：買方未按期付款，未及時辦理運輸手續，未及時開立信用狀，買方其他違反契約或法定義務的行為。解決方法則有：和解、調解、訴訟及商務仲裁四種，其中以買賣雙方私下和解為最省時、省錢，也不傷和氣，故買賣雙方在發出索賠信函時必須語氣婉轉外，亦應合情合理，先檢討自己有無疏失，而非推卸責任或作任何強詞奪理的敘述，接著再說明索賠的原因和要求。

索賠信包含三個要點：

- 第一要點：提及索賠的原因，如交貨遲延、貨物不符合契約約定、未及時開立信用狀等。
- 第二要點：詳細說明索賠的要求，如損害賠償金額、退貨、拒收、換貨等。
- 第三要點：敬候對方的答覆。

索賠信常用語句：

㈠索賠單字

claim v. & n.：索賠，賠償，賠償金

compensate v.：賠償，補償

to make a (one's) claim、to register a (one's) claim、 to file a (one's) claim、to lodge a (one's) claim、to raise a (one's) claim、to put in a (one's) claim、to bring up a (one's) claim：提出索賠

to make a claim with (against) sb.：向某方提出索賠

to make a claim for (on) sth.：就某事提出索賠

㈡索賠信常用語句

1. I'm afraid you should compensate us by 10% of the total amount of the contract.
   貴公司應賠償我方契約全部金額的 10%。

2. We regret for the loss you have suffered and agree to compensate you by USD500.
   我方對貴公司所遭受的損失深表歉意，同意賠償貴公司 500 美元。
   * suffered：遭受

3. We compensate you by 5% of the total value plus inspection fee.

我方賠償貴公司 5%的損失，另外加上商品檢驗費。

4. There are some different types of claims.

索賠有幾種不同的類型。

5. This is a claim on quality.

這是品質索賠。

6. We have already made a careful investigation of the case.

我方已經對這個索賠案件作了詳細的調查研究。

* investigation：調查、研究

7. I want to settle our claim on you for the 50 tons of ...(name of commodity), as per Sales Confirmation No. 123456.

我方想處理關於售貨確認書第 123456 號 50 噸……（商品）的索賠問題。

* settle：解決爭端

* as per：根據、按照

8. We are not in a position to entertain your claim.

我方不能接受貴公司提出的索賠要求。

* position ：立場、狀況

* are not in a position to：（處於不好的位置）意指無法、不能

* entertain：接受、考慮

9. But we regret our inability to accommodate your claim.

很抱歉我們不能接受貴公司的索賠。

* accommodate：迎合、遷就

10. Claims for incorrect material must be made within 60 days after arrival of the goods.

有關不合格材料的索賠問題必須在貨到後 60 天內提出。

11. We've given your claim our careful consideration.

我方已經就貴公司提出的索賠作了仔細研究。

12. We filed a claim with (against) you for the shortweight.

關於短重問題，我方已經向貴公司提出索賠。

* filed：正式提出

13. We have received your remittance in settlement of our claim.

我方已經收到貴公司理賠的匯款。

* remittance：匯款

* settlement：清償、解決

* in settlement of our claim：清償我方的索賠

14. I'll write to our home office to waive our claim immediately.

我方將立即寫信給總公司提出放棄索賠。

* waive：放棄

15. This is a claim on shortweight.

這是短重索賠。

16. This is a claim on delayed shipment.

這是延期裝運索賠。

17. Claim on shortweight is caused by packing damage or shortloading.

短重索賠是由包裝破損或短裝引起的。

* is caused by：由……引起

18. Claim on delayed shipment is that sellers fail to make the delivery according to time schedule.

延期裝運索賠是對賣方沒有按時裝運貨物而提出的索賠。

* fail to...：無法、疏忽

* delayed shipment：延期裝運
* according to：依照、依據

19. Claim on quality originates from inferior quality of goods or quality changes.

品質索賠是因貨物品質低劣或是品質改變。

* originates：產生於……、起自於……
* inferior：低劣

㈢抱怨、賠償常用語句

1. We have to complain to you about the damage in shipment which has caused us so much trouble.

我方不得不向貴公司抱怨，裝運的破損造成我方很大的麻煩。

2. We regret to inform you that the goods shipped per S.S. "Queen" arrived in such an unsatisfactory condition.

我方遺憾地告知貴公司由「皇后號」輪船運來的貨物令人十分不滿。

3. The importer has filed a complaint with our corporation about poor packing of the goods.

進口商因貨物的不良包裝向我方提出抱怨。

* filed：正式提出
* complaint：抱怨

4. We can assure you that such a thing will not happen again in future deliveries.

我方向貴公司保證這樣的事件在以後的出貨中不會再度發生。

* such a thing：這樣的事件

5. As regards inferior quality of your goods, we claim a compensation of USD100,000.

由於貴公司產品品質低劣，我方要求貴公司賠償 10 萬美元。

* As regards：關於
* inferior：低劣

6. We hope you would compensate us for the loss.

希望貴公司賠償我方損失。

7. In order to solve the problem, we ask for compensation for the loss.

為了解決問題，我方請求賠償所受的損失。

   * solve：解決

   * compensation：賠償

8. The claim is unfounded.

索賠理由不充分。

   * unfounded：無事實根據的、無理由的

9. We are not liable for the damage.

我方對損失沒有責任。

   * are liable for：有責任的

   * damage：損失

10. It is a case of force which is beyond our control.

這是人力無法控制的「不可抗力」事故。

   * beyond our control：超過我們的控制、人力無法控制的

11. The goods arrived at our port 10 days later than scheduled.

貨物比原先的計畫晚了 10 天才到達港口。

㈣結束語常用語句

1. We recommend this matter to your prompt attention.

我方建議貴公司立即針對此事回覆。

   * recommend：建議

2. We shall appreciated your prompt attention to the adjustment of this claim.

我方將感激貴公司對此要求的迅速處理。

   * adjustment：處理

3. Looking forward to your prompt action on this matter.

期待貴公司對於此事採取迅速的措施。

4. Please give this matter your immediate attention.

請貴公司立即回覆。

5. We must hear from you at once to avoid further action.

我方必須立即知悉貴公司的回覆，以避免採取進一步的行動。

* at once：立即

▶第六單元　學科英文題庫翻譯

1. We would be delighted to establish business relations with you.

我方很高興與貴方建立商業關係。

2. Your order No. A231 is now being processed and should be ready for dispatch by next week.

您的編號 A231 訂單正在處理中，預定在下星期出貨。

3. Please return the damaged goods. We will replace them free of charge.

請寄回損壞的物品，我方將免費更換。

4. Provided you can offer favorable quotations, we will place regular orders with you.

假如您能提供優惠的報價，我們將定期向您訂貨。

5. We will do everything we can to ensure early shipment.

我方將盡我們所能確保早日裝運。

6. You will understand that we must increase sales by distributing through as many outlets as possible.

貴公司應理解，我們必須藉由許多的暢貨中心來增加銷售量。

7. Can we send our representative to you with a model of the machine so he can give

you a <u>demonstration</u>?

我方可委派代表前往貴公司展示機器模型嗎?

8. We can send you a replacement, or if you like, we can <u>credit</u> your account.

我們可以寄給您替換品,或如果您願意,我們可以把退款存入您的帳戶。

9. Thank you for your enquiry <u>of</u> October 12 concerning DVD players.

謝謝您在 10 月 12 日關於 DVD 播放機的詢價信。

10. The new model has several additional <u>features</u> which will appeal to customers.

新的模型具有一些吸引客戶的特色。

11. As the photocopier is still under <u>warranty</u>, we'll repair it for free.

由於影印機仍在保固期限內,我們將免費修理。

12. We would like to know whether the firm is <u>reliable</u> in settling its accounts promptly.

我方想立刻知道工廠在結清帳款上是否可信賴?

13. As the time of shipment is fast approaching, we must ask you to fax the L/C and shipping <u>instructions</u> immediately.

由於裝運期即將來臨,我方必須要求您立刻傳真信用狀和裝運指示。

14. In regard to your invoice No. 23130 for $2,578, which we expected to be cleared two weeks ago, we still have not yet received your <u>remittance</u>.

關於您編號 23130 發票的 2,578 元,我們預期應在兩個禮拜前付清,至今仍未收到您們的匯款。

15. We trust that the <u>consignment</u> will reach you in perfect condition.

我們相信貨物到達您手中時會是理想的狀態。

16. Any information you provide will be treated in strict <u>confidence</u>.

您提供的任何資料將被保密處理。

17. We would be grateful if you would allow us an extension of three months to pay this invoice.

如果您允許我們延長三個月支付這張發票，我們將感激不盡。

18. The goods you inquired about are sold out, but we can offer you a substitute.

您詢問的物品已經售完，但我們可以提供您替代品。

19. We regret to inform you that our customers find your prices too high.

我方很遺憾的通知您，我們的顧客覺得您的價格太高了。

20. Owing to a fire in our warehouse, we have to postpone the shipping date to August 15.

由於我們的倉庫失火，所以必須延遲出貨日期至 8 月 15 日。

21. At the fair, we will exhibit some of our newly-developed products.

在展覽會上，我們將展示一些新開發的產品。

22. The package containing the dinner plates appeared to be in good condition.

含有餐盤的包裹看起來狀況很好。

23. We have learned from the Chamber of Commerce in Boston that you are a leading manufacturer of waterproof watches in Taiwan.

我方從波士頓商會得知，您在臺灣是防水手錶的領導製造商。

24. We enclose our credit note No. C35 for $ 15.75, which is a refund for the overcharge on invoice No. A321.

我們隨函附上編號 C35 的折讓單 15.75 元，這是編號 A321 發票所退還的多收款。

25. If you are not already represented here, we should be interested in acting as your sole

agents.

如果您在此地尚未有代理商，我方極有興趣成為您的獨家代理商。

26. The agency we are offering will be on a commission basis.

我們提供的代理業務採佣金制。

27. As this is our first transaction with you, we would be obliged if you could provide us with some references.

因為這是我們第一次與您交易，如果您可以提供我們一些備詢人，我們會很感激。

28. Payment will be made by bank transfer.

付款是透過銀行轉帳的。

29. You have chosen one of the most advanced and popular mobile phones available on the market today.

您所選的手機是目前市場上最先進的和最受歡迎的型式之一。

30. We provide a discount of 30% on quantities of not less than 200.

如果貨物數量超過200，我們提供30%的折扣。

31. We are a rapidly expanding multinational company.

我方是一個擴充迅速的多國企業。

32. Enclosed are our latest catalog and price list for your reference.

隨函附上我們最新的目錄和價目表供貴公司參考。

33. We have arranged with our bankers to open a letter of credit in your favor.

我方已經安排銀行簽發以貴公司為受益人的信用狀。

34. We are manufacturers of high quality office equipment.

我們是高品質辦公設備的製造商。

35. You will notice that the prices quoted are <u>extremely competitive</u> for a product of this quality.

您會發現這種品質的產品所報價格是非常具有競爭力的。

36. <u>Upon receipt of</u> your confirmation, we will execute the order.

一收到您的確認，我們將履行訂單。

37. <u>As</u> you can see from the enclosed catalogue, we offer a wide range of products.

就像在隨函目錄中您所見的，我方提供各式各樣的產品。

38. The broken teapots have been kept aside <u>in case</u> you need them to support a claim on your suppliers for compensation.

破掉的茶壺被置於一旁，以防您需要它作為向供應商要求賠償的證明。

39. <u>As soon as</u> shipment has been effected, we will advise you by fax.

一旦裝運後，我方將用傳真通知您。

40. If the quality of the goods comes up to our expectations, we can probably let you have <u>regular</u> orders.

如果貨物的品質達到我們的期望，我們或許可以給予貴公司經常性的訂單。

41. We have enclosed our price list but should point out that prices <u>are subject to change</u> as the market for raw materials is rather unstable at present.

隨函附上價目表，但我們必須指出價格可能會有所變化，因為目前原物料市場相當不穩定。

42. As this model is <u>in great demand</u>, we would recommend that you accept this offer as soon as possible.

由於此型式的需求很大，我們建議您盡快接受報價。

43. It would be appreciated if you could send some samples of the material.
我們將不勝感激，如果您能寄送一些原物料的樣品。

44. If you have any questions, please do not hesitate to let us know.
如果您有任何問題，請盡速讓我們知道。

45. We hope that you will find these terms satisfactory .
我們希望您覺得這些條款是令人滿意的。

46. We look forward to your prompt reply.
我們期望您的迅速答覆。

47. We have been exporting printers for 20 years.
我方出口印表機已經 20 年了。

48. We are importers in the textile trade and would like to get in touch with suppliers of this line.
本公司是紡織品貿易的進口商，想要與此產業的供應商聯絡。

49. We have quoted our most favorable prices.
我方所報的已是最優惠的價格。

50. We apologize for the delay and trust it will not cause you inconvenience .
我們為延遲而道歉，並且相信這不會造成貴公司的不便。

51. As requested, we are enclosing our catalogue and price list.
依照要求，我方隨函附入我們的目錄以及價目表。

52. Please confirm the order by email and send us the shipping information along with your invoice.
請用電郵確認訂單，並且將裝船資料一併附入您的發票。

53. Unfortunately, there is no manufacturer that we know of who can meet your needs.
不幸地，據我所知沒有製造商符合您的需求。

54. The inspector looked at the <u>certificate of origin</u> to check where the goods were produced.
檢驗人員檢驗原產地證明書，確認貨物是在哪裡製造的。

55. <u>C. C.</u> is usually written in an e-mail or at the end of a business letter before the names of the people who will receive a copy.
C.C.通常是寫在電郵裡或商業信函結尾的收信人姓名之前，他們將會收到副本。

56. This line has proved so popular that we regret to inform you that <u>it is out of stock</u>.
此貨物非常受歡迎，我們很遺憾地通知您沒有現貨。

57. Would you please <u>look into</u> this matter and send our order without further delay.
請您調查這件事情並盡速寄送訂單給我們。

58. Please <u>refer</u> to them for any information concerning our company.
請向他們詢問有關本公司的任何資料。

59. The distribution problem has finally been solved. <u>However</u>, another problem has arisen.
銷售的問題解決了，然而，另一個問題卻出現了。

60. Your claim has been passed on to our insurance company, who will <u>get in touch with you</u> soon.
您的索賠已經轉達給我方的保險公司，他們會盡速與您聯絡。

61. We specialize in <u>fashionable and affordable</u> footwear.
我們專門經營時髦且價格實惠的鞋子。

62. Our prices are relatively low in comparison with theirs.

我們的價格跟他們比，相對較低。

63. May we suggest that you visit our showrooms in Los Angeles where you can see a wide range of units?

我們能否建議您參觀位在洛杉磯的貨樣陳列室，您可以看見各式各樣的產品？

64. We are interested in importing Swiss cheese and would appreciate receiving your current catalog and export price list.

我們有興趣進口瑞士起士，並感謝如能收到您們當前的目錄和出口價目表。

65. The new model is much lighter than the old one.

新的模型比舊的輕得多。

66. The following is a list of our best-selling products.

下面列出我們最暢銷的商品。

67. Regarding the damaged goods, we have filed a claim with the insurance company.

關於損壞的貨物，我們已經向保險公司提出索賠。

68. To a Briton, 5/3/13 is 5 March 2016.

對英國人而言，5/3/13 是 2016 年 3 月 5 日。

69. Our prices are considerably lower than those of our competitors for goods of similar quality.

對於相似品質的貨物，我們的價格跟競爭對手比起來相對的低。

70. We sent you a fax on October 12 requesting some information about your notebook computers.

我們於 10 月 12 日傳真給您，詢問一些關於筆記型電腦的資訊。

71. We can supply from stock and will have no trouble meeting your delivery date.

我們可以立即交貨，同時不會延遲交貨日期。

72. We enclose our check for $1,530.75 in payment of your invoice number A531.

我們附上 1,530.75 元的支票，用以支付您編號 A531 的發票。

73. Three cases in the consignment were missing on arrival.

運送的三箱貨物於抵達時不見了。

74. In addition to the trade discount stated, we would allow you a special first-order discount of 3%.

除了所述的貿易折扣外，我們給予您特別的第一次訂貨折扣 3%。

75. This product is not only of the highest quality but also very reasonably priced.

這個產品不只是最高品質，而且是合理地訂價。

76. Under the circumstances, we have no choice but to cancel the order.

在這種情況下，我們別無選擇，只能取消訂單。

77. The term "middle of a month" in the letter of credit shall be construed as the 11th to the 20th.

信用狀條款「中旬」解釋為該月第 11 日到第 20 日。

78. This offer will be withdrawn if not accepted before June 15, 2016.

此報價如在 2016 年 6 月 15 日前沒有接受的話，將會被撤回。

79. We will grant you a 3% discount if your order value is over ￡15,000 for one shipment.

如果您每批貨物的訂單價值超過 15,000 元，我方會給貴公司 3%的折扣。

80. We have instructed our bankers to <u>amend</u> the L/C.

我們已經指示銀行修改信用狀。

81. Please <u>settle</u> the overdue payments immediately.

請立刻結清逾期的款項。

82. Our delivery will be a week early, so we'd like to <u>move up</u> the payment date as well.

我們的交貨日期將提前一個星期，所以也想提前付款日期。

83. We have the pleasure to introduce <u>ourselves</u> as an import agent.

我方很高興地自我介紹為一進口代理商。

84. Please open the relative <u>L/C</u> as soon as possible so we can arrange shipment without delay.

請盡快開發相關的信用狀，讓我方可立即安排裝貨。

85. According to UCP 600, the term "on or about June 5th" in the L/C shall be construed <u>as from May 31st to June 10th</u>.

根據 UCP 600 規定，信用狀條款「6 月 5 日前後」，應解釋為 5 月 31 日至 6 月 10 日。

86. We <u>specialize</u> in high quality bicycles.

我們專門經營高品質的腳踏車。

87. A: What do you do?

B: I'm a <u>sales assistant</u>.

您從事哪一行？

我是銷售助理。

88. A: I've got an appointment with Mr. Smith.

B: <u>When is he expecting you</u>?

我和史密斯先生有約。

他期待您何時去？

89. A: With less than three weeks for transit, they'd better go by air.

　B: Right. That way they'll arrive in time for the trade show.

運送時間少於三個禮拜，最好是用空運的方式。

對的。這樣貨物可及時抵達貿易展。

90. A: This clock comes with batteries, doesn't it?

　B: No. I'm afraid they're sold separately.

出售的時鐘有附帶電池，不是嗎？

不是。恐怕是分開來賣的。

91. A: How would you like your coffee?

　B: Black, please.

您想要什麼樣的咖啡？

請給我黑咖啡。

92. A: Where do you know Jack from?

　B: I used to work with him.

您是在何種情況下認識傑克的？

我曾與他共事過。

93. A: Can I speak to Mr. Johnson please?

　B: I'm sorry but he's not here right now. Can I take a message?

我可以和強森先生說話嗎？

抱歉，他現在不在這裡。有需要留言嗎？

94. Do you have A325 in stock?

A325 有現貨嗎？

95. We are pleased to quote as follows:

很高興報價如下：

96. Your payment is three months overdue.
   您的貨款已逾期三個月。

97. Since May 1 is a holiday, we will send your shipment on May 2.
   因為 5 月 1 日放假，所以我們會在 5 月 2 日送貨。

98. Because of your long association with our company, we will offer you a 25% discount off the list price.
   因貴方與本公司長期合作，我們將照定價打 75 折給您。

99. We are in urgent need of these goods.
   我們急需這些貨品。

100. It would be impossible for us to make any further reduction.
    我們不可能再降價。

101. In spite of the rise in raw material prices, we maintain our existing prices.
    儘管原物料價格上漲，我們仍維持原價。

102. The invoice will be sent to 179 Maple Street, the address you provided in your order.
    發票會寄至您訂單上所提供的地址：楓林街 179 號。

103. We are sending you our samples under separate cover.
    我們另外寄上樣品。

104. Please advise us by email once the goods have been shipped.
    一旦貨物裝船，請電郵告知。

105. Our supplier has informed us that the item is out of stock at present.

供應商告知該商品目前已無庫存。

106. We have to inform you that the model in question has already been discontinued.
該機種已停產，特此通知。

107. He asked you to reply to his message at the earliest possible time.
他要求您盡快回函。

108. Which of the following abbreviations is not related to companies?
下列哪一項簡寫與公司無關？

109. Which one is not a standard address abbreviation?
下列哪一項不是標準住址的簡寫？

110. Which of the following terms is not related to payment?
下列哪一項條件與付款無關？

第二節　勞動部勞力發展署測驗試題範例

一、試題範例

㈠完成下列翻譯（空格裡不只一字）：

①我方樂意與貴公司建立商業關係。

We would be delighted to _____ with you.

②付款將透過銀行轉帳。

Payment will be made by _____ .

③如您能寄一些材料樣本，將感激不盡。

It _____ if you could send some samples of the material.

④您的貨款已逾期三個月。

Your payment is _____ .

⑤儘管原物料價格上漲，我們仍維持原價。

_____ in raw material prices, we maintain our existing prices.

標準答案

題　號	答　案
①	establish business relations/enter into business relations
②	bank transfer.
③	would be appreciated
④	three months overdue.
⑤	In spite of the rise/Despite the rise

㈡臺灣貿易有限公司係一家出口貿易公司，專門經營汽車零件出口，今擬拓銷至海外市場，並已擬妥一封開發信，請於下列答案語群中，選出最適當之答案，並將答案代號填入答案紙，完成開發信之內容。（本題語群選項不可重複）

TAIWAN TRADING CO., LTD.

P.O. Box xxx-1966

Taipei, Taiwan

Tel: 886-2-2307-xxxx

Fax: 886-2-2307-xxxx

Date: July 25, 2006

Importadora Davis Ltda.

Diagonal Oriente 1704

Providencia Santiago,

Chile

Attn: Import Manager

Dear Sirs,

<u>Re: Auto Parts</u>

Through the courtesy of World Buyers Information, we have ___①___ of your esteemed name & address, and we take the liberty of introducing captioned products for you, hope these items will meet your ___②___ .

For your information, we have been manufacturing/exporting this ___③___ for many years, we have been enjoying a good sale of our products all over the world, and are now desirous of expanding our market to your end.

We enclose our newest catalogue as well as ___④___ for your reference. If our products are suitable or you find any size interesting, please let us know without hesitation, we assure you of our best service at all times.

We look forward to establishing ___⑤___ relationship with you soon and hope to receive your early reply.

Very truly yours,

Taiwan Trading Co., Ltd.

Calvin Lee

General Manager

CL/yy

Encl: Catalogue and Price List

答 案 代 號	答 案 語 群
A	inquiry
B	product
C	payment
D	price list
E	requirement
F	advice
G	business
H	quality
I	market
J	learned

標準答案

題號	①	②	③	④	⑤
答案	J	E	B	D	G

二、解析

答案代號	答案語群	中文
A	inquiry	詢價
B	product	產品
C	payment	付款
D	price list	價目表
E	requirement	所要求之產品
F	advice	通知
G	business	商業、業務
H	quality	品質
I	market	市場
J	learned	得知、獲悉

1. courtesy of：承蒙……的允許

2. we have learned of……：我方獲悉……

3. take the liberty of……：冒昧……

4. ...meet your requirement：……符合貴公司的需求

5. ...manufacturing/exporting this product for many years：……製造／出口此產品已多年

6. a good sale：銷售佳

7. all over the world：全世界

8. are desirous of：希望、渴望

9. expanding our market to your end：擴展我方市場至貴地

10. We enclose our newest catalogue as well as price list for your reference.
   我方隨函附上最新的目錄和價目表，敬供貴公司參考。

11. establishing business relationship with you soon...：盡速與貴公司建立業務關係

12. without hesitation：勿遲疑

13. look forward to：期望、盼望

第三節 練習題

一、開發信

(一) MINWANG TRADING CO., LTD.係一家出口貿易公司，專門經營輕工業產品出口，今擬拓銷至海外市場，並已擬妥一封開發信，請於下列答案語群中，選出最適當之答案，並將答案代號填入答案紙，完成開發信之內容。（本題語群選項不可重複）

答案代號	答案語群
A	claim
B	learned
C	establishing
D	catalogue
E	special
F	manufacturers
G	name
H	specific
I	discount
J	view
K	hope
L	distributor
M	general
N	quotations
O	effort
P	forward
Q	appreciate
R	favorable
S	business
T	merchandise

MINWANG TRADEING CO., LTD.

P.O. Box ××××-1234

Taipei City, Taiwan

Fax: 886-2-2331-××××

Tel: 886-2-2331-××××

Date: March 8, 20—

Tada Trading Co., Ltd.

Tokyo Tada Building, 211

Tokyo, Japan

Dear Sir or Madam,

We ___①___ from the International Department of Cathay United Bank that you are a reputable ___②___ in your area. We write this letter with a ___③___ to getting into business with you in near future.

We deal in the import and export of light industrial products for more than twenty years. With years of ___④___ we have expanded our ___⑤___ scope impressively and now we deal in nearly 100 kinds of ___⑥___ . We've succeeded in ___⑦___ trade relationship with many advanced ___⑧___ in France and have introduced a lot of excellent products abroad.

Enclosed please find our latest ___⑨___ together with price list for your initial reference.

We are looking ___⑩___ to your early reply.

Yours faithfully,

Minwang Trading Co., Ltd.

×××

Sales Manager

答案欄

題號	①	②	③	④	⑤	⑥	⑦	⑧	⑨	⑩
答案										

答案及解析：

標準答案

題號	①	②	③	④	⑤	⑥	⑦	⑧	⑨	⑩
答案	B	L	J	O	S	T	C	F	D	P

答案代號	答案語群	中文
A	claim	索賠
B	learned	獲悉
C	establishing	建立
D	catalogue	目錄
E	special	特別的
F	manufacturers	製造商
G	name	名字
H	specific	明確的
I	discount	折扣
J	view	視野
K	hope	希望
L	distributor	銷售者
M	general	一般的
N	quotations	報價單
O	effort	努力
P	forward	向前
Q	appreciate	感謝
R	favorable	有利的
S	business	業務
T	merchandise	商品

1. learned from...：從……獲悉

2. reputable distributor：信譽良好的銷售者

3. in your area：貴公司所在地區（貴地）

4. with a view to：為了……、以便……、目的在……（後接 Ving，較 in order to 正式）

5. getting into business with...：建立業務往來

6. in near future：最近、不久的將來

7. deal in：經營

8. light industrial products：輕工業產品

9. With years of effort：經過數年的努力

10. expanded our business scope：擴展我方的業務範圍

11. 100 kinds of merchandise：百種商品

12. succeeded in establishing trade relationship with...：成功的和……建立交易關係

13. advanced manufacturers：先進的製造商

14. Enclosed please find our latest catalogue：隨函附上最新產品目錄

15. for your initial reference：敬供貴公司作初步的參考

16. are looking forward to：期待、期望

(二) K TOP TRADING CO., LTD.係一家貿易公司，專門經營鐘錶出口，今擬拓銷至海外市場，並已擬妥一封開發信，請於下列答案語群中，選出最適當之答案，並將答案代號填入答案紙，完成開發信之內容。（本題語群選項不可重複）

答案代號	答案語群
A	apologize
B	specialized
C	acknowledge
D	gain
E	satisfactory
F	advantage
G	range
H	deal
I	reputation
J	distribution
K	suitable
L	approval
M	latest
N	opportunity
O	got
P	particular
Q	well
R	special
S	steady
T	handle

K TOP TRADING CO., LTD.

P.O. Box ×××-1591

Taipei, Taiwan

Tel: 886-2-5611-××××

Fax: 886-2-5611-××××

Date: March 19, 20—

Saracen Trading Co., Ltd.

Denso Hall, Kuwait

Dear Sir,

We have ___①___ your name from the CHAMBER OF COMMERCE and are glad to introduce ourselves to you as a ___②___ company handling light products.

Our firm, which is located in the South of Taiwan, a new established importing and exporting light products. By now, we have been doing business with customers from many countries, and enjoy a high ___③___ . As one of the biggest dealers in Taiwan, we ___④___ a wide ___⑤___ of clocks, such as traditional Chinese clocks, electric clocks and so on.

Our experience of doing business with foreign customers has enabled us to know that Chinese clocks are selling ___⑥___ because of their attractive design, fine quality and low price. So we are confident that our commodities will be proved to be quite ___⑦___ to your customers.

We are now taking this ___⑧___ to express our desire to establish direct business relations with you on the basis of equality and mutual benefit. For your selection, we are sending you a copy of our ___⑨___ catalogue that might be ___⑩___ for your market.

Yours faithfully,

K Top Trading Co., Ltd.

×××

Manager

答案欄

題號	①	②	③	④	⑤	⑥	⑦	⑧	⑨	⑩
答案										

答案及解析：

標準答案

題號	①	②	③	④	⑤	⑥	⑦	⑧	⑨	⑩
答案	O	B	I	T	T	G	Q	E	N	M	K

答案代號	答案語群	中文
A	apologize	道歉
B	specialized	專業的
C	acknowledge	承認
D	gain	得到
E	satisfactory	令人滿意的
F	advantage	利益
G	range	範圍
H	deal	處理、經營
I	reputation	信譽
J	distribution	分配
K	suitable	適合的
L	approval	同意
M	latest	最新的
N	opportunity	機會
O	got	獲悉
P	particular	特別的
Q	well	很好的
R	special	特別的
S	steady	穩定的
T	handle	經營

1. We have got your name from...：我方透過……獲悉貴公司大名

2. introduce ourselves to you a...：謹向貴公司介紹本公司為……

3. a specialized company：一家專業的公司

4. handling：經營

5. is located in...：位於……

6. enjoy a high reputation：享有很高的信譽

7. we handle a wide range of clocks：我方經營鐘錶的範圍很廣（種類很多）

   * deal in：經營

8. such as：例如

9. and so on：等等

10. selling well：暢銷、銷路佳

11. attractive design：引人注目的設計

12. be proved：被證實

13. be quite satisfactory to...：令……非常滿意的

14. taking this opportunity to...：藉此機會……

15. on the basis of equality and mutual benefit：基於平等互惠之利益

16. ...latest catalogue：最新的目錄

17. ...be suitable for your market：適合貴方市場

二、詢價信

（一）TAIPEI INTERNATIONAL CORP.係一家臺灣的貿易公司，專門經營傢俱出口，今收到一封來自美國 ZENLOON TRADING CO., LTD.的詢價信，請於下列答案語群中，選出最適當之答案，並將答案代號填入答案紙，完成詢價信之內容。（本題語群選項不可重複）

答案代號	答案語群
A	active
B	interesting
C	payment
D	regards
E	relations
F	studying
G	attention
H	competitive
I	regret
J	cooperation
K	detail
L	retailing
M	illustrated

答案代號	答案語群
N	manufacturers
O	unacceptable
P	interested
Q	Therefore
R	appreciated
S	delivery
T	Besides

ZENLOON TRADING CO., LTD.

131-10 Maple Avenue Flushing,

New York 11355 USA

TAIPEI INTERNATIONAL CORP.

P.O. Box ×××-7537

Taipei , Taiwan

Date: May 7, 20—

Dear Sirs,

Thank you for your letter of May 2 and we are glad to learn of your desire to establish business ___①___ with us.

Many inquiries have been received from ___②___ shops in our country about furniture and therefore we are sure that there would be ___③___ demands. After carefully studying your ___④___ catalogue, we wish to inform you that we are especially ___⑤___ in the Art No. T1234. We shall appreciate your quoting us the most ___⑥___ prices based on CIFC3 New York. ___⑦___ , we wonder whether you can effect shipment during June on purchase of quantities of not less than one 40' FCL. Our usual terms of ___⑧___ are by D/P at 60 days sight.

Thank you for all your ___⑨___ .

Your immediate attention to this matter will be highly ___⑩___ .

Yours sincerely,

Zenloon Trading Co., Ltd.

×××

Manager

答案欄

題號	①	②	③	④	⑤	⑥	⑦	⑧	⑨	⑩
答案										

答案及解析：

標準答案

題號	①	②	③	④	⑤	⑥	⑦	⑧	⑨	⑩
答案	E	L	A	M	P	H	T	C	J	R

答案代號	答案語群	中文
A	active	活躍的
B	interesting	有興趣的
C	payment	付款
D	regards	致意
E	relations	關係
F	studying	研究
G	attention	注意
H	competitive	有競爭力的
I	regret	遺憾
J	cooperation	合作
K	detail	明細
L	retailing	零售的
M	illustrated	圖示的
N	manufacturers	製造商
O	unacceptable	無法接受的
P	interested	有興趣的
Q	Therefore	因此
R	appreciated	感激的
S	delivery	交貨
T	besides	而且、除……之外

1. establish business relations with us：與貴公司建立業務關係

2. Many enquiries have been received from retailing shops...：我方已接到許多零售商對……的詢價

3. there would be active demands：將會有活躍的銷路（暢銷）

4. illustrated catalogue：圖示目錄

5. we are especially interested in...：我方對……特別感興趣

　* 人＋ be interested in...：某人對……有興趣

6. the most competitive prices：最有競爭力的價格

7. Besides：此外

8. not less than：至少

9. 40' FCL：40 呎整櫃

10. terms of payment：付款條件

11. Thank you for all your cooperation.：感謝貴公司的合作

12. Your immediate attention to this matter will be hightly appreciated.：貴公司對此事立即處理，我方將無限感激

㈡FORTTEK TRADING CO., LTD.係一家臺灣的貿易公司，專門經營手錶出口，今收到一封來自馬來西亞SCUBA INTERNATIONAL TRADING CORPORATION.的詢價信，請於下列答案語群中，選出最適當之答案，並將答案代號填入答案紙，完成詢價信之內容。（本題語群選項不可重複）

答案代號	答案語群
A	studying
B	delay
C	arbitration
D	following
E	state
F	past
G	place
H	awaited
I	wait
J	details
K	provide
L	pass

答案代號	答案語群
M	offer
N	rock-bottom
O	cheap
P	on
Q	like
R	want
S	agent
T	together

SCUBA INTERNATIONAL TRADING CORPORATION

Plot 564-C, Lorong Perusahaan Baru 2,

Prai Industrial Estate, 13600 Prai, Penang, Malaysia

Tel: 01-11 -4533×××

Fax : 01-11-4533×××

FORTTEK TRADING CO., LTD.

Date: March 30, 20—

P.O. Box ×××-1456

Dear Sir/Madam,

Thank you for your letter ___①___ with your catalogue. We are glad to learn that you could supply wrist watches, as we have received inquiries from our clients in this area. Therefore please let us have full ___②___ on your products so we can ___③___ on the information to them.

After carefully ___④___ your catalogue, we found the ___⑤___ items suitable:

Art. No. CH277, CH693

We would ___⑥___ to ___⑦___ an initial order against the above items for one 40' container each with shipment, please quote us your ___⑧___ price CIFC5 Vancouver. Will you please also ___⑨___ your earlier delivery date, your terms of payment, and discounts for regular purchases. Your soon reply is ___⑩___ with much appreciation.

Yours truly,

Scuba International Trading Corporation

×××

Manager

答案欄

題號	①	②	③	④	⑤	⑥	⑦	⑧	⑨	⑩
答案										

答案及解析：

標準答案

題號	①	②	③	④	⑤	⑥	⑦	⑧	⑨	⑩
答案	T	J	L	A	D	Q	G	N	E	H

答案代號	答案語群	中文
A	studying	研究、研讀
B	delay	延誤
C	arbitration	仲裁
D	following	如下
E	state	陳述、敘述
F	past	超過
G	place	v.訂貨
H	awaited	等候
I	wait	等候
J	details	明細
K	provide	提供
L	pass	傳遞
M	offer	v.提供、n.報價
N	rock-bottom	最低
O	cheap	便宜
P	on	×
Q	like	喜歡
R	want	想要
S	agent	代理人
T	together	一起

1. together with：和、與

2. are glad to...：高興、樂意……

3. clients：客戶

4. in this area：本地

5. Therefore：因此、所以

6. full details：全部的明細、完整的明細

7. pass on...：傳遞給……

8. studying your catalogue：研讀貴公司的目錄

9. the following items：下列項目

10. would like to：想要

11. place an initial order：初次下訂單

12. rock-bottom price：最低價

　　* 價錢高低：價格以 high、low 形容，商品以 dear (expensive)、cheap 形容

　　　如：The price is too high for us.

　　　　　The goods is so cheap.

13. state your earlier delivery date：陳述貴公司最早交貨日期

14. is awaited with：敬候

三、報價函

㈠ DARAY INTERNATIONAL CO., LTD. 係一家貿易公司，專門經營玩具出口，今擬對美國的 YIHCHUUAN TOY CO., LTD. 報價，並已擬妥一封報價信，請於下列答案語群中，選出最適當之答案，並將答案代號填入答案紙，完成報價信之內容。（本題語群選項不可重複）

答案代號	答案語群
A	looking
B	learned
C	quote
D	catalogue
E	enquiry
F	manufacturers
G	advantage
H	learn

答案代號	答案語群
I	reply
J	irrevocable
K	quotation
L	receipt
M	validity
N	Commodity
O	favor
P	reputable
Q	exhibit
R	valid
S	receiving
T	clients

DARAY INTERNATIONAL CO., LTD.

P.O. Box ×××-5689

Taipei City 100, Taiwan

Tel: 886-2-2391-××××

Fax: 886-2-2391-××××

April 12, 20—

YIHCHUUAN TOY CO., LTD.

9812 Whithorn Dr. Houston, N.Y. 77095, U.S.A

Dear Sirs,

Thank you for your ___①___ of March 7th. We are very glad to ___②___ that you are interested in our products. Recently we have received a large number of orders from our ___③___ and it seems that the demand is still increasing. We hope the same thing will happen in your market and are very glad to ___④___ as follows:

___⑤___ : Toy Car

　　　○ART.NO.111 USD 21. 17 /PIECE FOBC3 KEELUNG

　　　○ART.NO.222 USD 22. 27 /PIECE CFRC3 NEW YORK

　　　○ART.NO.333 USD 22. 38 /PIECE CIFC3 NEW YORK

Packing: Packed in cartons of 12 pieces each one.

Shipment: Shipment is to be effected within 30 days after ___⑥___ of the relevant L/C, but not later than May 31.

Insurance: To be covered by the seller for 110% of total invoice value against all risks and Strikes Risks.

Payment: By ___⑦___ sight letter of credit in our ___⑧___.

This quotation is ___⑨___ for 3 days and we are ___⑩___ forward to receiving your order.

Yours faithfully,

Daray International Trading Co., Ltd.

×××

Manager

答案欄

題號	①	②	③	④	⑤	⑥	⑦	⑧	⑨	⑩
答案										

答案及解析：

標準答案

題號	①	②	③	④	⑤	⑥	⑦	⑧	⑨	⑩
答案	E	H	T	C	N	L	J	O	R	A

答案代號	答案語群	中文
A	looking	期望
B	learned	獲悉
C	quote	v.報價
D	catalogue	目錄
E	enquiry	詢價信
F	manufacturers	製造商
G	advantage	利益

答案代號	答案語群	中文
H	learn	獲悉
I	reply	回覆
J	irrevocable	不可撤銷的
K	quotation	報價信
L	receipt	收到
M	validity	adj.有效的
N	Commodity	商品
O	favor	恩惠
P	reputable	有信譽的
Q	exhibit	展示
R	valid	v.有效
S	receiving	收到
T	clients	顧客、客戶

1. Thank you for your enquiry of March 7th.

   謝謝貴公司 3 月 7 日的詢價信。

2. We are very glad to learn...：我方非常高興獲悉……（be glad to ＋ v.）

3. Recently：最近

4. We have received a large number of orders from our clients.

   從我方的客戶接到大量的訂單。

5. it seems that：似乎、好像

6. ... are very glad to quote as follows：我方非常樂意給予如下報價（be glad to ＋ v.）

7. Commodity: Toy Car：商品：玩具車

8. ...after receipt of the relevant L/C：收到相關信用狀後……（或 after receiving the relevant L/C）

9. not later than：不超過

10. By irrevocable sight letter of credit in our favor.

    以我方為受益人的不可撤銷即期信用狀。

11. This quotation is valid for 3 days.

    本報價信有效期為 3 天。

12.... we are looking forward to receiving your order.：我方期盼能接到貴公司的訂單

（二）WESTERN TRADING COMPANY 係臺灣一家貿易公司，專門經營出口業務，今擬對泰國的 KINGHOSIN GENERAL TRADING CO., LTD. 報價，並已擬妥一封報價信，請於下列答案語群中，選出最適當之答案，並將答案代號填入答案紙，完成報價信之內容。（本題語群選項不可重複）

答案代號	答案語群
A	consider
B	instruct
C	advise
D	assure
E	furnish
F	emphasize
G	advantage
H	attractive
I	affect
J	pleasure
K	requested
L	reasonable
M	upon
N	sharp
O	specification
P	standard
Q	anticipating
R	expect
S	stage
T	in

WESTERN TRADING COMMPANY

P.O. Box 123-××××

Taipei, Taiwan

Date: May 12, 20—

KINGHOSIN GENERAL TRADING CO., LTD.

191/54, 57, 18th Floor, Cti Tower

Rachadpisedroad, Klongtoey,

Bangkok, Thailand

Dear Ms. Lee,

Thank you for your inquiry of May 7 and we are very please to hear from you again.

We wish to ___①___ that samples you ___②___ has be sent to you earlier today. Kindly inform us ___③___ receipt of the said samples. As to the relevant fee, in order to facilitate you to promote sales in the initial ___④___ , we ___⑤___ them to you free of charge. We believe through our mutual efforts, there will be active demand in your market.

We are now pleased to quote as follows:

Art.No.	Pc./ctn.	Mea.(cm)	G.W.(kg)	N.W.(kg)	Unit Price(USD)		
					FOBC3	CFRC3	CIFC3
FG002	12	50×50×30	37	35	7.11	7.69	7.72
RG012	12	50×50×30	38	36	7.37	8.01	8.04

Min. Qty: 40' FCL

Packing: To be packed in export ___⑥___ packing.

Shipment: To be shipped by end of June.

Payment: Payment shall be effected by T/T immediately after sale of goods.

Insurance: On CIF basis, effected by us covering 110% of the invoice value against ICC(A) .

This quotation is only valid for 10 days.

You are cordially invited to take ___⑦___ of this ___⑧___ offer. We are ___⑨___ a large order from the Thailand, and that will cause a ___⑩___ rise in price.

We look forward to receiving your order.

Yours sincerely,

Western Trading Company

×××

Manager

答案欄

題號	①	②	③	④	⑤	⑥	⑦	⑧	⑨	⑩
答案										

答案及解析：

標準答案

題號	①	②	③	④	⑤	⑥	⑦	⑧	⑨	⑩
答案	C	K	M	S	E	P	G	H	Q	N

答案代號	答案語群	中文
A	consider	認為、考慮
B	instruct	指示
C	advise	告知
D	assure	確保
E	furnish	提供
F	emphasize	強調
G	advantage	利益
H	attractive	有吸引力的
I	affect	影響
J	pleasure	樂意
K	requested	請求、要求
L	reasonable	合理的
M	upon	✕
N	sharp	敏銳的、激烈的
O	specification	規格
P	standard	標準
Q	anticipating	預期
R	expect	期望
S	stage	階段、時期
T	in	✕

1. advise：告知

2. requested：請求、要求

3. be sent to：寄出

4. upon receipt of...：一收到……

5. the said samples：該樣品、上述之樣品

6. As to...：至於

  * As to ＋事物，As for ＋人

7. in order to：為了……

8. facilitate：促進

9. in the initial stage：在初期

10. furnish：提供

11. free of charge：免費

12. mutual efforts：互相努力

13. active demand：暢銷

14. as follows：如下、如次

15. export standard packing：出口標準包裝

16. by end of June：6 月底之前

17. cordially：誠懇地、衷心地

18. take advantage of：利用

19. attractive offer：有吸引力的報價

20. anticipating：預期

21. a large order：大量訂單

22. a sharp rise in price：價格急遽上揚

四、催款信

GOLDEN LEAF TRADING CORPORATION為臺灣一家貿易公司，因交易對手J-SHARP INTERNATIONAL CORP.尚有尾款未付清，今擬向 J-SHARP INTERNATIONAL CORP.催款，並已擬妥一封催款信，請於下列答案語群中，選出最適當之答案，並將答案代號填入答案紙，完成催款信之內容。（本題語群選項不可重複）

答案代號	答案語群
A	waited
B	explain
C	balance
D	pay
E	cleared
F	concerning
G	opportunity
H	receipt
I	unless
J	attention
K	allow
L	alternative
M	of
N	cover
O	enclosed
P	remittance
Q	action
R	proceedings
S	recover
T	as

GOLDEN LEAF TRADING CORPORATION

P.O. Box 123-××××

Taipei, Taiwan

Tel: 886-2-2973-××××

Fax: 886-2-2973-××××

Date: May 31, 20—

J-SHARP INTERNATIONAL CORP.

200 Westlake Park Blvd.#1200

Houston, U.S.A.

Dear Mr. Theopolis,

I wrote to you on two occasions, March 21 and April 14,　①　the Account No. TYG99014 which now has an outstanding ② of USD21,120.00.

I have ③ three months for either a reply to ④ why the balance has not been ⑤ , or a remittance, but have received neither.

Although I am reluctant to take legal ⑥ to recover the amount, you leave me no ⑦ . Therefore, ⑧ I receive your ⑨ within the next 10 days, my solicitors will be instructed to start ⑩ to recover the debt.

Your sincerely,

Golden Leaf Trading Corporation

×××

Manager

答案欄

題號	①	②	③	④	⑤	⑥	⑦	⑧	⑨	⑩
答案										

答案及解析：

標準答案

題號	①	②	③	④	⑤	⑥	⑦	⑧	⑨	⑩
答案	F	C	A	B	E	Q	L	I	P	R

答案代號	答案語群	中文
A	waited	等待
B	explain	解釋
C	balance	餘額、尾款
D	pay	付款
E	cleared	結清
F	concerning	關於
G	opportunity	機會

答案代號	答案語群	中文
H	receipt	收據
I	unless	除非
J	attention	注意
K	allow	允許
L	alternative	選擇
M	of	×
N	cover	包含
O	enclosed	隨函附上
P	remittance	匯款
Q	action	行動
R	proceedings	訴訟
S	recover	收回
T	as	×

1. on two occasions：兩次
2. concerning：關於
3. outstanding balance of USD21,120.00：未償付的尾款 USD21,120.00
4. I have waited three months.
   我方已等待三個月了。
5. a reply to explain why the balance has not been cleared：回函解釋為什麼尾款尚未付清
6. I am reluctant to...：我方不願意……
7. take legal action：採取法律行動
8. recover the amount：收回欠款
9. you leave me no alternative：貴公司讓我方沒有選擇的餘地
10. unless：除非
11. I receive your remittance：我方接到貴公司的匯款
12. solicitors：事務律師
13. be instructed to：被指示、被吩咐
14. start proceedings：提出訴訟
15. recover the debt：收回債務

五、索賠函

　　LENOVO GROUP TRADING CO., LTD. 為臺灣一家貿易公司，因交易對手NITTO DENKO CORPORATION 所交貨物有部分破損，今擬向 NITTO DENKO CORPORATION 索賠，並已擬妥一封索賠信，請於下列答案語群中，選出最適當之答案，並將答案代號填入答案紙，完成索賠信之內容。（本題語群選項不可重複）

答案代號	答案語群
A	inspection
B	survey
C	find
D	regret
E	responsible
F	length
G	because
H	contents
I	confirmed
J	easy
K	settlement
L	claim
M	due
N	refer
O	end
P	identify
Q	on
R	by
S	follows
T	forward

LENOVO GROUP TRADING CO., LTD.

P.O. Box 123-×××××

Tel: 886-2-5973-×××××

Fax: 886-2-5973-×××××

Date: November 15, 20—

NITTO DENKO CORPORATION

6411 Ivy Lane, Suite 300, Grennbelt,

MD 20770, U.S.A

Dear Sirs,

We   ①   to sales contract No.546 covering the purchase of 200 metric tons of cement.

We telexed you   ②   November 7 informing you that the consignment arrived on October 20.

On   ③   , we found that 180 bags had burst and that the   ④   , estimated at 9000 kgs, had been irretrievably lost.

We proceeded to have a   ⑤   report made. The report has now   ⑥   our initial findings.

The report indicates that the loss was   ⑦   to the use of substandard bags for which you, the supplies, are   ⑧   .

 On the strength of the survey report, we hereby register our claim against you as   ⑨   :

Short delivered quantity	USD180
Survey charges	USD50
Total claimed	USD230

We enclose survey report No.TS6478 and look forward to early   ⑩   of the claim.

Yours faithfully,

Lenovo Group Trading Co., Ltd.

×××

Manager

答案欄

題號	①	②	③	④	⑤	⑥	⑦	⑧	⑨	⑩
答案										

答案及解析：

標準答案

題號	①	②	③	④	⑤	⑥	⑦	⑧	⑨	⑩
答案	N	Q	A	H	B	I	M	E	S	K

答案代號	答案語群	中文
A	inspection	檢驗
B	survey	公證
C	find	發現
D	regret	遺憾
E	responsible	責任
F	length	長度
G	because	因為
H	contents	含量、內容
I	confirmed	確認
J	easy	容易
K	settlement	清償
L	claim	索賠
M	due	由於
N	refer	有關、參考
O	end	結束
P	identify	定義
Q	on	×
R	by	×
S	follows	跟隨
T	forward	期望

1. refer to：有關、針對

2. 200 metric tons of cement：200 公噸的水泥。

3. We telexed you on November 7 ...：我們在 11 月 7 日所發給貴公司的電文……

4. consignment：(1)託售貨物；(2)寄售

5. On inspection：檢驗

6. burst：破裂

7. contents：含量

8. estimated ：估計

9. irretrievably lost：無法彌補的損失

10. proceeded to：著手進行

11. survey report：公證報告

12. The report has now confirmed our initial findings.

   這份報告確認我方初步的調查結果。

13. due to：由於

14. substandard bags：不合標準的袋子

15. you, the supplies, are responsible：由貴公司（即供應商）負責

16. register our claim：提出我方的索賠

17. as follows：如下、如次

18. look forward to early settlement of the claim ：期盼貴公司能盡快清償我方的索
    賠要求

貿易流程

第一節　貿易流程內容解析

　　一般而言，貿易流程會因貿易型態、貿易結算（付款）方式、貿易條件及政府法規而有所差異，詳見表1。

表1　影響貿易流程各項因素

常見貿易型態	常用貿易結算方式	常用貿易條件	常見政府法規
1. 直接貿易	1. 匯付	1. FOB	1. 簽證制度
2. 間接貿易	2. 信用狀	2. CFR	2. 報關制度
3. 商業方式貿易	3. 託收	3. CIF	3. 報檢制度
4. 易貨方式貿易			

　　依據勞動部勞動力發展署所公布測驗試題範例，貿易流程圖以直接貿易、商業方式貿易、信用狀結算方式及FOB、CFR、CIF三種貿易條件為架構，結合了物流加上金流的概念。

　　所謂金流，即指貿易結算方式，目前國際貿易常見結算方式有匯付、信用狀和託收三種。以進出口貿易總金額計算，匯付方式已接近80%左右，此一轉變與世界先進國家一致，主因為企業不再以信用風險為唯一考量因素，加入企業本身現金流量、財務操作等其他因素後，愈來愈多企業已改採匯付方式。

　　以下介紹三種結算方式的貿易流程。

一、信用狀結算方式的貿易流程（勞動部勞動力發展署公布試題範例）

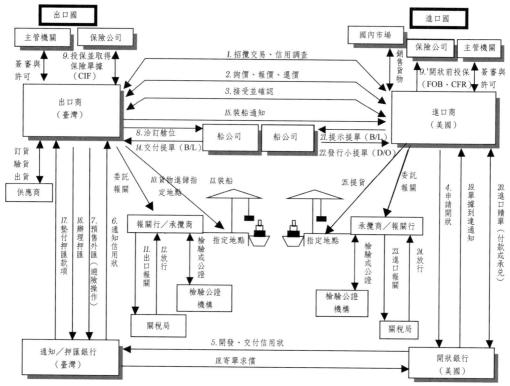

🎖️ 圖1　信用狀貿易流程圖

🎖️ 表2　信用狀結算方式貿易流程圖程序

1.	招攬交易、信用調查
2.	詢價、報價、還價
3.	接受並確認
4.	申請開狀
5.	開發、交付信用狀
6.	通知信用狀
7.	預售外匯（避險操作）
8.	洽訂艙位
9.	投保並取得保險單據（CIF）
9.'	開狀前投保（FOB、CFR）

10.	貨物進儲指定地點
11.	出口報關
12.	放行
13.	裝船
14.	交付提單（B/L）
15.	裝船通知
16.	辦理押匯
17.	墊付押匯款項
18.	寄單求償
19.	單據到達通知
20.	進口贖單（付款或承兌）
21.	提示提單（B/L）
22.	發行小提單（D/O）
23.	進口報關
24.	放行
25.	提貨

・解說

1. 招攬交易、信用調查

招攬交易：可透過出國拜訪、刊登廣告、寄發推銷函、參加展覽等方式。
信用調查：可透過往來銀行、中國輸出入銀行、徵信機構等管道。

2. 詢價、報價、還價

對於有興趣的商品，買方可進一步向賣方發函詢價，賣方則可根據買方需要的商品數量或其他條件進行報價，但在市場競爭激烈的今天，買方通常都同時向多家廠商詢價，在經過多方比價、還價後，慎選其中一家或一家以上的廠商合作。

3.接受並確認

買方接受報價，再經賣方最後確認，買賣契約即告成立。買賣契約一旦成立，雙方的權利義務也因而確定，賣方必須交付貨物，買方則必須支付貨款。

4.申請開狀

以信用狀為付款方式，買方必須先向往來銀行申請開發信用狀，買方若為首次申請開狀，應先申請外匯授信額度，再提供開狀申請書、輸入許可證或估價單、保險單正本及保險費收據副本（L/C 規定由國外廠商投保者免附）。開狀銀行受理買方之申請後，將依買方指示簽發信用狀。

5.開發、交付信用狀

開狀銀行開發信用狀後，一般都透過其在出口地之往來銀行通知信用狀。

6.通知信用狀

通知銀行接到國外開狀銀行開來之信用狀，就其外觀之真實性予以查對後，通知信用狀受益人前來領取。

7.預售外匯（避險操作）

賣方接受信用狀後，為避免未來因匯率變動而產生之外匯損失，可以先與銀行訂立遠期外匯交易，達成預售外匯之避險操作。

8.洽訂艙位

在 CIF 貿易條件下，賣方備妥貨物後，應向船公司洽訂艙位（Booking），由船公司發給裝貨單（Shipping Order；簡稱 S/O），裝貨單上會註明貨物進倉地點、結關日……，作為賣方辦理出口通關及裝船之文件。

9.投保並取得保險單據（CIF）

在 CIF 貿易條件下，賣方必須向保險公司投保貨物運輸保險，取得保險單（Insurance Policy）作為押匯文件。

9.'開狀前投保（FOB、CFR）

在 FOB、CFR 貿易條件下，賣方並無投保之義務，開狀銀行為保障其融資債權之安全性，通常會要求買方在申請開狀前，先投保貨物運輸保險。

10.貨物進儲指定地點

貨物於結關日（Closing Date）前運送到碼頭（或貨櫃場），經報關行現場人員確認無誤後，碼頭（或貨櫃場）便將進倉資料傳輸到海關，待海關查驗放行後，即可辦理裝船。

11.出口報關

報關行及碼頭（或貨櫃場）雙方均將資料傳輸到海關之後，由電腦依據報關人申報之 CCC 號列等因素判定以 C1（免審免驗）、C2（文件審核）或 C3（貨物查驗）方式通關。

12.放行

通關後若無其他問題即可放行，進行裝船作業。其中 C1 為電腦直接放行，C2 為文件審核→放行，C3 為貨物查驗→文件審核→放行。

13.裝船

海關放行後，貨物即可開始裝船，待裝船完成後，船上大副即在大副收據（Mate's Receipt；簡稱 M/R）上簽署並交予賣方。

14.交付提單（B/L）

待貨物完成裝船後，賣方憑大副收據並繳完船公司方面的費用，便可向船公司換取提單（Bill of Lading；簡稱 B/L）辦理出口押匯。

15.裝船通知

賣方在貨物裝船後發給買方有關貨物詳細裝運情況的通知，其目的在於讓買方做好籌措資金、付款、進口通關和提貨的準備，裝船通知應按契約或信用狀規定的時間發出。

16.辦理押匯

賣方依信用狀之規定，將貨物裝運出口後，備齊信用狀規定之匯票、商業發票、提單、保險單等有關貨運單據，向往來銀行申請押匯以貸得出口款項。

17.墊付押匯款項

出口押匯屬授信行為，押匯銀行於審單無誤後，扣除手續費、貼現息，將押匯款項墊付予賣方。

18.寄單求償

押匯銀行依信用狀指示，將相關貨運單據寄往開狀銀行或其指定銀行請求付款。

19.單據到達通知

開狀銀行通知買方貨運單據已達進口地。

20.進口贖單（付款或承兌）

買方付款（即期信用狀）或承兌（遠期信用狀）後，開狀銀行即將貨運單據交予買方。

21.提示提單（B/L）

買方向船公司提示提單，以換領小提單。

22.發行小提單（D/O）

船到目的港，買方繳清運費或相關費用後，即可憑提單（B/L）向船公司換發小提單（D/O），憑以辦理進口通關、提貨相關事宜。

23.進口報關

報關行將進口報關資料透過電子傳輸方式與關貿網路連線報關，由電腦依據報關人申報之 CCC 號列等因素判定以 C1（免審免驗）、C2（文件審核）或 C3（貨物查驗）方式通關。經海關查驗（或免驗）及繳納關稅後，海關即發出放行通知。

24.放行

C1為電腦直接放行，C2為文件審核→放行，C3為貨物查驗→文件審核→放行。

25.提貨

海關放行後，買方便可辦理提貨。

二、託收結算方式貿易流程

㈠付款交單（D/P）

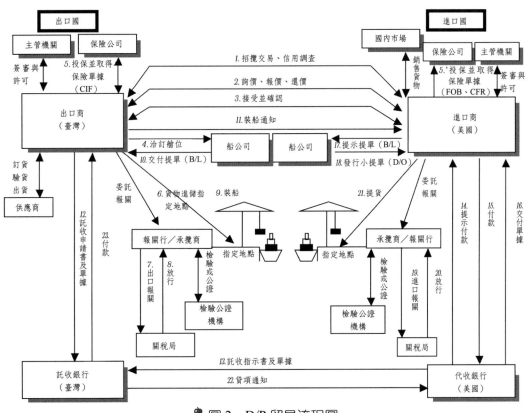

📖 圖 2　D/P 貿易流程圖

♟️表 3　D/P 方式貿易流程圖程序

1.	招攬交易、信用調查
2.	詢價、報價、還價
3.	接受並確認
4.	洽訂艙位
5.	投保並取得保險單據（CIF）
5.'	投保並取得保險單據（FOB、CFR）
6.	貨物進儲指定地點
7.	出口報關
8.	放行
9.	裝船
10.	交付提單（B/L）
11.	裝船通知
12.	託收申請書及單據
13.	託收指示書及單據
14.	提示付款
15.	付款
16.	交付單據
17.	提示提單（B/L）
18.	發行小提單（D/O）
19.	進口報關
20.	放行
21.	提貨
22.	貸項通知
23.	付款

(二) 承兌交單（D/A）

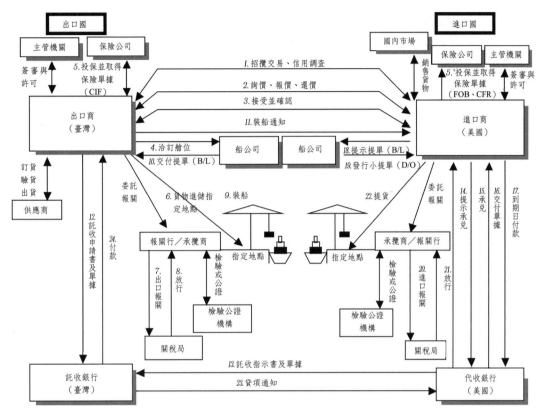

📖 圖 3　D/A 貿易流程圖

📖 表 4　D/A 方式貿易流程圖程序

1.	招攬交易、信用調查
2.	詢價、報價、還價
3.	接受並確認
4.	洽訂艙位
5.	投保並取得保險單據（CIF）
5.'	投保並取得保險單據（FOB、CFR）
6.	貨物進儲指定地點
7.	出口報關
8.	放行
9.	裝船

10.	交付提單（B/L）
11.	裝船通知
12.	託收申請書及單據
13.	託收指示書及單據
14.	提示承兌
15.	承兌
16.	交付單據
17.	到期日付款
18.	提示提單（B/L）
19.	發行小提單（D/O）
20.	進口報關
21.	放行
22.	提貨
23.	貸項通知
24.	付款

三、匯付結算方式貿易流程

匯付方式有電匯、信匯及票匯三種，其中以電匯最常見。付款方式則依交貨前後，分為交貨前付款，如 CWO、CIA；交貨後付款，如 CAD、Consignment、O/A、Instalment。下述貿易流程圖以電匯及 O/A 方式說明。

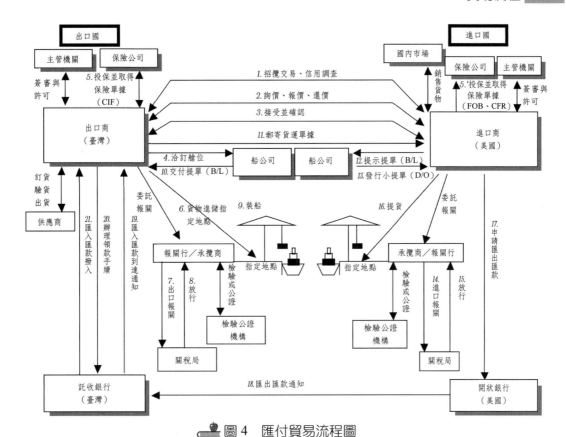

📖 圖 4　匯付貿易流程圖

📖 表 5　O/A 方式貿易流程圖程序

1.	招攬交易、信用調查
2.	詢價、報價、還價
3.	接受並確認
4.	洽訂艙位
5.	投保並取得保險單據（CIF）
5.'	投保並取得保險單據（FOB、CFR）
6.	貨物進儲指定地點
7.	出口報關
8.	放行
9.	裝船
10.	交付提單（B/L）
11.	郵寄貨運單據
12.	提示提單（B/L）
13.	發行小提單（D/O）

14.	進口報關
15.	放行
16.	提貨
17.	申請匯出匯款
18.	匯出匯款通知
19.	匯入匯款到達通知
20.	辦理領款手續
21.	匯入匯款撥入

第二節　勞動部勞動力發展署測驗試題範例

請依下列貿易流程圖，依序將①②③④⑤之步驟名稱填入答案欄內。

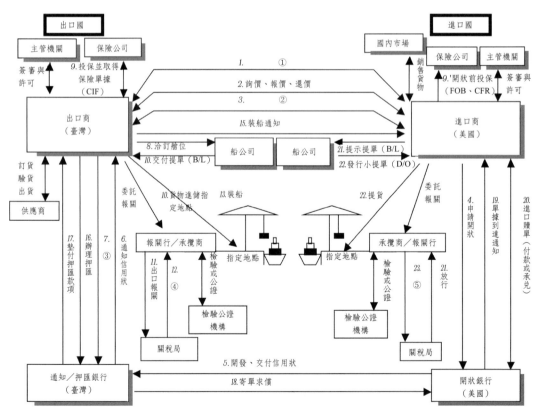

🍎 圖5　範例：貿易流程圖

🏆 標準答案

題　號	答　案
①	1. 招攬交易、信用調查
②	3. 接受並確認
③	7. 預售外匯（避險操作）
④	12. 放行
⑤	23. 進口報關

第三節　練習題

一、請依下列貿易流程圖，依序將①②③④⑤之步驟名稱填入答案欄內。

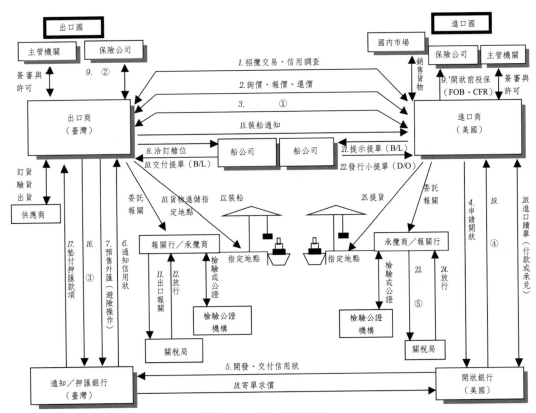

🏆 圖6　貿易流程圖

題　號	答　案
①	
②	
③	
④	
⑤	

二、請依下列貿易流程圖，依序將①②③④⑤之步驟名稱填入答案欄內。

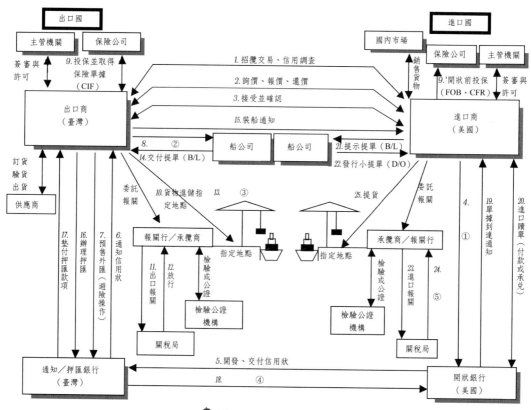

🍎 圖7　貿易流程圖

題　號	答　案
①	
②	
③	
④	
⑤	

三、請依下列貿易流程圖，依序將①②③④⑤之步驟名稱填入答案欄內。

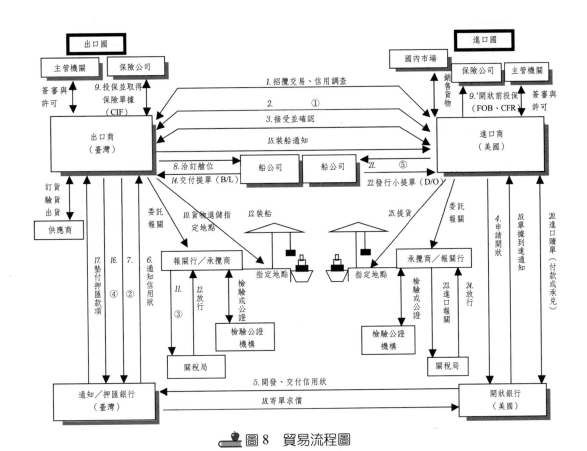

🍎 圖 8　貿易流程圖

題　號	答　案
①	
②	
③	
④	
⑤	

四、請依下列貿易流程圖，依序將①②③④⑤之步驟名稱填入答案欄內。

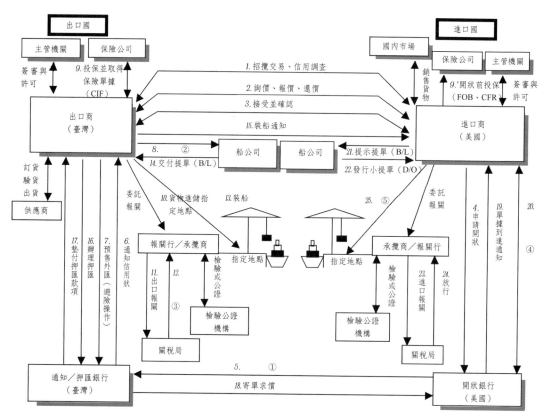

🍈 圖9　貿易流程圖

題　號	答　案
①	
②	
③	
④	
⑤	

五、請依下列貿易流程圖，依序將①②③④⑤之步驟名稱填入答案欄內。

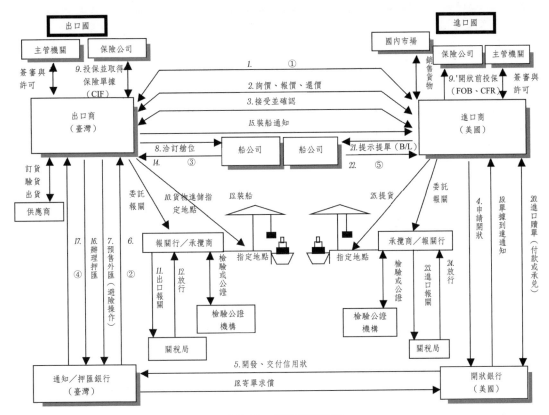

圖 10　貿易流程圖

題　號	答　案
①	
②	
③	
④	
⑤	

解　答

一、

題　號	答　案
①	3.接受並確認
②	9.投保並取得保險單據（CIF）
③	16.辦理押匯
④	19.單據到達通知
⑤	23.進口報關

二、

題　號	答　案
①	4.申請開狀
②	8.洽訂艙位
③	13.裝船
④	18.寄單求償
⑤	24.放行

三、

題　號	答　案
①	2.詢價、報價、還價
②	7.預售外匯（避險操作）
③	11.出口報關
④	16.辦理押匯
⑤	21.提示提單（B/L）

四、

題　號	答　案
①	5.開發、交付信用狀
②	8.洽訂艙位
③	12.放行
④	20.進口贖單（付款或承兌）
⑤	25.提貨

五、

題　號	答　案
①	1.招攬交易、信用調查
②	6.通知信用狀
③	14.交付提單（B/L）
④	17.墊付押匯款項
⑤	22.發行小提單（D/O）

出口價格核算

第一節　出口價格核算內容解析

一、報價數量核算

　　出口商作價格核算時，在不知客戶訂購數量的前提下，如以併櫃方式報價，則以客戶採購量須超過船公司規定的最低裝運量計算；如以整櫃方式報價，常使用的有 20 呎櫃和 40 呎櫃兩種，前者的有效容積約為 25CBM，後者的有效容積約為 50CBM，通常則按照貨櫃可容納的最大包裝數量來計算報價數量，以節省海運費。

　　根據產品的體積、包裝單位、銷售單位來計算報價數量：

【例 1】

　　產品 A 的包裝單位是 CARTON（箱），銷售單位是 SET（套），每箱裝 60 套，每箱體積為 0.164CBM。試分別計算產品 A 以併櫃、20 呎櫃及 40 呎櫃裝運出口時的報價數量。

貨櫃	併櫃（CFS）	20 呎整櫃	40 呎整櫃
最低裝運量	1 CBM	25 CBM	50 CBM

解：

　　1. 併櫃：

　　　　包裝數量＝ 1÷0.164 ＝ 6.098，進位取整數 7 CARTON（箱）

報價數量＝ $7 \times 60 = 420$ SET（套）

  2. 每 20 呎櫃：

包裝數量＝ $25 \div 0.164 = 152.439$，進位取整數 153 CARTON（箱）

報價數量＝ $153 \times 60 = 9{,}180$ SET（套）

  3. 每 40 呎櫃：

包裝數量＝ $50 \div 0.164 = 304.878$，進位取整數 305 CARTON（箱）

報價數量＝ $305 \times 60 = 18{,}300$ SET（套）

【例 2】

    產品 B 的包裝單位是 CARTON（箱），銷售單位是 CARTON（箱），每箱體積為 0.0095CBM。試分別計算產品 B 以併櫃、20 呎櫃及 40 呎櫃裝運出口時的報價數量。

貨櫃	併櫃（CFS）	20 呎整櫃	40 呎整櫃
最低裝運量	1 CBM	25 CBM	50 CBM

解：

  1. 併櫃：

包裝數量＝ $1 \div 0.0095 = 105.263$，進位取整數 106 CARTON（箱）

報價數量＝ 106 CARTON（箱）

  2. 20 呎整櫃：

包裝數量＝ $25 \div 0.0095 = 2{,}631.578$，進位取整數 2,632 CARTON（箱）

報價數量＝ 2,632 CARTON（箱）

  3. 40 呎整櫃：

包裝數量＝ $50 \div 0.0095 = 5{,}263.158$，進位取整數 5,264 CARTON（箱）

報價數量＝ 5,264 CARTON（箱）

注意：由於該產品的包裝單位和銷售單位相同，故此例的報價數量＝包裝數量。

二、貨品成本核算

    貨品成本又稱為基價（Base Price），是整個價格的核心。出口貨品的來源不外購進及自行製造，就專業出口商而言，這項貨品成本即為向國內製造商或其他供給者購入出口貨物所付的貨款。就從事直接出口的工廠而言，貨品成本即為出廠價格。

【例如】

產品 A，供應商報價為每套 NTD100，求採購 420 套的成本？

解：

採購成本＝NTD100×420＝NTD42,000 元

三、業務費用核算

業務費用（Handling Charges）包括包裝費、報檢費、報關費、倉儲費、國內運費、銀行手續費與押匯貼現息、推廣貿易服務費及商港服務費等。出口廠商會將常發生的出口費用加總，估算出業務費用占出口價格核算的固定比率展開報價。

四、海運費核算

出口交易中，採用 CFR、CIF 貿易條件時，出口商需核算海運費，而選擇併櫃、20 呎櫃或 40 呎櫃方式裝運，對海運費的支付是有差別的。實務上，出口商為減少海運費支出，對於貨物外包裝的尺寸、重量，貨物在貨櫃內的配裝、排放以及堆疊都有一定的研究，以利減低海運費。目前業界所採用之包裝尺寸單位有公制及英制兩種，其換算方式為：

> 1 呎＝12 吋
> 1 立方呎（CFT）＝1,728 立方吋（CFT；業界稱為「才」）
> 1 立方公尺（CBM）＝35.315 立方呎

【例如】

產品 A 及產品 B 出口到加拿大，貿易條件為 CIF Montreal。試分別計算產品 A 及產品 B 以併櫃、20 呎櫃及 40 呎櫃裝運出口時的每套（或每件）海運費。

產品資料：

產　品	A	B
包裝方式	30 SETS/ CTN	20PCS/CTN
包裝體積	40×40×40(cm)	20"×18"×15"(inch)

運費資料：

運費	併櫃（CFS）	20 呎整櫃	40 呎整櫃
	USD 70	USD 1,500	USD 2,500
最低裝運量	1 CBM	25 CBM	50 CBM

解：

1. 產品 A、產品 B 的體積：

(1)產品 A 的體積：

$0.4 \times 0.4 \times 0.4 = 0.064$ CBM

(2)產品 B 的體積：

$20 \times 18 \times 15 \div 1,728 = 3.13$ CFT

$3.13 \div 35.315 = 0.089$ CBM

2. 產品 A、產品 B 的海運費：

(1)產品 A 的海運費：

- 併櫃：

包裝數量 $= 1 \div 0.064 = 15.625$，進位取整數 16 CARTON（箱）

報價數量 $= 16 \times 30 = 480$ SET（套）

每套運費 = 每箱 0.064 CBM × 每 CBM 運費 USD70 ÷ 每箱 30 SETS=USD0.15

- 20 呎整櫃：

包裝數量 $= 25 \div 0.064 = 390.625$，進位取整數 391 CARTON（箱）

報價數量 $= 391 \times 30 = 11,730$ SET（套）

每套運費 $=$ USD1,500 $\div$ 11,730 $=$ USD0.13

- 40 呎整櫃：

包裝數量 $= 50 \div 0.064 = 781.25$，進位取整數 782 CARTON（箱）

報價數量 $= 782 \times 30 = 23,460$ SET（套）

每套運費 $=$ USD2,500 $\div$ 23,460 $=$ USD0.11

(2)產品 B 的海運費：

- 併櫃：

包裝數量 $= 1 \div 0.089 = 11.236$，進位取整數 12 CARTON（箱）

報價數量 $= 12 \times 20 = 240$ PIECE（件）

每件運費 = 每箱 0.089 CBM × 每 CBM 運費 USD70 ÷ 每箱 20=USD0.31

- 20 呎整櫃：

包裝數量 $= 25 \div 0.089 = 280.899$，進位取整數 281 CARTON（箱）

報價數量 $= 281 \times 20 = 5,620$ PIECE（件）

每件運費 $=$ USD1,500 $\div$ 5,620 $=$ USD0.27

- 40 呎整櫃：

包裝數量 $= 50 \div 0.089 = 561.798$，進位取整數 562 CARTON（箱）

報價數量 = 562×20 = 11,240 PIECE（件）

每件運費 = USD2,500÷11,240 =USD0.22

五、保險費核算

出口交易中，以 CIF 貿易條件成交的情況下，出口商需要先向保險公司查詢保險費率，用以核算保險費。其計算公式如下：

保險費 = 保險金額×保險費率

保險金額 = CIF 價格×（1＋保險加成率）

在國際貿易中，保險金額應以信用狀規定；倘信用狀未規定，則為 CIF 價格加計 10%（即保險加成為 10%）。

【例如】

產品A的CIF價格為USD8,937.6，進口商要求按成交價格的110%投保一切險，保險費率為0.8%。試計算出口商應付給保險公司的保險費用？

解：

保險金額 = USD8,937.6×110% = USD9,831.36

保險費 = USD9,831.36×0.8% = USD78.65

六、佣金核算

出口商給予買方（或代理商）的回扣或佣金，比率視雙方的約定而定。其計算方式如下：

佣金 = 報價條件 × 佣金率

【例如】

若 CIF=USD100，求 CIFC10 為多少？

解：

CIFC10 = USD100＋佣金

= USD100＋(CIFC10 × 10%)

= USD100÷(1 － 10%)

= USD111.11

七、利潤核算

預期利潤率的高低，通常視貨品種類、進口市場情形、交易數量、供求關係、買方信用、付款條件與手續繁簡而異，並無一定的準則。

八、FOB、CFR、CIF 報價核算

產品資料：

產　品	A	B
包裝方式	30 SETS/ CTN	20PC/CTN
包裝體積	40×40×40(cm)	20"×18"×15"(inch)
採購成本	NTD100/ SET	NTD150/PC

運費資料：

運費	併櫃（CFS）	20 呎整櫃	40 呎整櫃
	USD 70	USD 1,500	USD 2,500
最低裝運量	1 CBM	25 CBM	50 CBM

其他報價資料：

匯率：1USD=33.5NTD	利潤率：10%
保險費率：0.65%	業務費率：8%

報價核算操作：（下列運費之來源請參考四、海運費核算）

1. 產品 A 報價核算：

(1)併櫃方式報價：

FOB ＝ 成本 NTD100+業務費 8%+利潤 10%

＝ $(100 \div 33.5) \div (1 - 8\%) \div (1 - 10\%)$ ＝ USD3.61

CFR ＝ 成本 NTD100+運費 USD0.15+業務費 8%+利潤 10%

$$= (100 \div 33.5 + 0.15) \div (1 - 8\%) \div (1 - 10\%) = USD3.79$$

CIF＝成本NTD100＋運費USD0.15＋保費（$1.1 \times 0.65\%$）＋業務費8%＋利潤10%

$$= (100 \div 33.5 + 0.15) \div (1 - 1.1 \times 0.65\%) \div (1 - 8\%) \div (1 - 10\%) = USD3.81$$

CIFC5＝成本 NTD100＋運費 USD0.15＋保費（$1.1 \times 0.65\%$）＋

　　　業務費 8%＋利潤 10%＋佣金 5%

$$= (100 \div 33.5 + 0.15) \div (1 - 1.1 \times 0.65\%) \div (1 - 8\%) \div$$

$$(1 - 10\%) \div (1 - 5\%)$$

$$= USD4.01$$

(2) 20 呎整櫃方式報價：

CFR＝成本 NTD100＋運費 USD0.13＋業務費 8% ＋ 利潤 10%

$$= (100 \div 33.5 + 0.13) \div (1 - 8\%) \div (1 - 10\%) = USD3.76$$

CIF＝成本 NTD100＋運費 USD0.13＋保費（$1.1 \times 0.65\%$）

　　　＋業務費 8%＋利潤 10%

$$= (100 \div 33.5 + 0.13) \div (1 - 1.1 \times 0.65\%) \div (1 - 8\%) \div (1 - 10\%) = USD3.79$$

CIFC8＝成本 NTD100＋運費 USD0.13＋保費（$1.1 \times 0.65\%$）

　　　＋業務費 8%＋利潤 10%＋佣金 8%

$$= (100 \div 33.5 + 0.13) \div (1 - 1.1 \times 0.65\%) \div (1 - 8\%) \div$$

$$(1 - 10\%) \div (1 - 8\%)$$

$$= USD4.12$$

(3) 40 呎整櫃方式報價：

CFR＝成本 NTD100＋運費 USD0.11＋業務費 8%＋利潤 10%

$$= (100 \div 33.5 + 0.11) \div (1 - 8\%) \div (1 - 10\%) = USD3.74$$

CIF＝成本 NTD100＋運費 USD0.11＋保費（$1.1 \times 0.65\%$）

　　　＋業務費 8%＋利潤 10%

$$= (100 \div 33.5 + 0.11) \div (1 - 1.1 \times 0.65\%) \div (1 - 8\%) \div (1 - 10\%) = USD3.76$$

CIFC10＝成本 NTD100＋運費 USD0.11＋保費（$1.1 \times 0.65\%$）

　　　＋業務費 8%＋利潤 10%＋佣金 10%

$$= (100 \div 33.5 + 0.11) \div (1 - 1.1 \times 0.65\%) \div (1 - 8\%) \div$$

$$(1 - 10\%) \div (1 - 10\%)$$

$$= USD4.18$$

2.產品 B 報價核算：

(1)併櫃方式報價：

　　FOB = 成本 NTD150 + 業務費 8% + 利潤 10% = USD5.41

　　CFR = 成本 NTD150 + 運費 USD0.31 + 業務費 8% + 利潤 10%

　　　　= $(150 \div 33.5 + 0.31) \div (1-8\%) \div (1-10\%)$ = USD5.78

　　CIF = 成本 NTD150 + 運費 USD0.31 + 保費（$1.1 \times 0.65\%$）

　　　　＋業務費 8% + 利潤 10%

　　　　= USD5.82

　　CIFC5 = 成本 NTD150 + 運費 USD0.31 + 保費（$1.1 \times 0.65\%$）

　　　　　＋業務費 8% + 利潤 10% + 佣金 5%

　　　　　= USD6.13

(2) 20 呎整櫃方式報價：

　　CFR = 成本 NTD150 + 運費 USD0.27 + 業務費 8% + 利潤 10% = USD5.73

　　CIF = 成本 NTD150 + 運費 USD0.27 + 保費（$1.1 \times 0.65\%$）

　　　　＋業務費 8% + 利潤 10%

　　　　= USD5.78

　　CIFC8 = 成本 NTD150 + 運費 USD0.27 + 保費（$1.1 \times 0.65\%$）＋業務費 8%

　　　　　＋利潤 10% + 佣金 8%

　　　　　= USD6.28

(3) 40 呎整櫃方式報價：

　　CFR = 成本 NTD150 + 運費 USD0.22 + 業務費 8% + 利潤 10% = USD5.67

　　CIF = 成本 NTD150 + 運費 USD0.22 + 保費（$1.1 \times 0.65\%$）

　　　　＋業務費 8% + 利潤 10%

　　　　= USD5.71

　　CIFC10 = 成本 NTD150 + 運費 USD0.22 + 保費（$1.1 \times 0.65\%$）

　　　　　　＋業務費 8% + 利潤 10% + 佣金 10%

　　　　　　=USD6.35

第二節　勞動部勞動力發展署測驗試題範例

一、試題範例

根據以下資料，對貨號 A 與貨號 B 兩種以體積噸計算海運運費的貨物，分別以併櫃與整櫃運量，核算相關運費與報價。

產品資料：

型　　號	A	B
包裝方式	15 SET/箱（CTN）	12 PC/箱（CTN）
包裝尺寸	50×45×36(cm)	12"×15"×20" (inch)
採購成本	NTD200/ SET	NTD240/PC

運費資料：

運費	併櫃（CFS）	20 呎整櫃	40 呎整櫃
	USD 100	USD 2,500	USD 4,500
最低裝運量	1 CBM	25 CBM	50 CBM

其他報價資料：

匯率：1USD=33.5NTD	利潤率：10%
保險費率：0.13%	業務費率：5%

注意事項：

1. 核算要求：計算過程無法整除者，CBM 計算至小數點第 4 位，四捨五入後取 3 位；其餘請計算至小數點第 3 位，四捨五入後取 2 位。

2. 佣金計算方式：以所求報價條件本身為佣金計算基礎，如 FOB&C 與 CIF&C 分別為 FOB 與 CIF 為基礎之含佣價。

🏆 貨號 A：併櫃方式報價

題目	本測驗項目請依下列核算方式計算，作答時僅填入答案即可	單位
1. 每箱 CBM 數	$0.5 \times 0.45 \times 0.36 = 0.081$	CBM
2. 每盒（SET）運費	$0.081 \times 100 \div 15 = 0.54$	USD/SET
3. FOB 報價	$(200 \div 33.5) \div (1 - 5\%) \div (1 - 10\%) = 6.98$	USD/SET
4. CFR 報價	$(200 \div 33.5 + 0.54) \div (1 - 5\%) \div (1 - 10\%) = 7.61$	USD/SET
5. CIFC3 報價	$(200 \div 33.5 + 0.54) \div (1 - 1.1 \times 0.13\%) \div (1 - 5\%)$ $\div (1 - 10\%) \div (1 - 3\%) = 7.86$	USD/SET

🏆 貨號 B：40 呎整櫃方式報價

題目	本測驗項目請依下列核算方式計算，作答時僅填入答案即可	單位
1. 每箱才數	$12 \times 15 \times 20 \div 1,728 = 2.08$	才（CFT）
2. 每箱 CBM 數	$2.08 \div 35.315 = 0.059$	CBM
3. 40 呎櫃報價數量	$50 \div 0.059 = 847.46$，進位取整數 848 箱 $\times 12 = 10,176$	PC
4. 每 PC 運費	$4,500 \div 10,176 = 0.44$	USD/PC
5. CIF 報價	$(240 \div 33.5 + 0.44) \div (1 - 1.1 \times 0.13\%) \div (1 - 5\%) \div (1 - 10\%)$ $= 8.91$	USD/PC

二、解析

為方便讀者瞭解整個出口價格核算過程，將先以計算總表方式說明不同貨號、不同運送方式、不同貿易條件及含佣價格的核算方式，再依勞動部勞動力發展署公布的試題範例方式說明。

(一)貨號 A

🏆 貨號 A 出口價格核算計算總表

項次	項目	計算說明
1.	採購成本	NTD200/SET 匯率：1USD=33.5NTD
2.	業務費率	5%

項次	項目	計算說明
3.	利潤率	10%

FOB ＝ 採購成本業務費率利潤率

$$FOB = (200 \div 33.5) \div (1 - 5\%) \div (1 - 10\%) = 6.98 (\text{USD/SET})$$

項次	項目	計算說明
4.	海運費	(1)包裝方式：15 SET/箱（CTN） (2)包裝尺寸：50×45×36(cm)

併櫃 （1CBM/USD100）	20'櫃 （25CBM/USD2,500）	40'櫃 （50CBM/USD4,500）
1. 先計算每箱 CBM： 0.5×0.45×0.36 ＝ 0.081 CBM *2.* 再計算每套運費： 0.081×100÷15 ＝ 0.54/SET	*1.* 先計算每箱 CBM： 0.5×0.45×0.36 ＝ 0.081 CBM *2.* 再計算 20'櫃報價箱數 及套數： 25÷0.081 ＝ 308.64， 進位取整數為 309 CTN 309×15 ＝ 4,635 SET *3.* 最後計算每套運費： 2,500÷4,635=0.54/SET	*1.* 先計算每箱 CBM： 0.5×0.45×0.36 ＝ 0.081 CBM *2.* 再計算 40'櫃報價箱數 及套數： 50÷0.081 ＝ 617.28， 進位取整數為 618 CTN 618×15 ＝ 9,270 SET *3.* 最後計算每套運費： 4,500÷9,270=0.49/SET

CFR ＝ 採購成本＋海運費＋業務費率＋利潤率

併櫃	20'櫃	40'櫃
CFR = (200÷33.5 + 0.54)÷(1 − 5%) ÷(1 − 10%) = 7.61 (USD/SET)	CFR = (200÷33.5 + 0.54)÷(1 − 5%)÷ (1 − 10%) = 7.61 (USD/SET)	CFR = (200÷33.5 + 0.49)÷(1 − 5%)÷ (1 − 10%) = 7.56 (USD/SET)

項次	項目	計算說明
5.	保險費率	0.13%（因題目未給予保險金額，故依慣例以110%CIF 金額為基準）

CIF ＝ 採購成本＋海運費＋保險費＋業務費率＋利潤率

併櫃	20'櫃	40'櫃
CIF = (200÷33.5+0.54) ÷(1 − 1.1×0.13%) ÷(1 − 5%)÷(1 − 10%) = 7.63(USD/SET)	CIF = (200÷33.5+0.54) ÷(1 − 1.1×0.13%) ÷(1 − 5%)÷(1 − 10%) = 7.63(USD/SET)	CIF = (200÷33.5+0.49) ÷(1 − 1.1×0.13%) ÷(1 − 5%)÷(1 − 10%) = 7.57(USD/SET)

項次	項目	計算說明
6.	佣金率	3%

CIFC3 ＝ 採購成本＋海運費＋保險費＋業務費率＋利潤率＋佣金率

項次	項目	計算說明		
		併櫃	20'櫃	40'櫃
		CIFC3 = (200÷33.5 + 0.54)÷(1－1.1×0.13%) ÷(1－5%)÷(1－10%) ÷(1－3%) = 7.86(USD/SET)	CIFC3 = (200÷33.5 + 0.54)÷(1－1.1×0.13%) ÷(1－5%)÷(1－10%) ÷(1－3%) = 7.86(USD/SET)	CIFC3 = (200÷33.5 + 0.49)÷(1－1.1×0.13%) ÷(1－5%)÷(1－10%) ÷(1－3%) = 7.80(USD/SET)

貨號 A：20 呎貨櫃方式報價

題目	核算方式及答案	單位
1. 每箱 CBM 數	0.5×0.45×0.36= 0.081	CBM
2. 20 呎櫃報價數量	25÷0.081=308.64，進位取整數 309 箱×15 = 4,635	SET
3. 每盒（SET）運費	2,500÷4,635 = 0.54	USD/SET
4. CFR 報價	(200÷33.5＋0.54)÷(1－5%)÷(1－10%)= 7.61	USD/SET
5. CIFC3 報價	(200÷33.5＋0.54)÷(1－1.1×0.13%)÷(1－5%)÷ (1－10%)÷(1－3%) = 7.86	USD/SET

貨號 B：40 呎整櫃方式報價

題目	核算方式及答案	單位
1. 每箱 CBM 數	0.5×0.45×0.36= 0.081	CBM
2. 40 呎櫃報價數量	50÷0.081=617.28，進位取整數 618 箱×15 = 9,270	SET
3. 每盒（SET）運費	4,500÷9,270 = 0.49	USD/SET
4. FOB 報價	(200÷33.5)÷(1－5%)÷(1－10%)= 6.98	USD/SET
5. CIFC3 報價	(200÷33.5＋0.49)÷(1－1.1×0.13%)÷(1－5%)÷ (1－10%)÷(1－3%) = 7.80	USD/SET

(二)貨號 B

貨號 B 出口價格核算計算總表

項次	項目	計算說明
1.	採購成本	NTD240/PC 匯率：1USD=33.5NTD
2.	業務費率	5%

項次	項目	計算說明
3.	利潤率	10% 　FOB ＝ 採購成本＋業務費率＋利潤率 FOB ＝ (240÷33.5)÷(1－5%)÷(1－10%)= 8.38(USD/ PC)
4.	海運費	(1)包裝方式：12 PC/箱（CTN） (2)包裝尺寸：12"×15"×20"（inch） (3)換算公式：1 立方呎＝1,728 立方吋、1 CBM＝35.315 立方呎

併櫃（1CBM/USD100）	20'櫃（25CBM/ USD2,500）	40'櫃（50CBM/ USD4,500）
1. 先計算每箱 CBM： 12×15×20÷1,728 =2.08 2.08÷35.315=0.059 2.再計算每套運費： 0.059×100÷12 = 0.49/ PC	*1.* 先計算每箱 CBM： 12×15×20÷1,728 =2.08 2.08÷35.315=0.059 2.再計算 20'櫃報價箱數 及套數： 25÷0.059 ＝ 423.73， 進位取整數為 424 CTN 424×12＝5,088 PC 3.最後計算每套運費： 2,500÷5,088＝0.49/ PC	*1.* 先計算每箱 CBM： 12×15×20÷1,728 = 2.08 2.08÷35.315=0.059 2.再計算 40'櫃報價箱數 及件數： 50÷0.059 ＝ 847.46， 進位取整數為 848 CTN 848×12＝10,176 PC 3.最後計算每套運費： 4,500÷10,176＝0.44/ PC
CFR ＝ 採購成本＋海運費＋業務費率＋利潤率		
CFR ＝ (240÷33.5 ＋ 0.49)÷(1－5%)÷ (1－10%) ＝ 8.95(USD/ PC)	CFR ＝ (240÷33.5 ＋ 0.49)÷(1－5%)÷ (1－10%) ＝ 8.95 (USD/ PC)	CFR ＝ (240÷33.5 ＋ 0.44)÷(1－5%)÷ (1－10%) ＝ 8.89(USD/ PC)

項次	項目	計算說明
5.	保險費率	0.13%（因題目未給予保險金額，故依慣例以 110%CIF 金額為基準）

　CIF ＝ 採購成本＋海運費＋保險費＋業務費率＋利潤率

併櫃	20'櫃	40'櫃
CIF ＝ (240÷33.5＋0.49) ÷(1－1.1×0.13%) ÷(1－5%)÷(1－10%) ＝ 8.97(USD/ PC)	CIF ＝ (240÷33.5＋0.49) ÷(1－1.1×0.13%) ÷(1－5%)÷(1－10%) ＝ 8.97(USD/ PC)	CIF ＝ (240÷33.5＋0.44) ÷(1－1.1×0.13%) ÷(1－5%)÷(1－10%) ＝ 8.91(USD/SET)

項次	項目	計算說明
6.	佣金率	3%

　CIFC3 ＝ 採購成本＋海運費＋保險費＋業務費率＋利潤率＋佣金率

項次	項目	計算說明		
		併櫃	20'櫃	40'櫃
		CIFC3 = (240÷33.5+0.49)÷(1−1.1×0.13%)÷(1−5%)÷(1−10%)÷(1−3%) = 9.24 (USD/ PC)	CIFC3 = (240÷33.5+0.49)÷(1−1.1×0.13%)÷(1−5%)÷(1−10%)÷(1−3%) =9.24 (USD/ PC)	CIFC3 = (240÷33.5+0.44)÷(1−1.1×0.13%)÷(1−5%)÷(1−10%)÷(1−3%) = 9.18 (USD/ PC)

👑 貨號 B：併櫃方式報價

題目	核算方式及答案	單位
1. 每箱才數	12×15×20÷1,728=2.08	才（CFT）
2. 每箱 CBM 數	2.08÷35.315=0.059	CBM
3. 每 PC 運費	0.059×100÷12 = 0.49	USD/PC
4. CFR 報價	(240÷33.5+0.49)÷(1−5%)÷(1−10%) =8.95	USD/PC
5. CIFC3 報價	(240÷33.5+0.49)÷(1−1.1×0.13%)÷(1−5%)÷(1−10%)÷（1−3%）=9.24	USD/PC

👑 貨號 B：20 呎整櫃方式報價

題目	核算方式及答案	單位
1. 每箱才數	12×15×20÷1,728=2.08	才（CFT）
2. 每箱 CBM 數	2.08÷35.315=0.059	CBM
3. 20 呎櫃報價數量	25÷0.059 =423.73，進位取整數 424 箱×12 = 5,088	PC
4. 每 PC 運費	2,500÷5,088 = 0.49	USD/PC
5. CIFC3 報價	(240÷33.5+0.49)÷(1−1.1×0.13%)÷(1−5%)÷(1−10%)÷（1−3%）=9.24	USD/PC

第三節 練習題

一、根據以下資料，對貨號 A 與貨號 B 兩種以體積噸計算海運運費的貨物，分別以併櫃與整櫃運量，核算相關運費與報價，並填入答案欄內。

產品資料：

型　　號	A	B
包裝方式	20SET/箱（CTN）	16 PC/箱（CTN）
包裝尺寸	40×45×36(cm)	22"×20"×20" (inch)
採購成本	NTD150/ SET	NTD120/PC

運費資料：

運費	併櫃（CFS）	20 呎整櫃	40 呎整櫃
	USD 80	USD 2,000	USD 3,500
最低裝運量	1 CBM	25 CBM	50 CBM

其他報價資料：

匯率：1USD=33.25NTD	利潤率：6%
保險費率：0.85%	業務費率：5%

注意事項：

1. 核算要求：計算過程無法整除者，CBM計算至小數點第 4 位，四捨五入後取 3 位；其餘請計算至小數點第 3 位，四捨五入後取 2 位。

2. 佣金計算方式：以所求報價條件本身為佣金計算基礎，如 FOB&C 與 CIF&C 分別為 FOB 與 CIF 為基礎之含佣價。

貨號 A：併櫃方式報價

題目	答案	單位
1. 每箱 CBM 數		CBM
2. 每盒（SET）運費		USD/SET
3. FOB 報價		USD/SET
4. CFR 報價		USD/SET
5. CIFC3 報價		USD/SET

貨號 A：20 呎貨櫃方式報價

題目	答案	單位
1. 每箱 CBM 數		CBM
2. 20 呎櫃報價數量		SET
3. 每盒（SET）運費		USD/SET
4. CFR 報價		USD/SET
5. CIFC3 報價		USD/SET

貨號 A：40 呎貨櫃方式報價

題目	答案	單位
1. 每箱 CBM 數		CBM
2. 40 呎櫃報價數量		SET
3. 每盒（SET）運費		USD/SET
4. CFR 報價		USD/SET
5. CIFC3 報價		USD/SET

貨號 B：併櫃方式報價

題目	答案	單位
1. 每箱才數		才（CFT）
2. 每箱 CBM 數		CBM
3. 每 PC 運費		PC
4. FOB 報價		USD/PC
5. CIFC3 報價		USD/PC

📖 貨號 B：20 呎整櫃方式報價

題目	答案	單位
1. 每箱才數		才（CFT）
2. 每箱 CBM 數		CBM
3. 20 呎櫃報價數量		PC
4. 每 PC 運費		USD/PC
5. CIFC3 報價		USD/PC

📖 貨號 B：40 呎整櫃方式報價

題目	答案	單位
1. 40 呎櫃報價數量		PC
2. 每 PC 運費		USD/PC
3. CFR 報價		USD/PC
4. CIF 報價		USD/PC
5. CIFC3 報價		USD/PC

答案：

📖 貨號 A 出口價格核算計算總表

項次	項目	計算說明
1.	採購成本	NTD150/SET 匯率：1USD=33.25NTD
2.	業務費率	5%
3.	利潤率	6% FOB ＝ 採購成本＋業務費率＋利潤率 FOB =（150÷33.25）÷（1－5%）÷（1－6%）= 5.05(USD/SET)
4.	海運費	(1)包裝方式：20 SET ／箱（CTN） (2)包裝尺寸：40×45×36(cm)

項次	項目	計算說明

	併櫃 （1CBM/USD80）	20'櫃 （25CBM/USD2,000）	40'櫃 （50CBM/USD3,500）
1.先計算每箱 CBM： $0.4 \times 0.45 \times 0.36$ $= 0.065$ CBM 2.再計算每套運費： $0.065 \times 80 \div 20$ $= 0.26$/SET	1.先計算每箱 CBM： $0.4 \times 0.45 \times 0.36$ $= 0.065$ CBM 2.再計算 20'櫃報價箱數 及套數： $25 \div 0.065 = 384.62$， 進位取整數為 385 CTN $385 \times 20 = 7,700$ SET 3.最後計算每套運費： $2,000 \div 7,700 = 0.26$/SET	1.先計算每箱 CBM： $0.4 \times 0.45 \times 0.36$ $= 0.065$ CBM 2.再計算 40'櫃報價箱數 及套數： $50 \div 0.065 = 769.23$， 進位取整數為 770 CTN $770 \times 20 = 15,400$ SET 3.最後計算每套運費： $3,500 \div 15,400 = 0.23$/SET

CFR＝採購成本＋海運費＋業務費率＋利潤率

併櫃	20'櫃	40'櫃
CFR $= (150 \div 33.25 +$ $0.26) \div (1-5\%) \div$ $(1-6\%)$ $= 5.34$ (USD/SET)	CFR $= (150 \div 33.25 +$ $0.26) \div (1-5\%) \div$ $(1-6\%)$ $= 5.34$ (USD/SET)	CFR $= (150 \div 33.25 +$ $0.23) \div (1-5\%) \div$ $(1-6\%)$ $= 5.31$ (USD/SET)

項次	項目	計算說明
5.	保險費率	0.85%（因題目未給予保險金額，故依慣例以 110%CIF 金額為基準）

CIF＝採購成本＋海運費＋保險費＋業務費率＋利潤率

併櫃	20'櫃	40'櫃
CIF $= (150 \div 33.25 + 0.26)$ $\div (1 - 1.1 \times 0.85\%)$ $\div (1-5\%) \div (1-6\%)$ $= 5.39$(USD/SET)	CIF $= (150 \div 33.25 + 0.26)$ $\div (1 - 1.1 \times 0.85\%)$ $\div (1-5\%) \div (1-6\%)$ $= 5.39$(USD/SET)	CIF $= (150 \div 33.25 + 0.23)$ $\div (1 - 1.1 \times 0.85\%)$ $\div (1-5\%) \div (1-6\%)$ $= 5.36$(USD/SET)

項次	項目	計算說明
6.	佣金率	3%

CIFC3＝採購成本＋海運費＋保險費＋業務費率＋利潤率＋佣金率

併櫃	20'櫃	40'櫃
CIF $= (150 \div 33.25 +$ $0.26) \div (1-1.1 \times$ $0.85\%) \div (1-5\%) \div$ $(1-6\%) \div (1-3\%)$ $= 5.56$(USD/SET)	CIF $= (150 \div 33.25 +$ $0.26) \div (1-1.1 \times$ $0.85\%) \div (1-5\%) \div$ $(1-6\%) \div (1-3\%)$ $= 5.56$(USD/SET)	CIF $= (150 \div 33.25 +$ $0.23) \div (1-1.1 \times$ $0.85\%) \div (1-5\%) \div$ $(1-6\%) \div (1-3\%)$ $= 5.53$(USD/SET)

📖 貨號 A：併櫃方式報價

題目	答案	單位
1. 每箱 CBM 數	$0.4 \times 0.45 \times 0.36 = 0.065$	CBM
2. 每盒（SET）運費	$0.065 \times 80 \div 20 = 0.26$	USD/SET
3. FOB 報價	$(150 \div 33.25) \div (1 - 5\%) \div (1 - 6\%) = 5.05$	USD/SET
4. CFR 報價	$(150 \div 33.25 + 0.26) \div (1 - 5\%) \div (1 - 6\%) = 5.34$	USD/SET
5. CIFC3 報價	$(150 \div 33.25 + 0.26) \div (1 - 1.1 \times 0.85\%) \div$ $(1 - 5\%) \div (1 - 6\%) \div (1 - 3\%) = 5.56$	USD/SET

📖 貨號 A：20 呎貨櫃方式報價

題目	答案	單位
1. 每箱 CBM 數	$0.4 \times 0.45 \times 0.36 = 0.065$	CBM
2. 20 呎櫃報價數量	$25 \div 0.065 = 384.62$，進位取整數 385 箱 $\times 20 = 7,700$	SET
3. 每盒（SET）運費	$2,000 \div 7,700 = 0.26$	USD/SET
4. CFR 報價	$(150 \div 33.25 + 0.26) \div (1 - 5\%) \div (1 - 6\%) = 5.34$	USD/SET
5. CIFC3 報價	$(150 \div 33.25 + 0.26) \div (1 - 1.1 \times 0.85\%) \div$ $(1 - 5\%) \div (1 - 6\%) \div (1 - 3\%) = 5.56$	USD/SET

📖 貨號 A：40 呎貨櫃方式報價

題目	答案	單位
1. 每箱 CBM 數	$0.4 \times 0.45 \times 0.36 = 0.065$	CBM
2. 40 呎櫃報價數量	$50 \div 0.065 = 769.23$，進位取整數 770 箱 $\times 20 = 15,400$	SET
3. 每盒（SET）運費	$3,500 \div 15,400 = 0.23$	USD/SET
4. CFR 報價	$(150 \div 33.25 + 0.23) \div (1 - 5\%) \div (1 - 6\%) = 5.31$	USD/SET
5. CIFC3 報價	$(150 \div 33.25 + 0.23) \div (1 - 1.1 \times 0.85\%) \div$ $(1 - 5\%) \div (1 - 6\%) \div (1 - 3\%) = 5.53$	USD/SET

📖 貨號 B 出口價格核算計算總表

項次	項目	計算說明
1.	採購成本	NTD120/PC 匯率：1USD=33.25NTD
2.	業務費率	5%
3.	利潤率	6% FOB ＝ 採購成本＋業務費率＋利潤率

項次	項目	計算說明
		FOB = $(120 \div 33.25) \div (1 - 5\%) \div (1 - 6\%) = 4.04$ (USD/ PC)
4.	海運費	(1)包裝方式：16 PC/箱（CTN） (2)包裝尺寸：22"×20"×20" (inch) (3)換算公式：1 立方呎 = 1,728 立方吋、1 CBM = 35.315 立方呎

併櫃 （1CBM/USD80）	20'櫃 （25CBM/USD2,000）	40'櫃 （50CBM/USD3,500）
1. 先計算每箱 CBM： $22 \times 20 \times 20 \div 1,728$ $= 5.09$ $5.09 \div 35.315 = 0.144$ *2.* 再計算每套運費： $0.144 \times 80 \div 16$ $= 0.72 / $ PC	*1.* 先計算每箱 CBM： $22 \times 20 \times 20 \div 1,728$ $= 5.09$ $5.09 \div 35.315 = 0.144$ *2.* 再計算 20'櫃報價箱數 及套數： $25 \div 0.144 = 173.61$， 進位取整數為 174 CTN $174 \times 16 = 2,784$ PC *3.* 最後計算每套運費： $2,000 \div 2,784 = 0.72/ $ PC	*1.* 先計算每箱 CBM： $22 \times 20 \times 20 \div 1,728$ $= 5.09$ $5.09 \div 35.315 = 0.144$ *2.* 再計算 40'櫃報價箱數 及件數： $50 \div 0.144 = 347.22$， 進位取整數為 348 CTN $348 \times 16 = 5,568$ PC *3.* 最後計算每套運費： $3,500 \div 5,568 = 0.63/ $ PC

CFR ＝ 採購成本＋海運費＋業務費率＋利潤率

併櫃	20'櫃	40'櫃
CFR = $(120 \div 33.25 + 0.72) \div (1 - 5\%)$ $\div (1 - 6\%)$ $= 4.85$(USD/ PC)	CFR = $(120 \div 33.25 + 0.72) \div (1 - 5\%)$ $\div (1 - 6\%)$ $= 4.85$ (USD/ PC)	CFR = $(120 \div 33.25 + 0.63) \div (1 - 5\%)$ $\div (1 - 6\%)$ $= 4.75$ (USD/ PC)

項次	項目	計算說明
5.	保險費率	0.85%（因題目未給予保險金額，故依慣例以 110%CIF 金額為基準）

CIF ＝ 採購成本＋海運費＋保險費＋業務費率＋利潤率

併櫃	20'櫃	40'櫃
CIF = $(120 \div 33.25 + 0.72)$ $\div (1 - 1.1 \times 0.85\%)$ $\div (1 - 5\%) \div (1 - 6\%)$ $= 4.89$(USD/ PC)	CIF = $(120 \div 33.25 + 0.72)$ $\div (1 - 1.1 \times 0.85\%)$ $\div (1 - 5\%) \div (1 - 6\%)$ $= 4.89$(USD/ PC)	CIF = $(120 \div 33.25 + 0.63)$ $\div (1 - 1.1 \times 0.85\%)$ $\div (1 - 5\%) \div (1 - 6\%)$ $= 4.79$(USD/ PC)

項次	項目	計算說明
6.	佣金率	3%

CIFC3 ＝ 採購成本＋海運費＋保險費＋業務費率＋利潤率＋佣金率

項次	項目	計算說明		
		併櫃	20'櫃	40'櫃
		CIFC3 = (120÷33.25 + 0.72)÷(1 − 1.1×0.85%) ÷(1 − 5%)÷(1 − 6%)÷ (1 − 3%) = 5.04 (USD/ PC)	CIFC3 = (120÷33.25 + 0.72)÷(1 − 1.1×0.85%) ÷(1 − 5%)÷(1 − 6%)÷ (1 − 3%) = 5.04 (USD/ PC)	CIFC3 = (120÷33.25 + 0.63)÷(1 − 1.1×0.85%) ÷(1 − 5%)÷(1 − 6%)÷ (1 − 3%) = 4.94 (USD/ PC)

貨號 B：併櫃方式報價

題目	答案	單位
1. 每箱才數	$22 \times 20 \times 20 \div 1,728 = 5.09$	才（CFT）
2. 每箱 CBM 數	$5.09 \div 35.315 = 0.144$	CBM
3. 每 PC 運費	$0.144 \times 80 \div 16 = 0.72$	PC
4. FOB 報價	$(120 \div 33.25) \div (1 - 5\%) \div (1 - 6\%) = 4.04$	USD/PC
5. CIFC3 報價	$(120 \div 33.25 + 0.72) \div (1 - 1.1 \times 0.85\%) \div (1 - 5\%) \div$ $(1 - 6\%) \div (1 - 3\%) = 5.04$	USD/PC

貨號 B：20 呎整櫃方式報價

題目	答案	單位
1. 每箱才數	$22 \times 20 \times 20 \div 1,728 = 5.09$	才（CFT）
2. 每箱 CBM 數	$5.09 \div 35.315 = 0.144$	CBM
3. 20 呎櫃報價數量	25÷0.144=173.61，進位取整數 174 箱×16 = 2,784	PC
4. 每 PC 運費	$2,000 \div 2,784 = 0.72$	USD/PC
5. CIFC3 報價	$(120 \div 33.25 + 0.72) \div (1 - 1.1 \times 0.85\%) \div (1 - 5\%) \div$ $(1 - 6\%) \div (1 - 3\%) = 5.04$	USD/PC

🐔 貨號 B：40 呎整櫃方式報價

題目	答案	單位
1. 40 呎櫃報價數量	$50 \div 0.144 = 347.22$，進位取整數 348 箱 $\times 16 = 5,568$	PC
2. 每 PC 運費	$3,500 \div 5,568 = 0.63$	USD/PC
3. CFR 報價	$(120 \div 33.25 + 0.63) \div (1 - 5\%) \div (1 - 6\%) = 4.75$	USD/PC
4. CIF 報價	$(120 \div 33.25 + 0.63) \div (1 - 1.1 \times 0.85\%) \div (1 - 5\%) \div$ $(1 - 6\%) = 4.79$	USD/PC
5. CIFC3 報價	$(120 \div 33.25 + 0.63) \div (1 - 1.1 \times 0.85\%) \div (1 - 5\%) \div$ $(1 - 6\%) \div (1 - 3\%) = 4.94$	USD/PC

二、根據以下資料，對貨號 A 與貨號 B 兩種以體積噸計算海運運費的貨物，分別以併櫃與整櫃運量，核算相關運費與報價，並填入答案欄內。

產品資料：

型　　號	A	B
包裝方式	28SET/箱（CTN）	25 PC/箱（CTN）
包裝尺寸	50×55×65(cm)	25"×22"×20" (inch)
採購成本	NTD180/ SET	NTD200/PC

運費資料：

運費	併櫃（CFS）	20 呎整櫃	40 呎整櫃
	USD 100	USD 1,800	USD 3,200
最低裝運量	1 CBM	25 CBM	50 CBM

其他報價資料：

匯率：1USD=33.02NTD	利潤率：10%
保險費率：0.75%	業務費率：8%

注意事項：

1. 核算要求：計算過程無法整除者，CBM 計算至小數點第 4 位，四捨五入後取 3 位；其餘請計算至小數點第 3 位，四捨五入後取 2 位。

2. 佣金計算方式：以所求報價條件本身為佣金計算基礎，如 FOB&C 與 CIF&C 分別為 FOB 與 CIF 為基礎之含佣價。

♟ 貨號 A：併櫃方式報價

題目	答案	單位
1. 每箱 CBM 數		CBM
2. 每盒（SET）運費		USD/SET
3. FOB 報價		USD/SET
4. CFR 報價		USD/SET
5. CIFC5 報價		USD/SET

♟ 貨號 A：20 呎貨櫃方式報價

題目	答案	單位
1. 每箱 CBM 數		CBM
2. 20 呎櫃報價數量		SET
3. 每盒（SET）運費		USD/SET
4. CFR 報價		USD/SET
5. CIFC5 報價		USD/SET

♟ 貨號 A：40 呎貨櫃方式報價

題目	答案	單位
1. 每箱 CBM 數		CBM
2. 40 呎櫃報價數量		SET
3. 每盒（SET）運費		USD/SET
4. CFR 報價		USD/SET
5. CIFC5 報價		USD/SET

♟ 貨號 B：併櫃方式報價

題目	答案	單位
1. 每箱才數		才（CFT）
2. 每箱 CBM 數		CBM
3. 每 PC 運費		USD/PC
4. FOB 報價		USD/PC
5. CIFC5 報價		USD/PC

🔖 貨號 B：20 呎整櫃方式報價

題目	答案	單位
1. 每箱才數		才（CFT）
2. 每箱 CBM 數		CBM
3. 20 呎櫃報價數量		PC
4. 每 PC 運費		USD/PC
5. CIFC5 報價		USD/PC

🔖 貨號 B：40 呎整櫃方式報價

題目	答案	單位
1. 40 呎櫃報價數量		PC
2. 每 PC 運費		USD/PC
3. CFR 報價		USD/PC
4. CIF 報價		USD/PC
5. CIFC5 報價		USD/PC

答案：

🔖 貨號 A 出口價格核算計算總表

項次	項目	計算說明
1.	採購成本	NTD180/SET 匯率：1USD=33.02NTD
2.	業務費率	8%
3.	利潤率	10% **FOB ＝ 採購成本＋業務費率＋利潤率** FOB ＝ (180÷33.02)÷(1－8%)÷(1－10%)＝ 6.58(USD/SET)
4.	海運費	(1)包裝方式：28 SET/箱（CTN） (2)包裝尺寸：50×55×65(cm)

項次	項目	計算說明		
		併櫃（1CBM/USD100）	20'櫃（25CBM/USD1,800）	40'櫃（50CBM/USD3,200）
		1. 先計算每箱 CBM： 0.5×0.55×0.65 = 0.179 CBM *2.* 再計算每套運費： 0.179×100÷28 = 0.64/SET	*1.* 先計算每箱 CBM： 0.5×0.55×0.65 = 0.179 CBM *2.* 再計算 20'櫃報價箱數及套數： 25÷0.179 = 139.66，進位取整數為 140 CTN 140×28 = 3,920 SET *3.* 最後計算每套運費： 1,800÷3,920 = 0.46/SET	*1.* 先計算每箱 CBM： 0.5×0.55×0.65 = 0.179 CBM *2.* 再計算 40'櫃報價箱數及套數： 50÷0.179 = 279.33，進位取整數為 280 CTN 280×28 = 7,840 SET *3.* 最後計算每套運費： 3,200÷7,840 = 0.41/SET
		CFR ＝ 採購成本＋海運費＋業務費率＋利潤率		
		CFR = (180÷33.02 + 0.64)÷(1 − 8%)÷ (1 − 10%) = 7.36 (USD/SET)	CFR = (180÷33.02 + 0.46)÷(1 − 8%)÷ (1 − 10%) = 7.14 (USD/SET)	CFR = (180÷33.02 + 0.41)÷(1 − 8%)÷ (1 − 10%) = 7.08 (USD/SET)
5.	保險費率	0.75%（因題目未給予保險金額，故依慣例以 110%CIF 金額為基準）		
		CIF ＝ 採購成本＋海運費＋保險費＋業務費率＋利潤率		
		併櫃	20'櫃	40'櫃
		CIF = (180÷33.02＋0.64) ÷(1 − 1.1×0.75%) ÷(1 − 8%)÷(1 − 10%) = 7.42(USD/SET)	CIF = (180÷33.02＋0.46) ÷(1 − 1.1×0.75%) ÷(1 − 8%)÷(1 − 10%) = 7.20(USD/SET)	CIF = (180÷33.02＋0.41) ÷(1 − 1.1×0.75%) ÷(1 − 8%)÷(1 − 10%) = 7.14(USD/SET)
6.	佣金率	5%		
		CIFC5 ＝ 採購成本＋海運費＋保險費＋業務費率＋利潤率＋佣金率		
		併櫃	20'櫃	40'櫃
		CIFC5 = (180÷33.02 + 0.64)÷(1 − 1.1×0.75%) ÷(1 − 8%)÷(1 − 10%) ÷(1 − 5%) = 7.81(USD/SET)	CIFC5 = (180÷33.02 + 0.46)÷(1 − 1.1×0.75%) ÷(1 − 8%)÷(1 − 10%) ÷(1 − 5%) = 7.58(USD/SET)	CIFC5 = (180÷33.02 + 0.41)÷(1 − 1.1×0.75%) ÷(1 − 8%)÷(1 − 10%) ÷(1 − 5%) = 7.51(USD/SET)

📖 貨號 A：併櫃方式報價

題目	答案	單位
1. 每箱 CBM 數	$0.5 \times 0.55 \times 0.65 = 0.179$	CBM
2. 每盒（SET）運費	$0.179 \times 100 \div 28 = 0.64$	USD/SET
3. FOB 報價	$(180 \div 33.02) \div (1 - 8\%) \div (1 - 10\%) = 6.58$	USD/SET
4. CFR 報價	$(180 \div 33.02 + 0.64) \div (1 - 8\%) \div (1 - 10\%) = 7.36$	USD/SET
5. CIFC5 報價	$(180 \div 33.02 + 0.64) \div (1 - 1.1 \times 0.75\%) \div (1 - 8\%)$ $\div (1 - 10\%) \div (1 - 5\%) = 7.81$	USD/SET

📖 貨號 A：20 呎貨櫃方式報價

題目	答案	單位
1. 每箱 CBM 數	$0.5 \times 0.55 \times 0.65 = 0.179$	CBM
2. 20 呎櫃報價數量	$25 \div 0.179 = 139.66$，進位取整數 140 箱 $\times 28 = 3{,}920$	SET
3. 每盒（SET）運費	$1{,}800 \div 3{,}920 = 0.46$	USD/SET
4. CFR 報價	$(180 \div 33.02 + 0.46) \div (1 - 8\%) \div (1 - 10\%) = 7.14$	USD/SET
5. CIFC5 報價	$(180 \div 33.02 + 0.46) \div (1 - 1.1 \times 0.75\%) \div (1 - 8\%)$ $\div (1 - 10\%) \div (1 - 5\%) = 7.58$	USD/SET

📖 貨號 A：40 呎貨櫃方式報價

題目	答案	單位
1. 每箱 CBM 數	$0.5 \times 0.55 \times 0.65 = 0.179$	CBM
2. 40 呎櫃報價數量	$50 \div 0.179 = 279.33$，進位取整數 280 箱 $\times 28 = 7{,}840$	SET
3. 每盒（SET）運費	$3{,}200 \div 7{,}840 = 0.41$	USD/SET
4. CFR 報價	$(180 \div 33.02 + 0.41) \div (1 - 8\%) \div (1 - 10\%) = 7.08$	USD/SET
5. CIFC5 報價	$(180 \div 33.02 + 0.41) \div (1 - 1.1 \times 0.75\%) \div (1 - 8\%)$ $\div (1 - 10\%) \div (1 - 5\%) = 7.51$	USD/SET

📖 貨號 B 出口價格核算計算總表

項次	項目	計算說明
1.	採購成本	NTD200/PC
		匯率：1USD=33.02NTD
2.	業務費率	8%
3.	利潤率	10%
		FOB ＝ 採購成本＋業務費率＋利潤率

項次	項目	計算說明
		FOB = (200 ÷ 33.02) ÷ (1 − 8%) ÷ (1 − 10%)= 7.32 (USD/ PC)

4. 海運費

(1)包裝方式：25PC/箱（CTN）

(2)包裝尺寸：25"×22"×20" (inch)

(3)換算公式：1 立方呎 = 1,728 立方吋、1 CBM = 35.315 立方呎

併櫃 （1CBM/USD100）	20'櫃 （25CBM/USD1,800）	40'櫃 （50CBM/USD3,200）
1.先計算每箱 CBM： 25×22×20÷1,728 =6.37 6.37÷35.315=0.180 2.再計算每套運費： 0.180×100÷25 =0.72/ PC	1.先計算每箱 CBM： 25×22×20÷1,728 =6.37 6.37÷35.315= 0.180 2.再計算 20'櫃報價箱數 及套數： 25÷0.180 = 138.89， 進位取整數為 139 CTN 139×25 = 3,475 PC 3.最後計算每套運費： 1,800÷3,475 = 0.52/ PC	1.先計算每箱 CBM： 25×22×20÷1,728 =6.37 6.37÷35.315 = 0.180 2.再計算 40'櫃報價箱數 及件數： 50÷0.180 = 277.78， 進位取整數為 278CTN 278×25 = 6,950PC 3.最後計算每套運費： 3,200÷6,950 = 0.46/ PC

CFR = 採購成本＋海運費＋業務費率＋利潤率

併櫃	20'櫃	40'櫃
CFR = (200 ÷ 33.02 + 0.72) ÷ (1 − 8%) ÷ (1 − 10%) = 8.18(USD/ PC)	CFR = (200 ÷ 33.02 + 0.52) ÷ (1 − 8%) ÷ (1 − 10%) = 7.94(USD/ PC)	CFR = (200 ÷ 33.02 + 0.46) ÷ (1 − 8%) ÷ (1 − 10%) = 7.87 (USD/ PC)

5. 保險費率

0.75%（因題目未給予保險金額，故依慣例以 110%CIF 金額為基準）

CIF = 採購成本＋海運費＋保險費＋業務費率＋利潤率

併櫃	20'櫃	40'櫃
CIF = (200 ÷ 33.02 + 0.72) ÷ (1 − 1.1×0.75%) ÷ (1 − 8%) ÷ (1 − 10%) = 8.25(USD/ PC)	CIF = (200 ÷ 33.02 + 0.52) ÷ (1 − 1.1×0.75%) ÷ (1 − 8%) ÷ (1 − 10%) = 8.01(USD/ PC)	CIF = (200 ÷ 33.02 + 0.46) ÷ (1 − 1.1×0.75%) ÷ (1 − 8%) ÷ (1 − 10%) = 7.94 (USD/ PC)

6. 佣金率

5%

CIFC5 = 採購成本＋海運費＋保險費＋業務費率＋利潤率＋佣金率

項次	項目	計算說明		
		併櫃	20'櫃	40'櫃
		$CIFC5 = (200 \div 33.02 + 0.72) \div (1 - 1.1 \times 0.75\%)$ $\div (1 - 8\%) \div (1 - 10\%)$ $\div (1 - 5\%)$ $= 8.69(USD/PC)$	$CIFC5 = (200 \div 33.02 + 0.52) \div (1 - 1.1 \times 0.75\%)$ $\div (1 - 8\%) \div (1 - 10\%)$ $\div (1 - 5\%)$ $= 8.43(USD/PC)$	$CIFC5 = (200 \div 33.02 + 0.46) \div (1 - 1.1 \times 0.75\%)$ $\div (1 - 8\%) \div (1 - 10\%)$ $\div (1 - 5\%)$ $= 8.35(USD/PC)$

貨號 B：併櫃方式報價

題目	答案	單位
1. 每箱才數	$25 \times 22 \times 20 \div 1728 = 6.37$	才（CFT）
2. 每箱 CBM 數	$6.37 \div 35.315 = 0.180$	CBM
3. 每 PC 運費	$0.180 \times 100 \div 25 = 0.72$	USD/PC
4. FOB 報價	$(200 \div 33.02) \div (1 - 8\%) \div (1 - 10\%) = 7.32$	USD/PC
5. CIFC5 報價	$(200 \div 33.02 + 0.72) \div (1 - 1.1 \times 0.75\%) \div (1 - 8\%)$ $\div (1 - 10\%) \div (1 - 5\%) = 8.69$	USD/PC

貨號 B：20 呎整櫃方式報價

題目	答案	單位
1. 每箱才數	$25 \times 22 \times 20 \div 1728 = 6.37$	才（CFT）
2. 每箱 CBM 數	$6.37 \div 35.315 = 0.180$	CBM
3. 20 呎櫃報價數量	$25 \div 0.180 = 138.89$，進位取整數 139 箱 $\times 25 = 3,475$	PC
4. 每 PC 運費	$1,800 \div 3,475 = 0.52$	USD/PC
5. CIFC5 報價	$(200 \div 33.02 + 0.52) \div (1 - 1.1 \times 0.75\%) \div (1 - 8\%) \div$ $(1 - 10\%) \div (1 - 5\%) = 8.43$	USD/PC

📖 貨號 B：40 呎整櫃方式報價

題目	答案	單位
1. 40 呎櫃報價數量	$50 \div 0.180 = 277.78$，進位取整數 278 箱 $\times 25 = 6,950$	PC
2. 每 PC 運費	$3,200 \div 6,950 = 0.46$	USD/PC
3. CFR 報價	$(200 \div 33.02 + 0.46) \div (1 - 8\%) \div (1 - 10\%) = 7.87$	USD/PC
4. CIF 報價	$(200 \div 33.02 + 0.46) \div (1 - 1.1 \times 0.75\%) \div (1 - 8\%) \div$ $(1 - 10\%) = 7.94$	USD/PC
5. CIFC5 報價	$(200 \div 33.02 + 0.46) \div (1 - 1.1 \times 0.75\%) \div (1 - 8\%) \div$ $(1 - 10\%) \div (1 - 5\%) = 8.35$	USD/PC

三、根據以下資料，對貨號 A 與貨號 B 兩種以體積噸計算海運運費的貨物，分別以併櫃與整櫃運量，核算相關運費與報價，並填入答案欄內。

產品資料：

型　　號	A	B
包裝方式	10SET/箱（CTN）	6 PC/箱（CTN）
包裝尺寸	$62 \times 24 \times 46$(cm)	$27" \times 18" \times 11"$ (inch)
採購成本	NTD240/ SET	NTD480/PC

運費資料：

運費	併櫃（CFS）	20 呎整櫃	40 呎整櫃
	USD 100	USD 2,400	USD 4,200
最低裝運量	1 CBM	25 CBM	50 CBM

其他報價資料：

匯率：1USD=33. 20NTD	利潤率：8%
保險費率：0.75%	業務費率：6%

注意事項：

1. 核算要求：計算過程無法整除者，CBM 計算至小數點第 4 位，四捨五入後取

3 位；其餘請計算至小數點第 3 位，四捨五入後取 2 位。

2. 佣金計算方式：以所求報價條件本身為佣金計算基礎，如 FOB&C 與 CIF&C 分別為 FOB 與 CIF 為基礎之含佣價。

貨號 A：併櫃方式報價

題目	答案	單位
1. 每箱 CBM 數		CBM
2. 每盒（SET）運費		USD/SET
3. FOB 報價		USD/SET
4. CFR 報價		USD/SET
5. CIFC3 報價		USD/SET

貨號 A：20 呎貨櫃方式報價

題目	答案	單位
1. 每箱 CBM 數		CBM
2. 20 呎櫃報價數量		SET
3. 每盒（SET）運費		USD/SET
4. CFR 報價		USD/SET
5. CIFC3 報價		USD/SET

貨號 A：40 呎貨櫃方式報價

題目	答案	單位
1. 每箱 CBM 數		CBM
2. 40 呎櫃報價數量		SET
3. 每盒（SET）運費		USD/SET
4. CFR 報價		USD/SET
5. CIFC3 報價		USD/SET

📖 貨號 B：併櫃方式報價

題目	答案	單位
1. 每箱才數		才（CFT）
2. 每箱 CBM 數		CBM
3. 每 PC 運費		USD/PC
4. FOB 報價		USD/PC
5. CIFC3 報價		USD/PC

📖 貨號 B：20 呎整櫃方式報價

題目	答案	單位
1. 每箱才數		才（CFT）
2. 每箱 CBM 數		CBM
3. 20 呎櫃報價數量		PC
4. 每 PC 運費		USD/PC
5. CIFC3 報價		USD/PC

📖 貨號 B：40 呎整櫃方式報價

題目	答案	單位
1. 40 呎櫃報價數量		PC
2. 每 PC 運費		USD/PC
3. CFR 報價		USD/PC
4. CIF 報價		USD/PC
5. CIFC3 報價		USD/PC

答案：

📖 貨號 A 出口價格核算計算總表

項次	項目	計算說明
1.	採購成本	NTD240/SET 匯率：1USD=33.20NTD
2.	業務費率	6%

項次	項目	計算說明
3.	利潤率	8% **FOB ＝ 採購成本＋業務費率＋利潤率** FOB ＝（240÷33.20）÷（1－6%）÷（1－8%）＝ 8.36(USD/SET)

項次 4. 海運費

(1)包裝方式：10 SET/箱（CTN）

(2)包裝尺寸：62×24×46(cm)

併櫃 （1CBM/USD100）	20'櫃 （25CBM/USD2,400）	40'櫃 （50CBM/USD4,200）
1. 先計算每箱 CBM： 0.62×0.24×0.46 ＝ 0.068 CBM *2.* 再計算每套運費： 0.068×100÷10 ＝ 0.68/SET	*1.* 先計算每箱 CBM： 0.62×0.24×0.46 ＝ 0.068 CBM *2.* 再計算 20'櫃報價箱數及套數： 25÷0.068 ＝ 367.65， 進位取整數為 368 CTN 368×10 ＝ 3,680 SET *3.* 最後計算每套運費： 2,400÷3,680 ＝ 0.65/SET	*1.* 先計算每箱 CBM： 0.62×0.24×0.46 ＝ 0.068 CBM *2.* 再計算 40'櫃報價箱數及套數： 50÷0.068 ＝ 735.29， 進位取整數為 736 CTN 736×10 ＝ 7,360 SET *3.* 最後計算每套運費： 4,200÷7,360 ＝ 0.57/SET
CFR ＝ 採購成本＋海運費＋業務費率＋利潤率		
CFR ＝（240÷33.20＋ 0.68）÷（1－6%） ÷（1－8%） ＝ 9.15 (USD/SET)	CFR ＝（240÷33.20＋ 0.65）÷（1－6%） ÷（1－8%） ＝ 9.11 (USD/SET)	CFR ＝（240÷33.20＋ 0.57）÷（1－6%） ÷（1－8%） ＝ 9.02 (USD/SET)

項次 5. 保險費率

0.75%（因題目未給予保險金額，故依慣例以 110%CIF 金額為基準）

CIF ＝ 採購成本＋海運費＋保險費＋業務費率＋利潤率

併櫃	20'櫃	40'櫃
CIF ＝（240÷33.20＋0.68） ÷（1－1.1×0.75%） ÷（1－6%）÷（1－8%） ＝ 9.22(USD/ SET)	CIF ＝（240÷33.20＋0.65） ÷（1－1.1×0.75%） ÷（1－6%）÷（1－8%） ＝ 9.19(USD/ SET)	CIF ＝（240÷33.20＋0.57） ÷（1－1.1×0.75%） ÷（1－6%）÷（1－8%） ＝ 9.09(USD/ SET)

項次 6. 佣金率

3%

CIFC3 ＝ 採購成本＋海運費＋保險費＋業務費率＋利潤率＋佣金率

項次	項目	計算說明		
		併櫃	20'櫃	40'櫃
		CIFC3 = (240÷33.20 + 0.68)÷(1－1.1×0.75%) ÷(1－6%)÷(1－8%) ÷(1－3%) = 9.51(USD/SET)	CIFC3 = (240÷33.20 + 0.65)÷(1－1.1×0.75%) ÷(1－6%)÷(1－8%) ÷(1－3%) = 9.47(USD/SET)	CIFC3 = (240÷33.20 + 0.57)÷(1－1.1×0.75%) ÷(1－6%)÷(1－8%) ÷(1－3%) = 9.37(USD/SET)

📖 貨號 A：併櫃方式報價

題目	答案	單位
1. 每箱 CBM 數	0.62×0.24×0.46 = 0.068	CBM
2. 每盒（SET）運費	0.068×100÷10 = 0.68	USD/SET
3. FOB 報價	(240÷33.20)÷(1－6%)÷(1－8%) = 8.36	USD/SET
4. CFR 報價	(240÷33.20＋0.68)÷(1－6%)÷(1－8%) = 9.15	USD/SET
5. CIFC3 報價	(240÷33.20＋0.68)÷(1－1.1×0.75%)÷(1－6%) ÷(1－8%)÷(1－3%) = 9.51	USD/SET

📖 貨號 A：20 呎貨櫃方式報價

題目	答案	單位
1. 每箱 CBM 數	0.62×0.24×0.46 = 0.068	CBM
2. 20 呎櫃報價數量	25÷0.068 =367.65，進位取整數 368 箱×10 = 3,680	SET
3. 每盒（SET）運費	2,400÷3,680 = 0.65	USD/SET
4. CFR 報價	(240÷33.20＋0.65)÷(1－6%)÷(1－8%) = 9.11	USD/SET
5. CIFC3 報價	(240÷33.20＋0.65)÷(1－1.1×0.75%)÷(1－6%) ÷(1－8%)÷(1－3%) = 9.47	USD/SET

📖 貨號 A：40 呎貨櫃方式報價

題目	答案	單位
1. 每箱 CBM 數	0.62×0.24×0.46 = 0.068	CBM
2. 40 呎櫃報價數量	50÷0.068 = 735.29，進位取整數 736 箱×10 = 7,360	SET
3. 每盒（SET）運費	4,200÷7,360 = 0.57	USD/SET
4. CFR 報價	(240÷33.20＋0.57)÷(1－6%)÷(1－8%) = 9.02	USD/SET
5. CIFC3 報價	(240÷33.20＋0.57)÷(1－1.1×0.75%)÷(1－6%) ÷(1－8%)÷(1－3%) = 9.37	USD/SET

👑 貨號 B 出口價格核算計算總表

項次	項目	計算說明
1.	採購成本	NTD480/PC 匯率：1USD=33.20NTD
2.	業務費率	6%
3.	利潤率	8% **FOB ＝ 採購成本＋業務費率＋利潤率** FOB ＝ (480÷33.20)÷(1－6%)÷(1－8%)= 16.72 (USD/ PC)

項次	項目	計算說明
4.	海運費	(1)包裝方式：6PC/箱（CTN） (2)包裝尺寸：27"×18"×11" (inch) (3)換算公式：1 立方呎 = 1,728 立方吋、1 CBM = 35.315 立方呎

併櫃 （1CBM/USD100）	20'櫃 （25CBM/USD2,400）	40'櫃 （50CBM/USD4,200）
1. 先計算每箱 CBM： 27×18×11÷1,728 ＝3.09 3.09÷35.315＝0.087 *2.* 再計算每套運費： 0.087×100÷6 ＝1.45/ PC	*1.* 先計算每箱 CBM： 27×18×11÷1,728 ＝3.09 3.09÷35.315＝0.087 *2.* 再計算 20'櫃報價箱數 及套數： 25÷0.087 ＝ 287.36， 進位取整數為 288CTN 288×6＝1,728 PC *3.* 最後計算每套運費： 2,400÷1,728＝1.39/ PC	*1.* 先計算每箱 CBM： 27×18×11÷1,728 ＝3.09 3.09÷35.315＝0.087 *2.* 再計算 40'櫃報價箱數 及件數： 50÷0.087 ＝ 574.71， 進位取整數為 575CTN 575×6＝3,450PC *3.* 最後計算每套運費： 4,200÷3,450＝1.22/ PC
CFR ＝ 採購成本＋海運費＋業務費率＋利潤率		
CFR ＝ (480÷33.20＋ 　　　1.45)÷(1－6%) 　　　÷(1－8%) 　　　＝18.40(USD/ PC)	CFR ＝ (480÷33.20＋ 　　　1.39)÷(1－6%) 　　　÷(1－8%) 　　　＝18.33(USD/ PC)	CFR ＝ (480÷33.20＋ 　　　1.22)÷(1－6%) 　　　÷(1－8%) 　　　＝18.13(USD/ PC)

項次	項目	計算說明
5.	保險費率	0.75%（因題目未給予保險金額，故依慣例以 110%CIF 金額為基準） **CIF ＝ 採購成本＋海運費＋保險費＋業務費率＋利潤率**

項次	項目	計算說明		

		併櫃	20'櫃	40'櫃
		CIF = (480÷33.20+1.45) ÷(1－1.1×0.75%) ÷(1－6%)÷(1－8%) = 18.55 (USD/ PC)	CIF = (480÷33.20+1.39) ÷(1－1.1×0.75%) ÷(1－6%)÷(1－8%) = 18.48 (USD/ PC)	CIF = (480÷33.20+1.22) ÷(1－1.1×0.75%) ÷(1－6%)÷(1－8%) = 18.28 (USD/ PC)
6.	佣金率	3%		

CIFC3 ＝ 採購成本＋海運費＋保險費＋業務費率＋利潤率＋佣金率

併櫃	20'櫃	40'櫃
CIFC3 = (480÷33.20+1.45)÷(1－1.1×0.75%)÷(1－6%)÷(1－8%)÷(1－3%)= 19.12(USD/ PC)	CIFC3 = (480÷33.20+1.39)÷(1－1.1×0.75%)÷(1－6%)÷(1－8%)÷(1－3%)= 19.05(USD/ PC)	CIFC3 = (480÷33.20+1.22)÷(1－1.1×0.75%)÷(1－6%)÷(1－8%)÷(1－3%)= 18.85(USD/ PC)

貨號 B：併櫃方式報價

題目	答案	單位
1. 每箱才數	27×18×11÷1,728 = 3.09	才（CFT）
2. 每箱 CBM 數	3.09÷35.315 = 0.087	CBM
3. 每 PC 運費	0.087×100÷6 = 1.45	USD/PC
4. FOB 報價	(480÷33.20)÷(1－6%)÷(1－8%) = 16.72	USD/PC
5. CIFC3 報價	(480÷33.20+1.45)÷(1－1.1×0.75%)÷(1－6%)÷(1－8%)÷(1－3%) = 19.12	USD/PC

貨號 B：20 呎整櫃方式報價

題目	答案	單位
1. 每箱才數	27×18×11÷1,728 = 3.09	才（CFT）
2. 每箱 CBM 數	3.09÷35.315 = 0.087	CBM
3. 20 呎櫃報價數量	25÷0.087=287.36，進位取整數 288 箱×6 = 1,728	PC
4. 每 PC 運費	2,400÷1,728 = 1.39	USD/PC
5. CIFC3 報價	(480÷33.20+1.39)÷(1－1.1×0.75%)÷(1－6%)÷(1－8%)÷(1－3%) = 19.05	USD/PC

🏆 貨號 B：40 呎整櫃方式報價

題目	答案	單位
1. 40 呎櫃報價數量	$50 \div 0.087 = 574.71$，進位取整數 575 箱×6 = 3,450	PC
2. 每 PC 運費	$4,200 \div 3,450 = 1.22$	USD/PC
3. CFR 報價	$(480 \div 33.20 + 1.22) \div (1 - 6\%) \div (1 - 8\%) = 18.13$	USD/PC
4. CIF 報價	$(480 \div 33.20 + 1.22) \div (1 - 1.1 \times 0.75\%) \div (1 - 6\%) \div (1 - 8\%) = 18.28$	USD/PC
5. CIFC3 報價	$(480 \div 33.20 + 1.22) \div (1 - 1.1 \times 0.75\%) \div (1 - 6\%) \div (1 - 8\%) \div (1 - 3\%) = 18.85$	USD/PC

四、根據以下資料，對貨號 A 與貨號 B 兩種以體積噸計算海運運費的貨物，分別以併櫃與整櫃運量，核算相關運費與報價，並填入答案欄內。

產品資料：

型　號	A	B
包裝方式	6BAG／箱（CTN）	25 PC／箱（CTN）
包裝尺寸	92.5×48×17.5(cm)	30"×22"×15" (inch)
採購成本	NTD1,100/ SET	NTD350/PC

運費資料：

運費	併櫃（CFS）	20 呎整櫃	40 呎整櫃
	USD 130	USD3,000	USD 5,500
最低裝運量	1 CBM	25 CBM	50 CBM

其他報價資料：

匯率：1USD =33. 15NTD	利潤率：10%
保險費率： 1.05%	業務費率：5%

注意事項：

    1. 核算要求：計算過程無法整除者，CBM 計算至小數點第 4 位，四捨五入後取 3 位；其餘請計算至小數點第 3 位，四捨五入後取 2 位。

    2. 佣金計算方式：以所求報價條件本身為佣金計算基礎，如 FOB&C 與 CIF&C 分別為 FOB 與 CIF 為基礎之含佣價。

貨號 A：併櫃方式報價

題目	答案	單位
1. 每箱 CBM 數		CBM
2. 每袋（BAG）運費		USD/BAG
3. FOB 報價		USD/BAG
4. CFR 報價		USD/BAG
5. CIFC5 報價		USD/BAG

貨號 A：20 呎貨櫃方式報價

題目	答案	單位
1. 每箱 CBM 數		CBM
2. 20 呎櫃報價數量		BAG
3. 每袋（BAG）運費		USD/BAG
4. CFR 報價		USD/BAG
5. CIFC5 報價		USD/BAG

貨號 A：40 呎貨櫃方式報價

題目	答案	單位
1. 每箱 CBM 數		CBM
2. 40 呎櫃報價數量		BAG
3. 每袋（BAG）運費		USD/BAG
4. CFR 報價		USD/BAG
5. CIFC5 報價		USD/BAG

貨號 B：併櫃方式報價

題目	答案	單位
1. 每箱才數		才（CFT）
2. 每箱 CBM 數		CBM
3. 每 PC 運費		USD/PC
4. FOB 報價		USD/PC
5. CIFC5 報價		USD/PC

貨號 B：20 呎整櫃方式報價

題目	答案	單位
1. 每箱才數		才（CFT）
2. 每箱 CBM 數		CBM
3. 20 呎櫃報價數量		PC
4. 每 PC 運費		USD/PC
5. CIFC5 報價		USD/PC

貨號 B：40 呎整櫃方式報價

題目	答案	單位
1. 40 呎櫃報價數量		PC
2. 每 PC 運費		USD/PC
3. CFR 報價		USD/PC
4. CIF 報價		USD/PC
5. CIFC5 報價		USD/PC

答案：

貨號 A 出口價格核算計算總表

項次	項目	計算說明
1.	採購成本	NTD1,100/SET 匯率：1USD=33.15NTD
2.	業務費率	5%

項次	項目	計算說明
3.	利潤率	10% **FOB ＝ 採購成本＋業務費率＋利潤率** FOB ＝ $(1,100 \div 33.15) \div (1 - 5\%) \div (1 - 10\%)$ ＝ 38.81(USD/SET)
4.	海運費	(1)包裝方式：6 BAG/箱（CTN） (2)包裝尺寸：92.5×48×17.5(cm)

	併櫃 （1CBM/USD130）	20'櫃 （25CBM/USD3,000）	40'櫃 （50CBM/USD5,500）
	1. 先計算每箱 CBM： $0.925 \times 0.48 \times 0.175$ ＝ 0.078CBM 2. 再計算每袋運費： $0.078 \times 130 \div 6$ ＝ 1.69/BAG	1. 先計算每箱 CBM： $0.925 \times 0.48 \times 0.175$ ＝ 0.078CBM 2. 再計算 20'櫃報價箱數 及袋數： $25 \div 0.078 ＝ 320.51$， 進位取整數為 321 CTN $321 \times 6 = 1,926$ BAG 3. 最後計算每袋運費： $3,000 \div 1,926$ ＝ 1.56/BAG	1. 先計算每箱 CBM： $0.925 \times 0.48 \times 0.175$ ＝ 0.078CBM 2. 再計算 40'櫃報價箱數 及袋數： $50 \div 0.078 ＝ 641.03$， 進位取整數為 642 CTN $642 \times 6 = 3,852$ BAG 3. 最後計算每袋運費： $5,500 \div 3,852$ ＝ 1.43/BAG

CFR ＝ 採購成本＋海運費＋業務費率＋利潤率

併櫃	20'櫃	40'櫃
CFR ＝ $(1,100 \div 33.15$ $+ 1.69) \div (1 - 5\%)$ $\div (1 - 10\%)$ ＝ 40.79 (USD/BAG)	CFR ＝ $(1,100 \div 33.15$ $+ 1.56) \div (1 - 5\%)$ $\div (1 - 10\%)$ ＝ 40.63(USD/BAG)	CFR ＝ $(1,100 \div 33.15$ $+ 1.43) \div (1 - 5\%)$ $\div (1 - 10\%)$ ＝ 40.48(USD/BAG)

項次	項目	計算說明
5.	保險費率	1.05%（因題目未給予保險金額，故依慣例以 110%CIF 金額為基準） **CIF ＝ 採購成本＋海運費＋保險費＋業務費率＋利潤率**

併櫃	20'櫃	40'櫃
CIF ＝ $(1,100 \div 33.15 + 1.69)$ $\div (1 - 1.1 \times 1.05\%)$ $\div (1 - 5\%) \div (1 - 10\%)$ ＝ 41.26(USD/BAG)	CIF ＝ $(1,100 \div 33.15 + 1.56)$ $\div (1 - 1.1 \times 1.05\%)$ $\div (1 - 5\%) \div (1 - 10\%)$ ＝ 41.11 (USD/BAG)	CIF ＝ $(1,100 \div 33.15 + 1.43)$ $\div (1 - 1.1 \times 1.05\%)$ $\div (1 - 5\%) \div (1 - 10\%)$ ＝ 40.96(USD/BAG)

項次	項目	計算說明
6.	佣金率	5% **CIFC5 ＝ 採購成本＋海運費＋保險費＋業務費率＋利潤率＋佣金率**

項次	項目	計算說明		
		併櫃	20'櫃	40'櫃
		CIFC5 = (1,100÷33.15 + 1.69)÷(1 − 1.1×1.05%) ÷(1 − 5%)÷(1 − 10%) ÷(1 − 5%) = 43.43(USD/BAG)	CIFC5 = (1,100÷33.15 + 1.56)÷(1 − 1.1×1.05%) ÷(1 − 5%)÷(1 − 10%) ÷(1 − 5%) = 43.27 (USD/BAG)	CIFC5 = (1,100÷33.15 + 1.43)÷(1 − 1.1×1.05%) ÷(1 − 5%)÷(1 − 10%) ÷(1 − 5%) = 43.11 (USD/BAG)

貨號 A：併櫃方式報價

題目	答案	單位
1. 每箱 CBM 數	0.925×0.48×0.175 = 0.078	CBM
2. 每袋（BAG）運費	0.078×130÷6= 1.69	USD/BAG
3. FOB 報價	(1,100÷33.15)÷(1 − 5%)÷(1 − 10%) = 38.81	USD/BAG
4. CFR 報價	(1,100÷33.15＋1.69)÷(1 − 5%)÷(1 − 10%) =40.79	USD/BAG
5. CIFC5 報價	(1,100÷33.15＋1.69)÷(1 − 1.1×1.05%)÷(1 − 5%) ÷(1 − 10%)÷(1 − 5%) = 43.43	USD/BAG

貨號 A：20 呎貨櫃方式報價

題目	答案	單位
1. 每箱 CBM 數	0.925×0.48×0.175 = 0.078	CBM
2. 20 呎櫃報價數量	25÷0.078 = 320.51，進位取整數 321 箱×6＝1,926	BAG
3. 每袋（BAG）運費	3,000÷1,926 = 1.56	USD/BAG
4. CFR 報價	(1,100÷33.15＋1.56)÷(1 − 5%)÷(1 − 10%) = 40.63	USD/BAG
5. CIFC5 報價	(1,100÷33.15＋1.56)÷(1 − 1.1×1.05%)÷(1 − 5%)÷(1 − 10%)÷(1 − 5%) = 43.27	USD/BAG

貨號 A：40 呎貨櫃方式報價

題目	答案	單位
1. 每箱 CBM 數	0.925×0.48×0.175 = 0.078	CBM
2. 40 呎櫃報價數量	50÷0.078 = 641.03，進位取整數 642 箱×6＝3,852	BAG
3. 每袋（BAG）運費	5,500÷3,852 = 1.43	USD/BAG
4. CFR 報價	(1,100÷33.15＋1.43)÷(1 − 5%)÷(1 − 10%) = 40.48	USD/BAG
5. CIFC5 報價	(1,100÷33.15＋1.43)÷ ÷(1 − 1.1×1.05%)÷ (1 − 5%)÷(1 − 10%)÷(1 − 5%) = 43.11	USD/BAG

貨號 B 出口價格核算計算總表

項次	項目	計算說明
1.	採購成本	NTD350/PC 匯率：1USD=33.15NTD
2.	業務費率	5%
3.	利潤率	10% FOB ＝ 採購成本＋業務費率＋利潤率 FOB ＝ (350÷33.15)÷(1－5%)÷(1－10%)＝ 12.35(USD/ PC)

4.	海運費	(1)包裝方式：25PC/箱（CTN） (2)包裝尺寸：30"×22"×15" (inch) (3)換算公式：1 立方呎 ＝ 1,728 立方吋、1 CBM ＝ 35.315 立方呎

併櫃 （1CBM/USD130）	20'櫃 （25CBM/USD3,000）	40'櫃 （50CBM/USD5,500）
1. 先計算每箱 CBM： 30×22×15÷1,728 ＝ 5.73 5.73÷35.315 ＝ 0.162 2. 再計算每套運費： 0.162×130÷25 ＝ 0.84/ PC	1. 先計算每箱 CBM： 30×22×15÷1,728 ＝ 5.73 5.73÷35.315 ＝ 0.162 2. 再計算 20'櫃報價箱數 及套數： 25÷0.162 ＝ 154.32， 進位取整數為 155CTN 155×25 ＝ 3,875 PC 3. 最後計算每套運費： 3,000÷3,875 ＝ 0.77/ PC	1. 先計算每箱 CBM： 30×22×15÷1,728 ＝ 5.73 5.73÷35.315 ＝ 0.162 2. 再計算 40'櫃報價箱數 及件數： 50÷0.162 ＝ 308.64， 進位取整數為 309CTN 309×25 ＝ 7,725PC 3. 最後計算每套運費： 5,500÷7,725 ＝ 0.71/ PC
CFR ＝ 採購成本＋海運費＋業務費率＋利潤率		
CFR ＝ (350÷33.15＋ 0.84)÷(1－5%) ÷(1－10%) ＝ 13.33(USD/ PC)	CFR ＝ (350÷33.15＋ 0.77)÷(1－5%) ÷(1－10%) ＝ 13.25(USD/ PC)	CFR ＝ (350÷33.15＋ 0.71)÷(1－5%) ÷(1－10%) ＝ 13.18(USD/ PC)

5.	保險費率	1.05%（因題目未給予保險金額，故依慣例以 110%CIF 金額為基準） CIF ＝ 採購成本＋海運費＋保險費＋業務費率＋利潤率

項次	項目	計算說明

		併櫃	20'櫃	40'櫃
		CIF = (350÷33.15+0.84) ÷(1−1.1×1.05%) ÷(1−5%)÷(1−10%) = 13.49(USD/ PC)	CIF = (350÷33.15+0.77) ÷(1−1.1×1.05%) ÷(1−5%)÷(1−10%) = 13.40 (USD/ PC)	CIF = (350÷33.15+0.71) ÷(1−1.1×1.05%) ÷(1−5%)÷(1−10%) = 13.33 (USD/ PC)
6.	佣金率	5%		

CIFC5 ＝ 採購成本＋海運費＋保險費＋業務費率＋利潤率＋佣金率

併櫃	20'櫃	40'櫃
CIFC3 = (350÷33.15+ 0.84)÷(1−1.1×1.05%) ÷(1−5%)÷(1−10%) ÷(1−5%) = 14.20 (USD/ PC)	CIFC3 = (350÷33.15+ 0.77)÷(1−1.1×1.05%) ÷(1−5%)÷(1−10%) ÷(1−5%) = 14.11(USD/ PC)	CIFC3 = (350÷33.15+ 0.71)÷(1−1.1×1.05%) ÷(1−5%)÷(1−10%) ÷(1−5%) = 14.03(USD/ PC)

貨號 B：併櫃方式報價

題目	答案	單位
1. 每箱才數	30×22×15÷1,728 = 5.73	才（CFT）
2. 每箱 CBM 數	5.73÷35.315 = 0.162	CBM
3. 每 PC 運費	0.162×130÷25 = 0.84	USD/PC
4. FOB 報價	(350÷33.15)÷(1−5%)÷(1−10%) = 12.35	USD/PC
5. CIFC5 報價	(350÷33.15+0.84)÷(1−1.1×1.05%)÷(1−5%)÷ (1−10%)÷(1−5%) = 14.20	USD/PC

貨號 B：20 呎整櫃方式報價

題目	答案	單位
1. 每箱才數	30×22×15÷1,728 = 5.73	才（CFT）
2. 每箱 CBM 數	5.73÷35.315 = 0.162	CBM
3. 20 呎櫃報價數量	25÷0.162 = 154.32，進位取整數 155 箱×25 = 3,875	PC
4. 每 PC 運費	3,000÷3,875 = 0.77	USD/PC
5. CIFC5 報價	(350÷33.15+0.77)÷(1−1.1×1.05%)÷(1−5%)÷ (1−10%)÷(1−5%) = 14.11	USD/PC

📖 貨號 B：40 呎整櫃方式報價

題目	答案	單位
1. 40 呎櫃報價數量	$50 \div 0.162 = 308.64$，進位取整數 309 箱 $\times 25 = 7,725$	PC
2. 每 PC 運費	$5,500 \div 7,725 = 0.71$	USD/PC
3. CFR 報價	$(350 \div 33.15 + 0.71) \div (1 - 5\%) \div (1 - 10\%) = 13.18$	USD/PC
4. CIF 報價	$(350 \div 33.15 + 0.71) \div (1 - 1.1 \times 1.05\%) \div (1 - 5\%) \div$ $(1 - 10\%) = 13.33$	USD/PC
5. CIFC5 報價	$(350 \div 33.15 + 0.71) \div (1 - 1.1 \times 1.05\%) \div (1 - 5\%) \div$ $(1 - 10\%) \div (1 - 5\%) = 14.03$	USD/PC

五、根據以下資料，對貨號 A 與貨號 B 兩種以體積噸計算海運運費的貨物，分別以
併櫃與整櫃運量，核算相關運費與報價，並填入答案欄內。

產品資料：

型　　號	A	B
包裝方式	6SET/箱（CTN）	24 PC/箱（CTN）
包裝尺寸	62×48×60(cm)	21"×20"×19" (inch)
採購成本	NTD440/ SET	NTD720/PC

運費資料：

運費	併櫃（CFS）	20 呎整櫃	40 呎整櫃
	USD 65	USD1,780	USD 3,200
最低裝運量	1 CBM	25 CBM	50 CBM

其他報價資料：

匯率：1USD=33.10NTD	利潤率：7%
保險費率：0.95%	業務費率：8%

注意事項

1. 核算要求：計算過程無法整除者，CBM計算至小數點第 4 位，四捨五入後取 3 位；其餘請計算至小數點第 3 位，四捨五入後取 2 位。

2. 佣金計算方式：以所求報價條件本身為佣金計算基礎，如 FOB&C 與 CIF&C 分別為 FOB 與 CIF 為基礎之含佣價。

♟ 貨號 A：併櫃方式報價

題目	答案	單位
1. 每箱 CBM 數		CBM
2. 每盒（SET）運費		USD/SET
3. FOB 報價		USD/SET
4. CFR 報價		USD/SET
5. CIFC8 報價		USD/SET

♟ 貨號 A：20 呎貨櫃方式報價

題目	答案	單位
1. 每箱 CBM 數		CBM
2. 20 呎櫃報價數量		SET
3. 每盒（SET）運費		USD/SET
4. CFR 報價		USD/SET
5. CIFC8 報價		USD/SET

♟ 貨號 A：40 呎貨櫃方式報價

題目	答案	單位
1. 每箱 CBM 數		CBM
2. 40 呎櫃報價數量		SET
3. 每盒（SET）運費		USD/SET
4. CFR 報價		USD/SET
5. CIFC8 報價		USD/SET

🔖 貨號 B：併櫃方式報價

題目	答案	單位
1. 每箱才數		才（CFT）
2. 每箱 CBM 數		CBM
3. 每 PC 運費		USD/PC
4. FOB 報價		USD/PC
5. CIFC8 報價		USD/PC

🔖 貨號 B：20 呎整櫃方式報價

題目	答案	單位
1. 每箱才數		才（CFT）
2. 每箱 CBM 數		CBM
3. 20 呎櫃報價數量		PC
4. 每 PC 運費		USD/PC
5. CIFC8 報價		USD/PC

🔖 貨號 B：40 呎整櫃方式報價

題目	答案	單位
1. 40 呎櫃報價數量		PC
2. 每 PC 運費		USD/PC
3. CFR 報價		USD/PC
4. CIF 報價		USD/PC
5. CIFC8 報價		USD/PC

答案：

🔖 貨號 A 出口價格核算計算總表

項次	項目	計算說明
1.	採購成本	NTD440/SET 匯率：1USD=33.10NTD
2.	業務費率	8%

項次	項目	計算說明
3.	利潤率	7% **FOB ＝ 採購成本＋業務費率＋利潤率** FOB ＝ (440 ÷ 33.10) ÷ (1 − 8%) ÷ (1 − 7%) ＝ 15.54(USD/SET)

| 4. | 海運費 | (1)包裝方式：6 SET/箱（CTN）
(2)包裝尺寸：62×48×60(cm) |

併櫃 （1CBM/USD65）	20'櫃 （25CBM/USD1,780）	40'櫃 （50CBM/USD3,200）
1. 先計算每箱 CBM： 0.62×0.48×0.60 ＝ 0.179CBM *2.* 再計算每套運費： 0.179×65÷6 ＝ 1.94/SET	*1.* 先計算每箱 CBM： 0.62×0.48×0.60 ＝ 0.179CBM *2.* 再計算 20'櫃報價箱數及套數： 25÷0.179 ＝ 139.66， 進位取整數為 140 CTN 140×6 ＝ 840SET *3.* 最後計算每套運費： 1,780÷840 ＝ 2.12/SET	*1.* 先計算每箱 CBM： 0.62×0.48×0.60 ＝ 0.179CBM *2.* 再計算 40'櫃報價箱數及套數： 50÷0.179 ＝ 279.33， 進位取整數為 280CTN 280×6 ＝ 1,680 SET *3.* 最後計算每套運費： 3,200÷1,680 ＝ 1.90/SET
CFR ＝ 採購成本＋海運費＋業務費率＋利潤率		
CFR ＝ (440÷33.10＋ 1.94)÷(1−8%) ÷(1−7%) ＝ 17.80(USD/SET)	CFR ＝ (440÷33.10＋ 2.12)÷(1−8%) ÷(1−7%) ＝ 18.01(USD/SET)	CFR ＝ (440÷33.10＋ 1.90)÷(1−8%) ÷(1−7%) ＝ 17.76(USD/SET)

| 5. | 保險費率 | 0.95%（因題目未給予保險金額，故依慣例以 110%CIF 金額為基準） |

CIF ＝ 採購成本＋海運費＋保險費＋業務費率＋利潤率

併櫃	20'櫃	40'櫃
CIF ＝ (440÷33.10＋1.94) ÷(1−1.1×0.95%) ÷(1−8%)÷(1−7%) ＝ 17.99(USD/SET)	CIF ＝ (440÷33.10＋2.12) ÷(1−1.1×0.95%) ÷(1−8%)÷(1−7%) ＝ 18.20(USD/SET)	CIF ＝ (440÷33.10＋1.90) ÷(1−1.1×0.95%) ÷(1−8%)÷(1−7%) ＝ 17.94(USD/SET)

| 6. | 佣金率 | 8% |

CIFC8 ＝ 採購成本＋海運費＋保險費＋業務費率＋利潤率＋佣金率

項次	項目	計算說明		
		併櫃	20'櫃	40'櫃
		$CIFC8 = (440 \div 33.10 + 1.94) \div (1 - 1.1 \times 0.95\%)$ $\div (1 - 8\%) \div (1 - 7\%)$ $\div (1 - 8\%)$ $= 19.56\ (USD/SET)$	$CIFC8 = (440 \div 33.10 + 2.12) \div (1 - 1.1 \times 0.95\%)$ $\div (1 - 8\%) \div (1 - 7\%)$ $\div (1 - 8\%)$ $= 19.79(USD/SET)$	$CIFC8 = (440 \div 33.10 + 1.90) \div (1 - 1.1 \times 0.95\%)$ $\div (1 - 8\%) \div (1 - 7\%)$ $\div (1 - 8\%)$ $= 19.51(USD/SET)$

♟ 貨號 A：併櫃方式報價

題目	答案	單位
1. 每箱 CBM 數	$0.62 \times 0.48 \times 0.60 = 0.179$	CBM
2. 每盒（SET）運費	$0.179 \times 65 \div 6 = 1.94$	USD/SET
3. FOB 報價	$(440 \div 33.10) \div (1 - 8\%) \div (1 - 7\%) = 15.54$	USD/SET
4. CFR 報價	$(440 \div 33.10 + 1.94) \div (1 - 8\%) \div (1 - 7\%) = 17.80$	USD/SET
5. CIFC8 報價	$(440 \div 33.10 + 1.94) \div (1 - 1.1 \times 0.95\%) \div (1 - 8\%)$ $\div (1 - 7\%) \div (1 - 8\%) = 19.56$	USD/SET

♟ 貨號 A：20 呎貨櫃方式報價

題目	答案	單位
1. 每箱 CBM 數	$0.62 \times 0.48 \times 0.60 = 0.179$	CBM
2. 20 呎櫃報價數量	$25 \div 0.179 = 139.66$，進位取整數 140 箱 $\times 6 = 840$	SET
3. 每盒（SET）運費	$1,780 \div 840 = 2.12$	USD/SET
4. CFR 報價	$(440 \div 33.10 + 2.12) \div (1 - 8\%) \div (1 - 7\%) = 18.01$	USD/SET
5. CIFC8 報價	$(440 \div 33.10 + 2.12) \div (1 - 1.1 \times 0.95\%) \div (1 - 8\%)$ $\div (1 - 7\%) \div (1 - 8\%) = 19.79$	USD/SET

♟ 貨號 A：40 呎貨櫃方式報價

題目	答案	單位
1. 每箱 CBM 數	$0.62 \times 0.48 \times 0.60 = 0.179$	CBM
2. 40 呎櫃報價數量	$50 \div 0.179 = 279.33$，進位取整數 280 箱 $\times 6 = 1,680$	SET
3. 每盒（SET）運費	$3,200 \div 1,680 = 1.90$	USD/SET
4. CFR 報價	$(440 \div 33.10 + 1.90) \div (1 - 8\%) \div (1 - 7\%) = 17.76$	USD/SET
5. CIFC8 報價	$(440 \div 33.10 + 1.90) \div (1 - 1.1 \times 0.95\%) \div (1 - 8\%)$ $\div (1 - 7\%) \div (1 - 8\%) = 19.51$	USD/SET

♟貨號 B 出口價格核算計算總表

項次	項目	計算說明
1.	採購成本	NTD720/PC 匯率：1USD=33.10NTD
2.	業務費率	8%
3.	利潤率	7% **FOB ＝ 採購成本＋業務費率＋利潤率** FOB ＝ (720÷33.10)÷(1－8%)÷(1－7%)＝ 25.42 (USD/ PC)
4.	海運費	(1)包裝方式：24PC/箱（CTN） (2)包裝尺寸：21"×20"×19" (inch) (3)換算公式：1 立方呎＝1,728 立方吋、1 CBM＝35.315 立方呎

併櫃 （1CBM/USD65）	20'櫃 （25CBM/USD1,780）	40'櫃 （50CBM/USD3,200）
1.先計算每箱 CBM： 21×20×19÷1,728 ＝4.62 4.62÷35.315＝0.131 2.再計算每套運費： 0.131×65÷24 ＝0.35/ PC	1.先計算每箱 CBM： 21×20×19÷1,728 ＝4.62 4.62÷35.315＝0.131 2.再計算 20'櫃報價箱數 及套數： 25÷0.131 ＝ 190.83， 進位取整數為 191CTN 191×24＝4,584 PC 3.最後計算每套運費： 1,780÷4,584＝0.39/ PC	1.先計算每箱 CBM： 21×20×19÷1,728 ＝4.62 4.62÷35.315＝0.131 2.再計算 40'櫃報價箱數 及件數： 50÷0.131 ＝ 381.68， 進位取整數為 382CTN 382×24＝9,168PC 3.最後計算每套運費： 3,200÷9,168＝0.35/ PC
CFR ＝ 採購成本＋海運費＋業務費率＋利潤率		
CFR ＝ (720÷33.10＋ 0.35)÷(1－8%) ÷(1－7%) ＝ 25.83(USD/ PC)	CFR ＝ (720÷33.10＋ 0.39)÷(1－8%) ÷(1－7%) ＝ 25.88(USD/ PC)	CFR ＝ (720÷33.10＋ 0.35)÷(1－8%) ÷(1－7%) ＝ 25.83 (USD/ PC)

項次	項目	計算說明
5.	保險費率	0.95%（因題目未給予保險金額，故依慣例以 110%CIF 金額為基準） **CIF ＝ 採購成本＋海運費＋保險費＋業務費率＋利潤率**

項次	項目	計算說明		
		併櫃	20'櫃	40'櫃
		CIF = (720÷33.10+0.35) ÷(1−1.1×0.95%) ÷(1−8%)÷(1−7%) = 26.11 (USD/PC)	CIF = (720÷33.10+0.39) ÷(1−1.1×0.95%) ÷(1−8%)÷(1−7%) = 26.15(USD/PC)	CIF = (720÷33.10+0.35) ÷(1−1.1×0.95%) ÷(1−8%)÷(1−7%) = 26.11(USD/PC)
6.	佣金率	8%		
		CIFC8 = 採購成本＋海運費＋保險費＋業務費率＋利潤率＋佣金率		
		併櫃	20'櫃	40'櫃
		CIFC8 = (720÷33.10＋ 0.35)÷(1−1.1×0.95%) ÷(1−8%)÷(1−7%) ÷(1−8%) = 28.38(USD/PC)	CIFC8 = (720÷33.10＋ 0.39)÷(1−1.1×0.95%) ÷(1−8%)÷(1−7%) ÷(1−8%) = 28.43(USD/PC)	CIFC8 = (720÷33.10＋ 0.35)÷(1−1.1×0.95%) ÷(1−8%)÷(1−7%) ÷(1−8%) = 28.38(USD/PC)

📖 貨號 B：併櫃方式報價

題目	答案	單位
1. 每箱才數	21×20×19÷1,728 = 4.62	才（CFT）
2. 每箱 CBM 數	4.62÷35.315 = 0.131	CBM
3. 每 PC 運費	0.131×65÷24 = 0.35	USD/PC
4. FOB 報價	(720÷33.10)÷(1−8%)÷(1−7%) = 25.42	USD/PC
5. CIFC8 報價	(720÷33.10+0.35)÷(1−1.1×0.95%)÷(1−8%)÷ (1−7%)÷(1−8%) = 28.38	USD/PC

📖 貨號 B：20 呎整櫃方式報價

題目	答案	單位
1. 每箱才數	21×20×19÷1,728 = 4.62	才（CFT）
2. 每箱 CBM 數	4.62÷35.315 = 0.131	CBM
3. 20 呎櫃報價數量	25÷0.131=190.83，進位取整數 191 箱×24 = 4,584	PC
4. 每 PC 運費	1,780÷4,584 = 0.39	USD/PC
5. CIFC8 報價	(720÷33.10+0.39)÷(1−1.1×0.95%)÷(1−8%)÷ (1−7%)÷(1−8%) = 28.43	USD/PC

♟ 貨號 B：40 呎整櫃方式報價

題目	答案	單位
1. 40 呎櫃報價數量	$50 \div 0.131 = 381.68$，進位取整數 382 箱 $\times 24 = 9,168$	PC
2. 每 PC 運費	$3,200 \div 9,168 = 0.35$	USD/PC
3. CFR 報價	$(720 \div 33.10 + 0.35) \div (1 - 8\%) \div (1 - 7\%) = 25.83$	USD/PC
4. CIF 報價	$(720 \div 33.10 + 0.35) \div (1 - 1.1 \times 0.95\%) \div (1 - 8\%) \div (1 - 7\%) = 26.11$	USD/PC
5. CIFC8 報價	$(720 \div 33.10 + 0.35) \div (1 - 1.1 \times 0.95\%) \div (1 - 8\%) \div (1 - 7\%) \div (1 - 8\%) = 28.38$	USD/PC

商業信用狀分析

第一節　信用狀內容解析

一、信用狀格式

開狀銀行所開發之信用狀，依其送達通知銀行之方式，可分為兩種：

㈠郵遞方式

稱為郵遞信用狀（Mail L/C），開狀銀行將信用狀正本郵寄通知銀行再轉知受益人（出口商），費用較低廉，但遞送速度較電報為慢。

㈡電報方式

稱為電報信用狀（Cable L/C），開狀銀行將信用狀內容以電報送達通知銀行再轉知受益人，如以 Cable、Telegram、Telex 及 SWIFT 方式。電報方式又分為兩種：

1. 簡文電報（Brief Cable）方式

開狀銀行將信用狀內容中之主要事項，諸如申請人、受益人、信用狀號碼、金額等先行電報通知，然後再郵寄電報證實書（Cable Confirmation），出口商押匯時應同時備有 Brief Cable 及 Cable Confirmation 方可押匯。

2. 詳文電報（Full Cable）方式

開狀銀行將信用狀內容全部以電報送達，該全文電報除非註明另送 Cable Confirmation，則電報本身即視為正本（Operative Credit Instrument），出口商可單獨憑以押匯。

電報方式之信用狀格式，目前大多以 SWIFT 為主，SWIFT 環球銀行財務電信協會或環球銀行財務電訊系統（Society for Worldwide Interbank Financial Telecommunication），它是一套用於全世界各銀行間資訊傳遞、調撥資金、開發信用狀等一種高性能、低成本、安全、迅速、電文標準化，而且可以與各種電腦連續作業的電信系統。

(一) SWIFT 信用狀之特色

1. 自動核對密碼

SWIFT 其文尾部分會自動出現「密碼」，如密碼不符，開狀銀行發過來的信息就會自動被回拒。

2. 以數字代號引導信用狀內容

SWIFT 信用狀之內容，係以數字代號來引導。

(二) SWIFT 信用狀之電文代號及使用範圍

表 1　MT700 Issue of a Documentary Credit 跟單信用狀的開發

M/O	標示	欄位名稱
M	27	Sequence of Total 合計序號
M	40A	Form of Documentary Credit 跟單信用狀的類別
M	40E	Applicable Rules 適用規則
M	20	Documentary Credit Number 跟單信用狀號碼
O	23	Reference to Pre-Advice 預告的摘要
O	31C	Date of Issue 開狀日期
M	31D	Date and Place of Expiry 到期日及地點
M	32B	Currency Code, Amount 幣別代號及金額
O	51a	Applicant Bank 申請銀行
M	50	Applicant 申請人

M/O	標示	欄位名稱
M	59	Beneficiary 受益人
O	39A	Percentage Credit Amount Tolerance 信用狀金額上下寬容範圍之百分比
O	39B	Maximum Credit Amount 信用狀金額最大限度
O	39C	Additional Amounts Covered 附加金額之內容
M	41a	Available with... by 信用狀使用方式
O	42C	Drafts at... 匯票期限
O	42a	Drawee 付款銀行
O	42M	Mixed Payment Details 混合付款明細
O	42P	Deferred Payment Details 延期付款明細
O	43P	Partial Shipments 分批裝運
O	43T	Transhipment 轉運
O	44E	Port of Loading / Airport of Departure 裝運港口／機場
O	44F	Port of Discharge / Airport of Destination 卸貨港口／機場
O	44C	Latest Date of Shipment 最後裝運日期
O	44D	Shipment Period 裝運期間
O	45A	Description of Goods and/or Services 貨品名稱
O	46A	Documents Required 應具備的單據文件
O	47A	Additional Conditions 附加條件
O	71B	Charges 費用
O	48	Period for Presentation 提示期間
M	49	Confirmation Instructions 保兌指示
O	53a	Reimbursing Bank 補償銀行
O	78	Instructions to the Paying/Accepting/Negotiating Bank 給予付款／承兌／讓購銀行的指示
O	57a	Advise through Bank 收訊銀行以外的通知銀行
O	72	Sender to Receiver Information 銀行間的備註

M=Mandatory 必要項目；O=Optional 選列項目

二、信用狀內容

㈠郵遞信用狀

茲以所附郵遞信用狀，說明該信用狀內容如下：

<table>
<tr>
<td colspan="4" align="center">Chase Manhattan Bank
180 Canal St., New York, NY 10013 USA</td>
</tr>
<tr>
<td colspan="2" align="center">IRREVOCABLE DOCUMENTARY CREDIT</td>
<td colspan="2" align="center">Cable Address:</td>
</tr>
<tr>
<td align="center">DATE
May 11, 2018</td>
<td align="center">ADVISIED BY
☐ cable ☒ airmail</td>
<td align="center">of issuer
LC-123456</td>
<td align="center">of advising bank</td>
</tr>
<tr>
<td colspan="2">Advising Bank
COSMOS BANK , Taipei, Taiwan.</td>
<td colspan="2">Applicant
SUNRISE INC., Johnstown. N.Y. 11066</td>
</tr>
<tr>
<td colspan="2" rowspan="2">Beneficiary
HANNSTAR CO., LTD.
NO.100, KAO SHI RD., YANG-MEI TOWN-SHIP, TAOYUAN COUNTY 200,TAIWAN, R.O.C.</td>
<td colspan="2">Amount
USD10,800.00 (U.S. DOLLARS TEN THOU-SAND EIGHT HUNDRED ONLY)</td>
</tr>
<tr>
<td colspan="2">Expiry Date
July 11, 2018</td>
</tr>
<tr>
<td colspan="4">
Dear Sir(s),
We hereby issue in your favor this documentary credit which is available by negotiation of your drafts at sight drawn on us for100% invoice value bearing the clause "Drawn under Chase Manhattan Bank Credit No. LC-123456"
Accompanied by the following documents :
1. Commercial Invoice in triplicate.
2. Full set of clean on board Bills of Lading issued to the order of Chase Manhattan Bank, and marked "FREIGHT PREPAID" and notify buyer.
3. Insurance policy or certificate in negotiable form for full CIF value plus 10 percent covering institute cargo clauses (A), institute war clauses (cargo) and institute strikes clauses (cargo).
4. Packing List in triplicate.
Covering: PROCESSING LEATHER GLOVES   CIF NEW YORK
        evidencing shipment not later than July 15, 2018.
Special Instructions:
1. All banking charges outside U.S.A. are for account of beneficiary.
2. The credit is restricted to the advising bank for negotiation.
3. This credit is only transferable in your country.
4. Documents must be presented for negotiation within 10 days after B/L date.
</td>
</tr>
</table>

SHIPMENT FROM **KEELUNG** TO **NEW YORK**	PARTIAL SHIPMENTS **permitted**	TRANSHIPMENT **prohibited**
The amount of each draft negotiated with date of negotiation must be endorsed hereon by the negotiating bank. We hereby agree with you and with negotiating banks and bankers that drafts drawn under and in compliance with the terms of this credit shall to the drawee.	ADVISING BANK'S NOTIFICATION This is an Irrevocable Letter of Credit of the above mentioned Issuer and is transmitted to you without any responsibility or engagement on our part.	
Authorized Signature-Issuing Bank	Place, Date, Name, and Signature of Advising Bank	

解析：

1.

Chase Manhattan Bank 開狀銀行 180 Canal St., New York, NY 10013 USA			
IRREVOCABLE DOCUMENTARY CREDIT 不可撤銷、跟單信用狀		**CREDIT NUMBER** 信用狀編號	
DATE 開狀日期 May11, 2018	**ADVISIED BY** ☐ cable ☒ airmail	of issuer LC-123456	of advising bank
Advising Bank 通知銀行 COSMOS BANK , Taipei, Taiwan.		**Applicant** 開狀申請人 SUNRISE INC., Johnstown. N.Y. 11066	
Beneficiary 受益人 HANNSTAR CO., LTD. NO.100, KAO SHI RD., YANG-MEI TOWNSHIP, TAOYUAN COUNTY 200, TAIWAN, R.O.C.		**Amount** 金額 USD10,800.00 (U.S. DOLLARS TEN THOUSAND EIGHT HUNDRED ONLY)	
		Expiry Date 有效期限 July 11, 2018	

2.匯票條款

　　We hereby issue in your favor this documentary credit which is available by negotiation of your drafts at sight drawn on us for100% invoice value bearing the clause "Drawn under Chase Manhattan Bank Credit No. LC-123456"

　　(1)匯票發票人：

　　　　We hereby issue in your favor this documentary credit which is available by negotiation of your drafts.

其意為我行（開狀銀行）簽發以貴方為受益人的信用狀，貴方有權開具匯票以讓購方式兌款。此即表明受益人得開發匯票兌款，故受益人為匯票發票人。

(2)匯票付款人：

drawn on ＋匯票付款人，drawn on us 即以我行（開狀銀行）為匯票付款人。

UCP600 第六條規定：「信用狀之簽發，不可要求以申請人為匯票之付款人。」

(3)匯票付款期限：

付款期限	匯票種類	信用狀種類
at sight	即期匯票	即期信用狀
at ×××days after sight	遠期匯票	遠期信用狀

(4)匯票金額：

表示方式	意義	備註
for full invoice value	匯票金額即為發票金額	
90% invoice value	匯票金額是發票金額的 90%	可能使用兩種付款方式，如 CWO10%、L/C90%

(5)匯票發票條款（Drawn Clause）：

Bearing the clause "Drawn under Chase Manhattan Bank Credit No. LC-123456".

其意為規定受益人應於匯票上註明該匯票係依據 Chase Manhattan Bank 所開發第 LC-123456 號信用狀簽發，其目的為便於開狀銀行查核。

3.運送單據（Shipping Documents）種類

(1)商業發票（Commercial Invoice）：

Commercial Invoice in triplicate.

商業發票三份。

(2)提單（Bill of Lading）：

Full set of clean on board ocean Bills of Lading issued to the order of Chase Manhattan Bank, and marked "FREIGHT PREPAID" and notify buyer.

全套清潔已裝船提單，提單受貨人由 Chase Manhattan Bank 指定，並註明運費預付，貨到通知人為買方。

*Full set 全套：代表受益人押匯時需提示全套正本提單。

*Clean 清潔：代表受益人押匯時需提示清潔提單。

*On board 裝船：代表受益人押匯時需提示已裝船提單。

*to the order... 可轉讓提單：即提單受貨人由 Chase Manhattan Bank 指定， Chase Manhattan Bank 可將提單以背書方式轉讓。

*notify buyer：貨到被通知人為買方。

*Freight Prepaid：運費預付

支付運費方式：

種類	支付運費	貿易條件
Freight Prepaid 運費預付	Exporter	CFR、CIF
Freight Collect 運費後付	Importer	FOB、FAS

(3)保險單據（Insurance Policy or Certificate）：

Insurance policy or certificate in negotiable form for full CIF value plus 10% covering institute cargo clauses (A), institute war clauses (cargo) and institute strikes clauses (cargo).

①保險單據種類：

Insurance policy or certificate：保險單或保險證明書皆可。

②保險金額：

full CIF value plus 10%：CIF 金額加 10%為保險金額。

③保險種類：

institute cargo clauses (A), institute war clauses (cargo) and institute strikes clauses (cargo)：協會貨物條款 A 款險、戰爭險及罷工險。

(4)包裝單據（Packing List）：

Packing List in triplicate.

包裝單（或裝箱單）三份。

4.運送單據份數

依 UCP600 第十七條之規定：

(1)信用狀規定每一種單據至少須提示一份正本。

(2)信用狀要求提示單據副本,則提示正本或副本皆被允許。

(3)信用狀如使用「in duplicate」(一式兩份)、「in two folds」(兩份)、「in two copie」(兩份)等複式單據時,則提示一份正本及其餘份數為副本者即可。

(4)單據份數之表示:

一份	original	1 fold	1 copy
二份	duplicate	2 folds	2 copies
三份	triplicate	3 folds	3 copies
四份	quadruplicate	4 folds	4 copies
五份	quintuplicate	5 folds	5 copies
六份	sextuplicate	6 folds	6 copies
七份	septuplicate	7 folds	7 copies

5.貨物敘述(Covering……)

通常 Covering……或 Evidencing shipment of……後加貨物敘述。

6.運送條款

(1)裝運地、目的地、可否分批裝運、可否轉運:

SHIPMENT FROM KEELUNG TO NEW YORK	PARTIAL SHIPMENTS permitted	TRANSHIPMENT prohibited
Shipment from 裝運地 To 目的地	可否分批裝運: 允許	可否轉運: 禁止

信用狀如未禁止分批裝運及轉運時,一律視為可以分批裝運及轉運。

(2)最後裝船期限:

Shipment not later than July 15, 2018.

最後裝船期限為 2018 年 7 月 15 日。

7.特別條款(Special Instruction)

(1)銀行費用的歸屬:

All banking charges outside U.S.A. are for account of beneficiary.

美國地區以外銀行費用均由受益人負擔。

(2)限制押匯的規定：

The credit is restricted to the advising bank for negotiation.

①本信用狀限在通知銀行押匯。

②故本信用狀為限押信用狀，限押銀行為通知銀行。

(3)信用狀轉讓的規定：

This credit is only transferable in your country.

①本信用狀可在受益人所在國家轉讓。

②故本信用狀為可轉讓信用狀。

(4)貨運單據提示期限的規定：

Documents must be presented for negotiation within10 days after B/L date.

①提示單據的期限是提單日後 10 天內。

②提示單據期限除必須在提單日後 10 天內，也必須在信用狀的有效期限內。

③如信用狀並無規定運送單據簽發日後之特定期間時，則以運送單據簽發日後 21 天內提示。

(二) SWIFT 信用狀

茲以所附 SWIFT 信用狀，說明該信用狀內容如下：

ISSUE OF A DOCUMENTARY CREDIT　　　　PAGE 00001

FUNC SWPR3

UMR 00569900

MSGACK　DWS765I　AUTH OK, KEY　B1960421D73591E7, BKCHCNBJ GUMAJPJT RECORD

BASIC HEADER　　　　　　　F　01　BKCHCNBJA300 7499 555888

APPLICATION HEADER 0 700 1650 020518 GUMAJPJTAXXX 1157 209685 020518 0948 N

*GUNMA BANK, LTD.,

*TOKYO

ISSUER HEADER　　　　　　BANK, PRIORITY 113;

　　　　　　　　　　　　　　　　　MSR USER REF, 108;

40A(FORM OF DOCUMENTARY CREDIT)：IRREVOCABLE

20 (DOCUMENTARY CREDIT NUMBER)：01-193851-4

31C (DATE OF ISSUE): 180403

40E(APPLICABLE RULES): UCP LATEST LATEST

3ID(DATE AND PLACE OF EXPIRY): 180505 TAIWAN

50(APPLICANT): NICHIMEN CORPORATION

                OSAKA, 530, JAPAN, P.O. BOX CENTRAL NO.18

59(BENEFICIARY): TAIWAN GARMENT CORP.,

                NO.567 DA AN RD., TAIPEI, TAIWAN

32B (CURRENCY CODE, AMOUNT): USD7,850

41D(AVAILABLE WITH...BY...): ANY BANK BY NEGOTIATION

42C(DRAFTS AT...): SIGHT FOR FULL INVOICE VALUE

42A(DRAWEE): GUNMA BANK, LTD.

43P(PARTIAL SHIPMENTS): PROHIBITED

43T(TRANSHIPMENT): PROHIBITED

44E(PORT OF LOADING): KEELUNG

44F(PORT OF DISCHARGE): OSAKA

44C (LATEST DATE OF SHIPMENT): 180425

45A(SHIPMENT OF GOODS): 6MM 80 PCT POLYESTER QUANTITY:1,800 LBS AT CIF OSAKA.

46B(DOCUMENTS REQUIRED):

  +SIGNED COMMERCIAL INVOICE IN TRIPLICATE.

  +SIGNED PACKING LIST IN TRIPLICATE

  +FULL SET（3/3）CLEAN ON BOARD BILLS OF LADING MADE OUT TO ORDER AND BLANK ENDORSED, MARKED "FREIGHT PREPAID" AND NOTIFY APPLICANT.

  + INSURANCE POLICIES/ CERTIFICATES IN DUPLICATE, ENDORSED IN BLANK FOR 110PCT OF INVOICE VALUE COVERING INSTITUTE CARGO CLAUSES (A) AND INSTITUTE WAR CLAUSES WITH CLAIMS PAYABLE AT DESTINATION IN THE CURRENCY OF THIS CREDIT.

47A(ADDITIONAL CONDITIONS):

  +3 PCT MORE OR LESS ON AMOUNT AND QUANTITY ACCEPTABLE

71B (CHARGES): ALL BANKING CHARGES OUTSIDE JAPAN INCLUDING ADVISING CHARGES IF ANY ARE FOR ACCOUNT OF BENEFICIARY.

48 (PERIOD FOR PRESENTATION): DOCUMENTS TO BE PRESENTED WITHIN 7 DAYS AFTER THE DATE OF ISSUANCE OF SHIPPING DOCUMENTS BUT WITHIN THE VALIDITY OF THE CREDIT.

49(CONFIRMATION INSTRUCTIONS): WITHOUT

解析：

40A(FORM OF DOCUMENTARY CREDIT)： IRREVOCABLE 為不可撤銷信用狀。

20 (DOCUMENTARY CREDIT NUMBER)：01-193851-4 為信用狀編號。

31C (DATE OF ISSUE): 180403 信用狀開狀日期為 2018 年 4 月 3 日。

40E(APPLICABLE RULES)：UCP LATEST VERSION 適用最新 UCP 版本。

3ID(DATE AND PLACE OF EXPIRY)：180505 TAIWAN 信用狀有效期限為臺灣時間 2018 年 5 月 5 日。

50(APPLICANT)：NICHIMEN CORPORATION OSAKA, 530, JAPAN, P.O. BOX CENTRAL NO.18 為開狀申請人。

59(BENEFICIARY)：TAIWAN GARMENT CORP., NO.567 DA AN RD., TAIPEI, TAIWAN 為信用狀受益人。

32B (CURRENCY CODE, AMOUNT)：USD7,850 為信用狀金額。

41D(AVAILABLE WITH...BY...)：ANY BANK BY NEGOTIATION 為未限押信用狀，受益人可向任何銀行押匯。

信用狀之使用方式可分為：

1. 讓購方式（By Negotiation）

(1)未限押：ANY BANK BY NEGOTIATION
(2)限押：×××BANK BY NEGOTIATION

2. 付款方式（By Payment）

(1)即期付款：×××BANK BY PAYMENT
(2)延期付款：×××BANK BY DEFERRED PAYMENT

3. 承兌方式（By Acceptance）

×××BANK BY ACCEPTANCE

42C(DRAFTS AT------)：SIGHT FOR FULL INVOICE VALUE 即期匯票，匯票金額同發票金額。

42A(DRAWEE)：GUNMA BANK, LTD.為匯票付款人。

43P(PARTIAL SHIPMENTS)：PROHIBITED 禁止分批裝運。信用狀如未禁止時，一律視為可分批裝運。

43T(TRANSHIPMENT)：PROHIBITED 禁止轉運。信用狀如未禁止時，一律視為可以轉運。

44E(PORT OF LOADING.)：KEELUNG 為裝運港。

44F(PORT OF DISCHARGE)：OSAKA 為卸貨港。

44C (LATEST DATE OF SHIPMENT)：180425 最後裝船期限為 2018 年 4 月 25 日，此日期不因任何原因順延。

45A(SHIPMENT OF GOODS)：6MM 80 PCT POLYESTER QUANTITY:1,800 LBS AT CIF OSAKA 裝運貨物為 6MM 80 PCT POLYESTER 數量為 1,800 磅，貿易條件為 CIF OSAKA

46B(DOCUMENTS REQUIRED)：應提示單據。

+SIGNED COMMERCIAL INVOICE IN TRIPLICATE.簽署商業發票三份。

+SIGNED PACKING LIST IN TRIPLICATE.簽署包裝單三份

+FULL SET（3/3）CLEAN ON BOARD BILLS OF LADING MADE OUT TO OR-DER AND BLANK ENDORSED, MARKED "FREIGHT PREPAID" AND NOTIFY APPLICANT.

全套三份清潔已裝船提單，受貨人待指定，須以空白背書方式轉讓，提單上應註明運費預付，且以申請人為貨到被通知人。

1. 提單份數

(1) Full Set B/L（全套提單）：

代表受益人押匯時需提示全套正本提單。

(2) 2/3 Set B/L（2/3 套提單）：

代表船公司發行三份正本提單，受益人押匯時只需提示兩份正本提單。

2. 提單種類

(1)裝船或備運提單：

銀行只接受裝船提單（On Board B/L）。

(2)清潔或不清潔提單：

銀行只接受清潔提單（Clean B/L）。

(3)指示式或記名式提單：

銀行只接受指示式提單，提單受貨人待指定（To Order）。

3.提單背書

(1)空白背書（Blank Endorsement）：

僅由背書人簽名，而不記載被背書人姓名。

(2)記名背書（Special Endorsement）：

除由背書人簽名外，尚須記載被背書人姓名。

4.貨到被通知人（Notify Party）

申請人。

5.運費

(1) Freight Prepaid：

運費預付，貿易條件為 CIF 時，由出口商支付運費。

(2) Freight Collect：

運費到付，貿易條件為 FOB 時，由進口商支付運費。

+INSURANCE POLICIES/CERTIFICATES IN DUPLICATE, ENDORSED IN BLANK FOR 110PCT OF INVOICE VALUE COVERING INSTITUTE CARGO CLAUSES (A) AND INSTITUTE WAR CLAUSES WITH CLAIMS PAYABLE AT DESTINATION IN THE CURRENCY OF THIS CREDIT.

兩份保險單或保險證明書，空白背書，保險金額為 110%發票金額，保險種類為協會貨物條款 A 款險及戰爭險，理賠地點為目的地，幣別與信用狀相同。

(1)保險單據：保險單或保險證明書皆可。

(2)空白背書（Endorsed in Blank）。

(3)保險金額：110%CIF 金額。

(4)保險種類：協會貨物條款 A 款險及戰爭險。

(5)理賠地點：目的地。

(6)理賠幣別：與信用狀相同。

47A(ADDITIONAL CONDITIONS)：+3 PCT MORE OR LESS ON AMOUNT AND QUANTITY ACCEPTABLE 金額及數量允許 3%上下之增減。

71B (CHARGES)：ALL BANKING CHARGES OUTSIDE JAPAN. INCLUDING ADVISING CHARGES IF ANY ARE FOR ACCOUNT OF BENEFICIARY. 日本境外之銀行費用，包含通知手續費在內，由受益人負擔。

48(PERIOD FOR PRESENTATION)：DOCUMENTS TO BE PRESENTED WITHIN 7 DAYS AFTER THE DATE OF ISSUANCE OF SHIPPING DOCUMENTS BUT WITHIN THE VALIDITY OF THE CREDIT. 提示單據期限必須在運送單據簽發日後 7 天之內，並在信用狀有效期限內。

提示單據期限必須同時符合下述兩項條件：

(1)信用狀有效期限。

(2)運送單據簽發日後特定期間內，如信用狀並無規定運送單據簽發日後之特定期間時，則以運送單據簽發日後 21 天內提示。

49(CONFIRMATION INSTRUCTIONS)：WITHOUT 無保兌之指示。

第二節 勞動部勞動力發展署測驗試題範例解析

一、試題範例

請依所附完整信用狀之內容，回答所列問題，並將正確答案填入答案紙。

MEGA INTERNATIONAL COMMERCIAL BANK
TAIPEI, TAIWAN

＊＊＊ AUTH. CORRECT WITH CURRENT KEY ＊＊＊

FIN UAK   {1：F21 ICBCTWTPA×××1808130031}

{4：{177：Date and Time (YYMMDDHHMM)：090620 1420}

  {451：acceptance/rejection   0}}

⋯⋯⋯⋯⋯⋯⋯⋯⋯⋯⋯⋯⋯⋯⋯⋯⋯⋯⋯⋯⋯⋯⋯⋯⋯⋯⋯

{1：FIN MESSAGE/Session/OSN   F01 ICBCTWTPA×××1808130031}

{2：Output Message Type   700 issue of a documentary credit

  Input Time/MIR   1501 090620 MRMDUS33

  Received from   HSBC BANK USA , NEW YORK

  Output Date/time   090620 1420

Priority/Delivery   Normal

....

: 40A   FORM OF DOCUMENTARY CREDIT

IRREVOCABLE

: 20   DOCUMENTARY CREDIT NUMBER

DC MTN 562462

: 31C   DATE OF ISSUE

090620

: 31D   DATE AND PLACE OF EXPIRY

090920 IN COUNTRY OF OPENING BANK

: 50   APPLICANT

ABC.USA.INC

100 LAGUNA RD. LOS ANGELES CA. 90024 , USA

: 59   BENEFICIARY

XYZ CO., LTD.

P.O. BOX 10000 TAIPEI, TAIWAN

: 32B   CURRENCY CODE, AMOUNT

USD204,516.89

: 41D   AVAILABLE WITH...BY...

ANY BANK BY NEGOTIATION

: 42C   DRAFTS AT...

SIGHT FOR 100PCT OF INVOICE VALUE

: 42D   DRAWEE

ISSUING BANK

: 43P   PARTIAL SHIPMENTS

ALLOWED

: 43T   TRANSHIPMENT

NOT ALLOWED

: 44E   PORT OF LOADING

KEELUNG, TAIWAN

: 44F   PORT OF DISCHARGE

LOS ANGELES

: 44C LATEST DATE OF SHIPMENT

090910

: 45A SHIPMENT OF (GOODS)

ELECTRIC RESISTANCE WELDED PIPE, CFR LOS ANGELES

: 46A DOCUMENTS REQUIRED

1. 3/3 ORIGINAL CLEAN SHIPPED ON BOARD BILLS OF LADING MARK-ED FREIGHT PREPAID, CONSIGNED TO OUR ORDER NOTIFY APPLI-CANT.

2. MANUALLY COMMERCIAL INVOICES IN THREE COPIES.

3. PACKING LIST IN ONE ORIGINAL AND ONE COPY.

: 47A ADDITIONAL CONDITIONS

＊ INSURANCE COVERED BY THE APPLICANT

＊ A USD25.00 FEE WILL BE DEDUCTED IF PROCEEDS ARE REMITTED VIA WIRE TRANSFER.

: 48 PERIOD FOR PRESENTATION

DOCUMENTS TO BE PRESENTED WITHIN 10 DAYS AFTER THE DATE OF ISSUANCE OF SHIPPING DOCUMENTS BUT WITHIN THE VALIDITY OF THE CREDIT.

: 71B CHARGES

ALL BANKING CHARGES OUTSIDE USA INCLUDING ADVISING CHARGES ARE FOR ACCOUNT OF BENEFICIARY.

: 49 CONFIRMATION INSTRUCTIONS

WITHOUT

: 72 SENDER TO RECEIVER INFORMATION

THIS CREDIT IS SUBJECT TO UCP (2007 REVISION) ICC PUBLICATION NO.600

{5：{MAC：32CABC93}AUTHENTICATION SUCCESSFUL WITH PRI-MARY KEY}

＊ END

參考題目與答案

信用狀當事人（請寫出英文抬頭）		
開狀銀行	HSBC BANK USA, NEW YORK	
受益人	XYZ CO., LTD. P.O. BOX 10000 TAIPEI, TAIWAN	
匯票付款人	HSBC BANK USA, NEW YORK	
信用狀種類		
是否為保兑信用狀？	☐ 是	☒ 否
是否為即期信用狀？	☒ 是	☐ 否
是否為可轉讓信用狀？	☐ 是	☒ 否
信用狀相關期限		
開狀日期	2009 年 6 月 20 日	
信用狀有效期限及地點	2009 年 9 月 20 日於開狀銀行國家	
最後裝運期限	2009 年 9 月 10 日	
運送相關規定		
起運地	KEELUNG, TAIWAN	
運費給付方式	☒預付	☐到付
是否可分批裝運	☒是	☐否
提示單據種類、份數、規定		
B/L 份數 CONSIGNEE	三份正本 TO ORDER OF HSBC BANK USA, NEW YORK	
包裝單份數	一份正本，一份副本	

二、解析

信用狀欄位說明

MEGA INTERNATIONAL COMMERCIAL BANK TAIPEI, TAIWAN	通知銀行
＊＊＊ AUTH.CORRECT WITH CURRENT KEY ＊＊＊	本信用狀經系統內現行的辨識鍵證實正確
FIN UAK {1：F21 ICBCTWTPA×××1808130031}	最後確認，表示本信用狀已被系統接受
{4：{177：Date and Time (YYMMDDHHMM)：090620 1420}	收到信用狀的時間與地點
{451：acceptance/rejection 0}}	系統接受或拒絕本信用狀
{1：FIN MESSAGE/Session/OSN F01 ICBCTWTPA×××1808130031}	此為最後電文
{2：Output Message Type 700 issue of a documentary credit	本信用狀為 MT700 跟單信用狀
Input Time/MIR 1501 090620 MRMDUS33	收到本信用狀時間
Received from HSBC BANK USA, NEW YORK	開狀銀行
Output Date/time 090620 1420	系統內列印出本信用狀的日期及時間
Priority/Delivery Normal	此為正常信用狀
：40A FORM OF DOCUMENTARY CREDIT IRREVOCABLE	不可撤銷信用狀
：20 DOCUMENTARY CREDIT NUMBER DC MTN 562462	信用狀號碼
：31C DATE OF ISSUE 090620	開狀日期為 2009 年 6 月 20 日
：31D DATE AND PLACE OF EXPIRY 090920 IN COUNTRY OF OPENING BANK	信用狀有效期限及地點為開狀銀行所在地時間 2009 年 9 月 20 日
：50 APPLICANT ABC.USA.INC 100 LAGUNA RD. LOS ANGELES CA. 90024, USA	申請人
：59 BENEFICIARY XYZ CO., LTD. P.O. BOX 10000 TAIPEI, TAIWAN	受益人
：32B CURRENCY CODE, AMOUNT USD204,516.89	信用狀金額為 204,516.89 美元

: 41D	AVAILABLE WITH...BY... ANY BANK BY NEGOTIATION	受益人可向任何銀行押匯，為未限押信用狀
: 42C	DRAFTS AT... SIGHT FOR 100PCT OF INVOICE VALUE	即期匯票，金額為 100%商業發票金額
: 42D	DRAWEE ISSUING BANK	付款銀行為開狀銀行
: 43P	PARTIAL SHIPMENTS ALLOWED	允許分批裝運
: 43T	TRANSHIPMENT NOT ALLOWED	不允許轉運
: 44E	PORT OF LOADING KEELUNG, TAIWAN	裝船港
: 44F	PORT OF DISCHARGE LOS ANGELES	卸貨港
: 44C	LATEST DATE OF SHIPMENT 090910	最遲裝船日為 2009 年 9 月 10 日
: 45A	SHIPMENT OF (GOODS) ELECTRIC RESISTANCE WELDED PIPE , CFR LOS ANGELES	裝運貨物為 ELECTRIC RESISTANCE WELDED PIPE 貿易條件為 CFR LOS ANGELES
: 46A	DOCUMENTS REQUIRED *1.* 3/3 ORIGINAL CLEAN SHIPPED ON BOARD BILLS OF LADING MARKED FREIGHT PREPAID, CONSIGNED TO OUR ORDER NOTIFY APPLICANT. *2.* MANUALLY COMMERCIAL INVOICES IN THREE COPIES. *3.* PACKING LIST IN ONE ORIGINAL AND ONE COPY.	所需單據： *1.*三份正本清潔、已裝船提單，註記運費預付，提單受貨人由開狀銀行指定，貨到通知人為申請人。 *2.*手簽商業發票三份。 *3.*包裝單一份正本、一份副本。
: 47A	ADDITIONAL CONDITIONS ＊ INSURANCE COVERED BY THE APPLICANT. ＊ A USD25.00 FEE WILL BE DEDUCTED IF PROCEEDS ARE REMITTED VIA WIRE TRANSFER.	附加條件： ＊保險由開狀申請人負擔。 ＊如經由電匯求償，則匯付的款項中將扣除 25 美元的費用。

: 48 PERIOD FOR PRESENTATION DOCUMENTS TO BE PRESENTED WITHIN 10 DAYS AFTER THE DATE OF ISSUANCE OF SHIPPING DOCUMENTS BUT WITHIN THE VALIDITY OF THE CREDIT.	提示單據期限為貨運單據簽發日後 10 天之內，但必須在信用狀有效期限內。
: 71B CHARGES ALL BANKING CHARGES OUTSIDE USA INCLUDING ADVISING CHARGES ARE FOR ACCOUNT OF BENEFICIARY.	美國地區以外之銀行費用，包含通知費用在內由受益人負擔。
: 49 CONFIRMATION INSTRUCTIONS WITHOUT	無保兌指示。
: 72 SENDER TO RECEIVER INFORMATION THIS CREDIT IS SUBJECT TO UCP (2007 REVISION) ICC PUBLICATION NO.600	本信用狀依國際商會所公布600號刊物信用狀統一慣例（2007 修訂版）規定。
{5：{MAC：32CABC93}AUTHENTICATION SUCCESSFUL WITH PRIMARY KEY}	本信用狀經辨識鍵證實成功。

第三節　練習題

一、試依所附信用狀回答下述題目：

MT700. DATE=180522 ARR.TIME=0303 REF. NO. IN11765
SENDER: CITI BANK N.V.

SEQUENCE OF TOTAL	27：1/1
FORM OF DOC. CREDIT	40A：IRREVOCABLE
DOC. CREDIT NUMBER	20：AB147258
DATE OF ISSUE	31C：180518
APPLICABLE RULES	40E：UCP LATEST VERSION
DATE AND PLACE OF EXPIRY	31D：180630
APPLICANT	50：BOUTONE CO., LTD.
BENEFICIARY	59：CHEN HAM IMPORT/EXPORT CO.
AMOUNT	32B：USD83,220.00
AVAILABLE WITH/BY	41D：ANY BANK BY NEGOTIATION

DRAFTS AT	42C : 30 DAYS SIGHT
DRAWEE	42D : CITI BANK N.V.
PARTIAL SHIPMENTS	43P : PROHIBITED
TRANSHIPMENT	43T : PROHIBITED
PORT OF LOADING	44E : KEELUNG
PORT OF DISCHARGE	44F : NEW YORK
LATEST DATE OF SHIPMEDT	44C: 180617

DESCRIPTION OF GOODS AND/OT SERVICES 45A:

PRODUCT IS TO BE SHIPPED IN TWO CONTAINERS.

P/O NO	GLOVE BRAND	NO. OF CASES	UNIT PRICE	AMOUNT
123	SYSCOMED VINYL EXAM	1,900	21.90	41,610.00
456	SYSCOMED VINYL EXAM	1,900	21.90	41,610.00
			TOTAL	USD83,220.00

THE GLOVES SIZE MIX FOR EACH SHIPMENT MUST BE IN ACCORDANCE
WITH THE PURCHASE ORDER LISTED ABOVE.

TERM OF DELIVERY : FOB KEELUNG

DOCUMENTS REQUIRED 46A :

   +SIGNED COMMERCIAL INVOICE IN TRIPLICATE.

   +PACKING LIST IN TRIPLICATE.

   +FULL SET CLEAN ON BOARD BILLS OF LADING MADE

    OUT TO ORDER OF CITI BANK N.V. NOTIFY: APPLICANT MARKED

    "FREIGHT COLLECT"

ADDITIONAL CONDITIONS 47A:

   (1) ALL DOCUMENTS MUST BE PRESENTED IN THE ENGLISH

      LANGUAGE UNLESS OTHERWISE STATED.

   (2) INSURANCE(MARINE, WAR, FIRE AND OTHER USUAL RISKS)

      TO BE COVERED BY THE APPLICANT.

   (3) A DISCREPANCY FEE OF USD75.00 WILL BE DEDUCTED FROM

      PROCEEDS IF DOCUMENTS ARE RECEIVED WITH DISCREPANCIES.

CHARGES 71B:

   ALL BANK CHARGES OUTSIDE THE U.S.A. AND ANY

DISCREPANCY, AMENDMENT AND CABLE CHARGES ARE FOR THE BENEFI-CIARY'S ACCOUNT.

CONFIRMATION INSTRUCTIONS 49:

WITHOUT

INSTRUCTIONS TO THE PAYING/ACCEPTING/NEGOTIATING BANK 78:

DOCUMENTS ARE TO BE SENT TO CITI BANK N.V. IN ONE LOT BY DHL OR SIMILAR COURIER SERVICE.

(一)請完成下述信用狀分析單：

信用狀當事人（請寫出英文抬頭）		
開狀銀行		
通知銀行		☐未註明
申請人		
受益人		
匯票付款人		
限押銀行		☐無
補償銀行		☐無
信用狀種類（請勾選）		
是否為可撤銷信用狀？	☐是	☐否
是否為保兌信用狀？	☐是	☐否
是否為即期信用狀？	☐是	☐否
是否為限押信用狀？	☐是	☐否
是否為可轉讓信用狀？	☐是	☐否
信用狀相關期限（請填 YYYY/MM/DD）		
開狀日期		
信用狀有效期限及地點		☐未註明地點
最後裝運期限		
提示單據期限	裝運日後_____天且不超過信用狀有效期限	
匯票期限	☐即期	☐遠期_____天

運送相關規定		
提單受貨人（英文）		
提單被通知人（英文抬頭）		
起運地		
目的地		
運費預付或到付	□預付	□到付
可否分批裝運	□可	□否
可否轉運	□可	□否

提示單據種類與規定		
提示單據種類（請勾選）	份數	其他規定
□商業發票		
□包裝單		
提單（□海運□空運）		背書方式： □未註明
□保險單據		保險金額： 保險種類：
□產地證明書		
□檢驗證明書		
□受益人證明書		
□其他（請依序註明） 1. 2. 3.		

信用狀其他內容	
信用狀號碼	
貿易條件	□未註明
契約／訂單／預期發票號碼	□未註明
信用狀金額	
最高押匯金額	
求償銀行求償方式	寄單次數： 寄單方式： □未註明

㈡請選擇正確答案：

(　　) 1. 本張信用狀為　①即期信用狀　②遠期信用狀　③可轉讓信用狀　④限押信用狀。

(　　) 2. 本張信用狀為　①不可撤銷、限押及遠期信用狀　②不可撤銷、即期及未限押信用狀　③不可轉讓、讓購及無保兌信用狀　④不可轉讓、遠期及保兌信用狀。

(　　) 3. 本張信用狀之匯票到期日為　①裝船日後 30 天付款　②承兌日後 30 天付款　③契約日後 45 天付款　④發票日後 30 天付款。

(　　) 4. 本張信用狀規定提示單據之期限為　①只須在信用狀有效期限內提示即可　②只須在運送單據簽發日後 21 天內提示即可　③必須在運送單據簽發日後 21 天內或不超過信用狀有效期限內提示　④必須在運送單據簽發日後 21 天內但不超過信用狀有效期限內提示。

(　　) 5. 本張信用狀上所規定之匯票付款人為　① ANY BANK　② CITI BANK N. V.　③ BOUTONE CO., LTD.　④ CHEN HAM IMPORT/EXPORT CO.。

(　　) 6. 本張信用狀上規定商業發票需提示幾份？　①兩份　②三份　③四份　④五份。

(　　) 7. 依本張信用狀有關分批裝運及轉運之規定為　①可分批裝運、可轉運　②可分批裝運、不可轉運　③不可分批裝運、可轉運　④不可分批裝、不可轉運。

(　　) 8. 本張信用狀之提單受貨人為　①由開狀銀行指定　②開狀銀行　③待指定　④申請人。

(　　) 9. 本張信用狀有關瑕疵費用，由何方負擔？　①開狀申請人　②押匯銀行　③開狀銀行　④受益人。

(　　) 10. 本張信用狀上有關裝運之規定，下列敘述何者正確？　① NEW YORK 為裝運港　②運費由出口商支付　③最後裝船期限為 2018 年 6 月 17 日　④ KEELUNG 為卸貨港。

解答：

　　(一)信用狀分析單：

信用狀當事人（請寫出英文抬頭）		
開狀銀行	CITI BANK N.V.	
通知銀行		☒未註明
申請人	BOUTONE CO., LTD.	
受益人	CHEN HAM IMPORT/EXPORT CO.	
匯票付款人	CITI BANK N.V.	
限押銀行		☒無
補償銀行		☒無
信用狀種類（請勾選）		
是否為可撤銷信用狀？	☐是	☒否
是否為保兌信用狀？	☐是	☒否
是否為即期信用狀？	☐是	☒否
是否為限押信用狀？	☐是	☒否
是否為可轉讓信用狀？	☐是	☒否
信用狀相關期限（請填 YYYY/MM/DD）		
開狀日期	2018/05/18	
信用狀有效期限及地點	2018/06/30	☒未註明地點
最後裝運期限	2018/06/17	
提示單據期限	裝運日後__21__天且不超過信用狀有效期限	
匯票期限	☐即期	☒遠期見票日後 30 天
運送相關規定		
提單受貨人（英文）	TO ORDER OF CITI BANK N.V.	
提單被通知人（英文抬頭）	BOUTONE CO., LTD.	
起運地	KEELUNG	
目的地	NEW YORK	
運費預付或到付	☐預付	☒到付
可否分批裝運	☐可	☒否
可否轉運	☐可	☒否

提示單據種類與規定		
提示單據種類（請勾選）	份數	其他規定
☒商業發票	三份	
☒包裝單	三份	
提單（☒海運□空運）	全套	背書方式： ☒未註明
□保險單據		保險金額： 保險種類：
□產地證明書		
□檢驗證明書		
□受益人證明書		
□其他（請依序註明） 1. 2. 3.		
信用狀其他內容		
信用狀號碼	AB147258	
貿易條件	FOB KEELUNG	□未註明
契約／訂單／預期發票號碼	P/O123、P/O456	□未註明
信用狀金額	USD83,220.00	
最高押匯金額	USD83,220.00	
求償銀行求償方式	寄單次數：一次 寄單方式：DHL 或快遞	□未註明

（二）正確答案：

1	2	3	4	5
②	③	②	④	②
6	7	8	9	10
②	④	①	④	③

（三）補充說明：

　　瑕疵費用（Discrepancy Fee）：依 UCP600 規定，只要單據有瑕疵時，開狀銀行即可拒付。但實務上，開狀銀行皆會先詢問申請人是否接受，若該瑕疵業經開狀銀行與申請人接受時，開狀銀行都會在所應付款項中扣除處理單據瑕疵之費用。

　　本信用狀有關瑕疵費用之敘述有兩項：

1. A DISCREPANCY FEE OF USD75.00 WILL BE DEDUCTED FROM PROCEEDS IF DOCUMENT ARE RECEIVED WITH DISCREPACIES.

所收到之單據如有瑕疵，將從所付之款項中扣除 75 美元之瑕疵費用。

2. ALL BANK CHARGES OUTSIDE THE U.S.A. AND ANY DISCREPANCY, AMENDMENT AND CABLE CHARGES ARE FOR THE BENEFICIARY'S ACCOUNT.

美國境外所有的銀行手續費以及瑕疵費用、信用狀修改費用、電報費用皆由受益人負擔。

二、試依所附信用狀回答下述題目：

DBA BANK

FORM OF DOC. CREDIT	*40 A:	IRREVOCABLE
DOC. CREDIT NUMBER	*20:	N3 AMOLO00284
DATE OF ISSUE	31 C:	180610
APPLICABLE RULES	*40 E:	UCP LATEST VERSION
DATE AND PLACE OF EXPIRY	*31 D:	DATE 180810 PLACE U.S.A.
APPLICANT	*50:	ALPHA TIRE IMPORTATION SERESFORD HOUSEBELLOZANNE ROAD ST. HELIER, JERSEY JE2 3JW CHANNEL ISLANDS, U.S.A.
BENEFICIARY	*59:	FORCEMAN INTERNATIONAL TRADING CO. LTD., NO.1, LANE 170, YUYAN ROAD, TAIPEI, TAIWAN.
AMOUNT	*32 B:	CURRENCY USD AMOUNT148,442.40
AVAILABLE WITH/BY	*41 D:	ANY BANK BY NEGOTIATION
DRAFTS AT…	*42 C:	SIGHT FOR FULL INVOICE VALUE
DRAWEE	*42 A:	DBA BANK, NEW YORK, U.S.A.
PARTIAL SHIPMENTS	43 P:	PROHIBITED
TRANSHIPMENT	43 T:	PERMITTED
PORT OF LOADING	44 E:	KEELUNG

PORT OF DISCHARGE	44 F:	NEW YORK
LATEST DATE OF SHIPMENT	44 C:	180715

DESCRIPT OF GOODS 45 A: 3121 PCS OF PNEUMATIC RUBBER TIRES
CIFC5 NEW YORK

DETAILS OF CHARGES 71 B: ALL CHARGES OUTSIDE THE U.S.A. ARE
FOR ACCOUNT OF BENEFICIARY.

PRESENTATION PERIOD 48: WITHIN 2 DAYS AFTER SHIPMENT, BUT
IN ANY EVENT WITHIN THE VALIDITY
OF THE CREDIT.

DOCUMENTS REQUIRED 78 B: + 2/3 SET CLEAN ON BOARD BILL OF
LADING TO ORDER OF SHIPPER BLANK
ENDORSED AND MARKED "FREIGHT
PREPAID" AND 1/3 ORIGINAL BILL OF
LADING SENT TO THE APPLICANT.
+ INSURANCE POLICY OR CERTIFICATE
FOR 110PCT OF INVOICE VALUE COVER-
ING ALL RISKS AND WAR RISKS AS PER
ICC DATED 1/1/2016
+ COMMERCIAL INVOICE IN 4 COPIES.
+ PACKING LIST IN 4 COPIES.

Trailer (Order is <AUT:> <ENC:> <CHK:> <TNG:> <PDE:>...)
MAC:1CBB6271
CHK:76AF95AE1F59

(一)請完成下述信用狀分析單:

信用狀當事人（請寫出英文抬頭）		
開狀銀行		
通知銀行		☐未註明
申請人		
受益人		
匯票付款人		
限押銀行		☐無
補償銀行		☐無
信用狀種類（請勾選）		
是否為可撤銷信用狀？	☐是	☐否
是否為保兌信用狀？	☐是	☐否
是否為即期信用狀？	☐是	☐否
是否為限押信用狀？	☐是	☐否
是否為可轉讓信用狀？	☐是	☐否
信用狀相關期限（請填 YYYY/MM/DD）		
開狀日期		
信用狀有效期限及地點		☐未註明地點
最後裝運期限		
提示單據期限	裝運日後_____天且不超過信用狀有效期限	
匯票期限	☐即期	☐遠期_____天
運送相關規定		
提單受貨人（英文）		
提單被通知人（英文抬頭）		
起運地		
目的地		
運費預付或到付	☐預付	☐到付
可否分批裝運	☐可	☐否
可否轉運	☐可	☐否

提示單據種類與規定			
提示單據種類（請勾選）	份數	其他規定	
□商業發票			
□包裝單			
提單（□海運□空運）		背書方式：	□未註明
□保險單據		保險金額： 保險種類：	
□產地證明書			
□檢驗證明書			
□受益人證明書			
□其他（請依序註明） 1. 2.			
信用狀其他內容			
信用狀號碼			
貿易條件			□未註明
契約／訂單／預期發票號碼			□未註明
信用狀金額			
最高押匯金額			
求償銀行求償方式	寄單次數： 寄單方式：		□未註明

(二)請選擇正確答案：

（　　）1. 本張信用狀為　①即期信用狀、保兌信用狀　②限押信用狀、遠期信用狀　③讓購信用狀、不可撤銷信用狀　④可轉讓信用狀、未限押信用狀。

（　　）2. 本張信用狀所要求提示的匯票是　①即期匯票　②銀行匯票　③遠期匯票　④承兌交單匯票。

（　　）3. 本張信用狀受益人所提示之保險單，其保險種類為　①全險及罷工險　②水漬險及戰爭險　③平安險及罷工險　④全險及戰爭險。

（　　）4. 本張信用狀規定受益人可以在何銀行押匯？　①開狀銀行　②通知銀行　③限押銀行　④任何銀行。

（　　）5. 本張信用狀項下之提單應由何者背書？　① ANY BANK　② DBA BANK, NEW YORK, U.S.A　③ FORCEMAN INTERNATIONAL TRADING CO.,

LTD.　④ ALPHA TIRE IMPORTATION。

（　）*6.* 本張信用狀所要求提示單據之期限為　①在信用狀有效期限內即可　②貨運單據簽發日後 2 日內即可　③貨運單據簽發日後 2 日內且必須在信用狀有效期限內　④貨運單據簽發日後 21 日內即可。

（　）*7.* 本張信用狀的匯票付款人為　① ANY BANK　② DBA BANK, NEW YORK, U.S.A　③ FORCEMAN INTERNATIONAL TRADING CO., LTD.　④ ALPHA TIRE IMPORTATION。

（　）*8.* 本張信用狀有關提單之份數，下列何者不正確？　①受益人裝船後寄送一份副本提單給申請人　②全套提單有三份正本　③受益人押匯時需提示兩份正本提單　④提貨時只需一份正本提單即可。

（　）*9.* 本張信用狀對分批裝運的規定是　①未規定　②禁止　③允許　④由託運人決定。

（　）*10.* 本張信用狀所提示的提單為　①空白抬頭之提單　②由託運人指示之提單　③由開狀銀行指示之提單　④記名受貨人之提單。

解答：

　　㈠信用狀分析單：

信用狀當事人（請寫出英文抬頭）		
開狀銀行	DBA BANK, NEW YORK, U.S.A.	
通知銀行		☒未註明
申請人	ALPHA TIRE IMPORTATION	
受益人	FORCEMAN INTERNATIONAL TRADING CO., LTD.	
匯票付款人	DBA BANK, NEW YORK, U.S.A.	
限押銀行		☒無
補償銀行		☒無
信用狀種類（請勾選）		
是否為可撤銷信用狀？	☐是	☒否
是否為保兌信用狀？	☐是	☒否
是否為即期信用狀？	☒是	☐否
是否為限押信用狀？	☐是	☒否
是否為可轉讓信用狀？	☐是	☒否

信用狀相關期限（請填 YYYY/MM/DD）			
開狀日期	2018/06/10		
信用狀有效期限及地點	2018/08/10　美國		☐未註明地點
最後裝運期限	2018/07/15		
提示單據期限	裝運日後＿2＿天且不超過信用狀有效期限		
匯票期限	☒即期		☐遠期＿＿＿＿天
運送相關規定			
提單受貨人（英文）	TO ORDER OF SHIPPER		
提單被通知人（英文抬頭）	未註明		
起運地	KEELUNG		
目的地	NEW YORK		
運費預付或到付	☒預付		☐到付
可否分批裝運	☐可		☒否
可否轉運	☒可		☐否
提示單據種類與規定			
提示單據種類（請勾選）	份數	其他規定	
☒商業發票	四份		
☒包裝單	四份		
提單（☒海運☐空運）	2/3套	背書方式：空白背書	☐未註明
☒保險單據	一份【註】	保險金額：110%發票金額 保險種類：全險、戰爭險	
☐產地證明書			
☐檢驗證明書			
☐受益人證明書			
☐其他（請依序註明） 1. 2. 3.			
信用狀其他內容			
信用狀號碼	N3 AMOLO00284		
貿易條件	CIFC5 NEW YORK		☐未註明
契約／訂單／預期發票號碼			☒未註明
信用狀金額	USD148,442.40		
最高押匯金額	USD148,442.40		
求償銀行求償方式	寄單次數： 寄單方式：		☒未註明

【註】依UCP600第二十八條規定：若保險單據表明簽發之正本超過一份時，所有正本均須提示。

(二)正確答案：

1	2	3	4	5
③	①	④	④	③
6	7	8	9	10
③	②	①	②	②

(三)補充說明：

擔保提貨&副提單背書：由於國際海運發達，時有進口貨物已到埠而信用狀項下之運送單據尚未寄達開狀銀行。進口商為節省海關倉儲費用或因業務上之急需，要求開狀銀行向航運公司簽發擔保提貨書（Letter of Guarantee）。進口商即以擔保提貨書向船公司換領提貨單，憑以報關提貨，此即擔保提貨；或直接以收到出口商所寄發之副提單（Duplicate B/L）要求開狀銀行背書，以便換領提貨單辦理報關提貨，此即副提單背書。

本信用狀中提及 2/3 SET CLEAN ON BOARD BILL OF LADING TO ORDER OF SHIPPER BLANK ENDORSED AND MARKED "FREIGHT PREPAID" AND 1/3 ORIGINAL BILL OF LADING SENT TO THE APPLICANT.可知受益人押匯時只需提供兩份正本提單，剩下一份正本提單通常被要求直接寄給申請人，以便申請人需要時可辦理副提單背書，而所謂副提單（Duplicate B/L），係指第二份正本提單，並非影本或副本的涵義。

三、試依所附信用狀回答問題：

:27　　:SEQUENCE OF TOTAL
　　　　1/2

:40A　:FORM OF DOC. CREDIT
　　　　IRREVOCABLE

:20　　:DOCUMENTARY CREDIT NUMBER
　　　　915FIM000711

:31C　:DATE OF ISSUE
　　　　180215

:40E　:APPLICABLE RULES
　　　　UCP LATEST VERSION

: 31D   : DATE AND PLACE OF EXPIRY

180502 IN THE BENEFICIARY'S COUNTRY

: 51A   : APPLICANT BANK

CHASE MANHATTAN BANK

: 50   : APPLICANT

SADA TECHNOLOGY EXPRESS, INC.

131-10 MAPLE AVENUE FLUSHING, NEW YORK 11335 U.S.A.

: 59   : BENEFICIARY

DARAY INTERNATIONAL CO., LTD.

8F, 153 NEI HU ROAD TAIPEI, TAIWAN

: 32B   : CURRENCY CODE, AMOUNT

USD52,500.00

: 39B   : MAX. CREDIT AMOUNT

NOT EXCEEDING

: 41A   : AVAILABLE WITH⋯BY⋯

ANY BANK BY NEGOTIATION

: 42C   : DRAFTS AT⋯

30 DAYS AFTER SIGHT

: 42A   : DRAWEE

CHASE MANHATTAN BANK

: 43P   : PARTIAL SHIPMENTS

ALLOWED

: 43T   : TRANSHIPMENT

NOT ALLOWED

: 44E   : PORT OF LOADING

KEELUNG PORT

: 44F   : PORT OF DISCHARGE

NEW YORK

: 44C   : LATEST DATE OF SHIPMENT

180425

: 45A   : SHIPMENT (OF GOODS)

+ POWER TILLER M-81

AS PER PURCHASE ORDER NO.123456

CIF NEW YORK INCOTERMS 2010

：46A ：DOCUMENTS REQUIRED

+ SIGNED COMMERCIAL INVOICE IN THREE COPIES

+ FULL SET OF ORIGINAL CLEAN ON BOARD BILLS OF LADING, ISSUING TO ORDER AND BLANK ENDORSED, MARKED "FREIGHT PREPAID" NOTIFY：APPLICANT WITH FULL NAME AND ADDRESS

+ PACKING LIST IN THREE COPIES

+ INSURANCE POLICIES OR CERTIFICATES IN DUPLICATE ENDORSED IN BLANK, FOR FULL CIF INVOICES VALUE PLUS 10% COVERING ICC(A)

+ BENEFICIARY'S CERTIFICATE STATING THAT ONE SET OF NON-NE-GOTIABLE SHIPPING DOCUMENTS HAVE BEEN SENT TO APPLI-CANT BY COURIER

：71B ：CHARGES

ALL BANKING CHARGES AND COMMISSIONS OUTSIDE THE U.S.A. ARE FOR BENEFICIARY'S ACCOUNT

：48 ：PERIOD FOR PRESENTATION

DOCUMENTS TO BE PRESENTED WITHIN SEVEN DAYS AFTER THE DATE OF SHIPMENT BUT WITHIN THE VALIDITY OF THE CREDIT.

：78 ：INSTRUCTIONS

A) PLS SEND DOCUMENTS TO CHASE MANHATTAN BANK P.O. BOX 12567 NEW YORK, U.S.A.

B) DISCREPANCY FEES FOR USD90.00 WILL BE IMPOSED FOR EACH SET OF DISCREPANT DOCUMENTS PRESENTED UNDER THIS DOC. CREDIT

C) REIMBURSEMENT AFTER RECEIPT OF CORRECT DOCUMENTS AT OUR COUNTERS, WE'LL CREDIT YOU AS PER YOUR INSTRUCTION

(一)請完成下述信用狀分析單：

信用狀當事人（請寫出英文抬頭）		
開狀銀行		
通知銀行		□未註明
申請人		
受益人		
匯票付款人		
限押銀行		□無
補償銀行		□無
信用狀種類（請勾選）		
是否為可撤銷信用狀？	□是	□否
是否為保兌信用狀？	□是	□否
是否為即期信用狀？	□是	□否
是否為限押信用狀？	□是	□否
是否為可轉讓信用狀？	□是	□否
信用狀相關期限（請填 YYYY/MM/DD）		
開狀日期		
信用狀有效期限及地點		□未註明地點
最後裝運期限		
提示單據期限	裝運日後_____天且不超過信用狀有效期限	
匯票期限	□即期	□遠期_____天
運送相關規定		
提單受貨人（英文）		
提單被通知人（英文抬頭）		
起運地		
目的地		
運費預付或到付	□預付	□到付
可否分批裝運	□可	□否
可否轉運	□可	□否
提示單據種類與規定		
提示單據種類（請勾選）	份數	其他規定
□商業發票		
□包裝單		
提單（□海運□空運）	背書方式：	□未註明

□保險單據	保險金額：
	保險種類：
□產地證明書	
□檢驗證明書	
□受益人證明書	
□其他（請依序註明） *1.* *2.* *3.*	
信用狀其他內容	
信用狀號碼	
貿易條件	□未註明
契約／訂單／預期發票號碼	□未註明
信用狀金額	
最高押匯金額	
求償銀行求償方式	寄單次數：　　　　　　　　　　　□未註明 寄單方式：

（二）請選擇正確答案：

（　）*1.* 本張信用狀為　①即期、不可轉讓信用狀　②不可撤銷、不可轉讓信用狀　③遠期、可轉讓信用狀　④不可撤銷、可轉讓信用狀。

（　）*2.* 依本張信用狀規定，匯票到期日為　①見票後 30 天　②提示單據後 30 天　③提單日後 30 天　④出票日後 30 天。

（　）*3.* 本張信用狀上所規定提示的提單，其受貨人為　① APPLICANT　② BENE-FICIARY　③ CHASE MANHATTAN BANK　④ TO ORDER。

（　）*4.* 本張信用狀項下之提單應由何者背書？　① ANY BANK　② CHASE MAN-HATTAN BANK　③ DARAY INTERNATIONAL CO., LTD.　④ SADA TECH-NOLOGY EXPRESS, INC.。

（　）*5.* 本張信用狀所規定提示單據之期限為　①貨運單據簽發日後 7 日內　②貨運單據簽發日後 7 日內且必須在信用狀有效期限內　③貨運單據簽發日後 21 日內且必須在信用狀有效期限內　④在信用狀有效期限內即可。

（　）*6.* 依本張信用狀內容，下列敘述何者正確？　①商業發票提示一份正本、兩份副本即可　②保險種類為(C)款險　③不可分批裝運、可轉運　④押匯金額可增減 3%。

（　　）7. 本張信用狀上有關運送之規定，下列敘述何者正確？　①KEELUNG為裝運港　②最後裝船期限為2018年5月2日　③運費由進口商支付　④貨到被通知人為DARAY INTERNATIONAL CO., LTD.。

（　　）8. 本張信用狀規定進口地以外之各項銀行費用由何者負擔？　①申請人　②開狀銀行　③受益人　④通知銀行。

（　　）9. 依本張信用狀規定，下列何者為銀行所接受之提單種類？　①全套、備運、清潔、指示式　②全套、裝運、清潔、記名式　③一份、裝運、清潔、記名式　④全套、裝運、清潔、指示式。

（　　）10. 依本張信用狀規定，押匯時不需提示下列何種單據？　①包裝單、提單　②商業發票、保險單　③受益人證明書　④產地證明書。

解答：

　　㈠信用狀分析單：

信用狀當事人（請寫出英文抬頭）		
開狀銀行	CHASE MANHATTAN BANK	
通知銀行		☒未註明
申請人	SADA TECHNOLOGY EXPRESS, INC.	
受益人	DARAY INTERNATIONAL CO., LTD.	
匯票付款人	CHASE MANHATTAN BANK	
限押銀行		☒無
補償銀行		☒無
信用狀種類（請勾選）		
是否為可撤銷信用狀？	☐是	☒否
是否為保兌信用狀？	☐是	☒否
是否為即期信用狀？	☐是	☒否
是否為限押信用狀？	☐是	☒否
是否為可轉讓信用狀？	☐是	☒否
信用狀相關期限（請填 YYYY/MM/DD）		
開狀日期	2018/02/15	
信用狀有效期限及地點	2018/05/02 臺灣	☐未註明地點
最後裝運期限	2018/04/25	
提示單據期限	裝運日後　7　天且不超過信用狀有效期限	
匯票期限	☐即期	☒遠期　見票日後30　天

運送相關規定		
提單受貨人（英文）	TO ORDER	
提單被通知人（英文抬頭）	SADA TECHNOLOGY EXPRESS, INC.	
起運地	KEELUNG	
目的地	NEW YORK	
運費預付或到付	☒預付	☐到付
可否分批裝運	☒可	☐否
可否轉運	☐可	☒否
提示單據種類與規定		
提示單據種類（請勾選）	份數	其他規定
☒商業發票	三份	
☒包裝單	三份	
提單（☒海運☐空運）	全套	背書方式：空白背書 ☐未註明
☒保險單據	兩份	保險金額：110%CIF 發票金額 保險種類：A 款險
☐產地證明書		
☐檢驗證明書		
☒受益人證明書		
☐其他（請依序註明） 1. 2. 3.		
信用狀其他內容		
信用狀號碼	915FIM000711	
貿易條件	CIF NEW YORK INCOTERMS 2010	☐未註明
契約／訂單／預期發票號碼	123456	☐未註明
信用狀金額	USD52,500.00	
最高押匯金額	USD52,500.00	
求償銀行求償方式	寄單次數： 寄單方式：	☒未註明

(二)正確答案：

1	2	3	4	5
②	①	④	③	②
6	7	8	9	10
①	①	③	④	④

四、試依所附信用狀回答問題：

MT700

FO1FCBKTWTPAXXX3289223094

07202328991006GBCBUS6LAXXX47051326499910070928N

27	SEQUENCE OF TOTAL: 1/1

40B　　FORM OF DOCUMENTARY CREDIT：IRREVOCABLE、TRANSFERABLE

21　　　DOCUMENTARY CREDIT NUMBER：523056120

31C　　DATE OF ISSUE：180228

40E　　APPLICABLE RULES：UCP LATEST VERSION

31D　　DATE AND PLACE OF EXPIRY：180423 AT NEGOTIATION BANK'S COUNTER

51A　　APPLICANT BANK：BANK OF AMERICA, N.A.

50　　　APPLICANT：WESTLAKE INTERNATIONAL CORP.
　　　　　　　　　　1230MARKET LOOP
　　　　　　　　　　SOUTHLAKE, TX 1235620

59　　　BENEFICIARY：ZENLOON CO., LTD.
　　　　　　　　　　NO. 123, TIEN YUH STREET
　　　　　　　　　　TAIPEI , TAIWAN R.O.C.

32B　　CURRENCY CODE, AMOUNT：USD12,000.00

39A　　PERCENTAGE CREDIT AMOUNT TOLERANCE：3/3

41D　　AVAILABLE WITH...BY...：ANY BANK BY NEGOTIATION

42B　　DRAFTS AT...：60 DAYS AFTER DATE

42D　　DRAWEE: BANK OF AMERICA, N.A.

43P　　PARTIAL SHIPMENTS：ALLOWED

43T   TRANSHIPMENT :   ALLOWED

44E   PORT OF LOADING: HONG KONG

44F   PORT OF DISCHARGE: DALLAS, TX

44C   LATEST DATE OF SHIPMENT :   180413

45A   SHIPMENT OF GOODS :

HARDWOOD FURNITURE MV-123, AS PER P/O NO.THF12530

FREE ON BOARD HONG KONG INCOTERMS 2010

46A   DOCUMENTS REQUIRED :

+ORIGINAL AND 3 COPIES OF COMMERCIAL INVOICE.

+ORIGINAL AND 3 COPIES OF PACKING LIST.

+FULL SET OF CLEAN ON BOARD BILLS OF LADING CONSIGNED TO THE ORDER OF BANK OF AMERICA, N.A., MARKED "FREIGHT COLLECT" INDICATING NOTIFY : LIANG INTERNATIONAL CO., LTD. ATTN: SHARITA POPPELL, 900 UNIVERSITY BLVS., N. STE 500, JACKSONVILLE, FL. 32211.

+INSPECTION CERTIFICATE MUST BE ISSUED BY SALLY WANG OF WES-

TLAKE INTERNATIONAL CORP.

+BENEFICIARY'S CERTIFICATE CERTIFYING THAT ONE SET OF NON-NEGOTIABLE DOCUMENTS HAVE BEEN SENT TO APPLICANT BY COURIER SERVICE WITHIN 3 DAYS AFTER SHIPMENT EFFECTED.

47A   ADDITIONAL CONDITIONS :

+INSURANCE IN COVER BY BUYER.

+PLUS OR MINUS THREE PERCENT IN QUANTITY AND AMOUNT IS ALLOWED.

+BILLS OF LADING MUST INDICATE WESTLAKE INTERNATIONAL CORP. AS SHIPPER.

71B   CHARGES :

+ALL BANKING CHARGES OUTSIED U.S.A. ARE FOR ACCOUNT OF BENEFICIARY.

+A DISCREPANT FEE OF USD90.00.

48　　　(PERIOD FOR PRESENTATION):

　　　　DOCUMENTS TO BE PRESENTED WITH 10 DAYS AFTER THE DATE OF

　　　　SHIPMENT BUT WITHIN THE VALIDITY OF THE CREDIT.

49　　　(CONFIRMATION INSTRUCTIONS): WITHOUT

　　　㈠請完成下述信用狀分析單：

信用狀當事人（請寫出英文抬頭）		
開狀銀行		
通知銀行		□未註明
申請人		
受益人		
匯票付款人		
限押銀行		□無
補償銀行		□無
信用狀種類（請勾選）		
是否為可撤銷信用狀？	□是	□否
是否為保兌信用狀？	□是	□否
是否為即期信用狀？	□是	□否
是否為限押信用狀？	□是	□否
是否為可轉讓信用狀？	□是	□否
信用狀相關期限（請填 YYYY/MM/DD）		
開狀日期		
信用狀有效期限及地點		□未註明地點
最後裝運期限		
提示單據期限	裝運日後_____天且不超過信用狀有效期限	
匯票期限	□即期	□遠期_____天
運送相關規定		
提單受貨人（英文）		
提單被通知人（英文抬頭）		
起運地		
目的地		
運費預付或到付	□預付	□到付
可否分批裝運	□可	□否
可否轉運	□可	□否

提示單據種類與規定		
提示單據種類（請勾選）	份數	其他規定
□商業發票		
□包裝單		
提單（□海運□空運）		背書方式：　　　　　　　　　　□未註明
□保險單據		保險金額： 保險種類：
□產地證明書		
□檢驗證明書		
□受益人證明書		
□其他（請依序註明） 1. 2. 3.		
信用狀其他內容		
信用狀號碼		
貿易條件		□未註明
契約／訂單／預期發票號碼		□未註明
信用狀金額		
最高押匯金額		
求償銀行求償方式		寄單次數： 寄單方式：　　　　　　　　　　□未註明

（二）請選擇正確答案：

（　　）*1.* 本張信用狀為　①即期、不可轉讓信用狀　②不可撤銷、不可轉讓信用狀　③遠期、可轉讓信用狀　④不可撤銷、保兌信用狀。

（　　）*2.* 本張信用狀的有效期限及地點為　① 2018 年 3 月 28 日開狀銀行櫃檯　② 2018 年 4 月 23 日押匯銀行櫃檯　③ 2018 年 4 月 13 日開狀銀行櫃檯　④ 2018 年 3 月 28 日押匯銀行櫃檯。

（　　）*3.* 依本張信用狀規定，匯票到期日為　①提單日後 60 天　②發票日後 60 天　③提示單據後 60 天　④見票後 60 天。

（　　）*4.* 本張信用狀交易使用之貿易條件為　①FOB HONG KONG　②FCA HONG KONG　③ CIF DALLAS, TX　④ FAS HONG KONG。

（ ） 5. 本張信用狀所規定提示的提單，其託運人應為 ① LIANG INTERNA-TIONAL CO., LTD. ② ZENLOON CO., LTD. ③ WESTLAKE INTERNA-TIONAL CORP. ④ BANK OF AMERICA, N.A.。

（ ） 6. 本張信用狀所規定提示的提單，其受貨人為 ① APPLICANT ② BENE-FICIARY ③ TO ORDER BANK OF AMERICA, N.A. ④ TO ORDER。

（ ） 7. 本張信用狀所規定提示單據之期限為 ①運送單據簽發日後 10 日內 ②運送單據簽發日後 10 日內且必須在信用狀有效期限內 ③運送單據簽發日後 21 日內且必須在信用狀有效期限內 ④在信用狀有效期限內即可。

（ ） 8. 依本張信用狀內容，下列敘述何者錯誤？ ①商業發票提示一份正本、兩份副本即可 ②由買方負責投保 ③押匯金額可增減 2% ④提單必須標示「運費到付」字樣。

（ ） 9. 依本張信用狀規定，有關提示單據之敘述，下列何者正確？ ①提單必須為全套、清潔、裝運、記名式 ②檢驗證明書及受益人證明書皆必須由受益人簽發 ③包裝單、商業發票至少必須提示一份正本 ④匯票種類為銀行匯票、遠期匯票。

（ ） 10. 依本張信用狀規定，押匯時不需提示下列何種單據？ ①包裝單、商業發票 ②檢驗證明書 ③受益人證明書 ④產地證明書。

解答：

　　(一)信用狀分析單：

信用狀當事人（請寫出英文抬頭）		
開狀銀行	BANK OF AMERICA, N.A.	
通知銀行		☒未註明
申請人	WESTLAKE INTERNATIONAL CORP.	
受益人	ZENLOON CO., LTD.	
匯票付款人	BANK OF AMERICA, N.A.	
限押銀行		☒無
補償銀行		☒無

信用狀種類（請勾選）		
是否為可撤銷信用狀？	☐是	☒否
是否為保兌信用狀？	☐是	☒否
是否為即期信用狀？	☐是	☒否
是否為限押信用狀？	☐是	☒否
是否為可轉讓信用狀？	☒是	☐否
信用狀相關期限（請填 YYYY/MM/DD）		
開狀日期	2018/03/28	
信用狀有效期限及地點	2018/04/23 押匯銀行櫃檯	☐未註明地點
最後裝運期限	2018/06/17	
提示單據期限	裝運日後___10___天且不超過信用狀有效期限	
匯票期限	☐即期	☒遠期___發票日後60___天
運送相關規定		
提單受貨人（英文）	TO ORDER BANK OF AMERICA, N.A.	
提單被通知人（英文抬頭）	LIANG INTERNATIONAL CO., LTD.	
起運地	HONG KONG	
目的地	DALLAS, TX	
運費預付或到付	☐預付	☒到付
可否分批裝運	☒可	☐否
可否轉運	☒可	☐否

提示單據種類與規定		
提示單據種類（請勾選）	份數	其他規定
☒商業發票	四份	一份正本、三份副本
☒包裝單	四份	一份正本、三份副本
提單（☒海運☐空運）	全套	背書方式：　　　　　　　　　　　☒未註明
☐保險單據		保險金額： 保險種類：
☐產地證明書		
☒檢驗證明書		必須由 WESTLAKE INTERNATIONAL CORP.的 SALLY WANG 簽發
☒受益人證明書		受益人必須在裝運後3天內將一套不可轉讓單據以快遞方式寄給申請人
☐其他（請依序註明） 1. 2. 3.		

信用狀其他內容		
信用狀號碼	523056120	
貿易條件	FOB HONG KONG INCOTERMS 2010	□未註明
契約／訂單／預期發票號碼	THF12530	□未註明
信用狀金額	USD12,000.00	
最高押匯金額	USD12,360.00	
求償銀行求償方式	寄單次數： 寄單方式：	☒未註明

(二)正確答案：

1	2	3	4	5
③	②	②	①	③
6	7	8	9	10
③	②	①	③	④

五、試依所附信用狀回答問題：

27(SEQUENCE OF TOTAL): 1/1

40A(FORM OF DOCUMENTARY CREDIT) : IRREVOCABLE

20 (DOCUMENTARY CREDIT NUMBER) : 23-235023-123

31(DATE OF ISSUE): 180103

40E(APPLICABLE RULES): UCP LATEST VERSION

3ID(DATE AND PLACE OF EXPIRY): 180303 TAIWAN

50(APPLICANT): GENOVATE COMPANY, LIMITED, FRANCE

59(BENEFICIARY): CHUNG KUO COMPANY, LIMITED, TAIWAN

32B(CURRENCY CODE, AMOUNT): USD23,100.00

39A(PERCENTAGE CREDIT AMOUNT TOLERANCE): 03/03

41D(AVAILABLE WITH...BY...): ANY BANK BY NEGOTIATION

42C(DRAFTS AT...): SIGHT

42A(DRAWEE): DE CAISSE NATIONALE CREDIT AGRICOLE

43P(PARTIAL SHIPMENTS): PROHIBITED

43T(TRANSHIPMENT): PROHIBITED

44E(PORT OF LOADING) :YANTIAN PORT/CHINA

44F(PORT OF DISCHARGE): BORDEAUX PORT/ FRANCE

44C (LATEST DATE OF SHIPMENT): 180220

45A(SHIPMENT OF GOODS): S/C NO.: ET1233205 16PC KITCHENWARE 2,000 SETS AT CIF BORDEAUX

46B(DOCUMENTS REQUIRED):

+SIGNED COMMERCIAL INVOICE IN QUADRUPLICATE

+SIGNED PACKING LIST IN QUADRUPLICATE

+2/3 SET ORIGINAL OF CLEAN ON BOARD BILLS OF LADING MADE OUT TO ORDER AND BLANK ENDORSED, MARKED "FREIGHT PREPAID" AND THIS L. C. NUMBER

+ INSURANCE POLICIES/ CERTIFICATES IN DUPLICATE, ENDORSED IN BLANK FOR 110PCT OF INVOICE VALUE COVERING INSTITUTE CARGO CLAUSES ALL RISKS. WAR CLAUSES AND SRCC WITH CLAIMS PAYABLE AT DESTINATION IN THE CURRENCY OF THE DRAFTS IRRESPECTIVE OF PERCENTAGE

+ BENEFICIARY'S CERTIFICATE CERTIFYING THAT ONE COPY OF INVOICE, PACKING LIST PLUS 1/3 SET ORIGINAL OF B/L HAVE BEEN SENT TO APPLICANT BY COURIER SERVICES IMMEDIATELY AFTER SHIPMENT DATE

47A(ADDITIONAL CONDITIONS):

+ DISCREPANCY FEE OF USD 90.00 WILL BE DEDUCTED FROM THE PROCEEDS OF ANY DRAWING IF DISCREPANT DOCUMENTS ARE PRESNTED

+ 3 PCT MORE OR LESS ON AMOUNT AND QUANTITY ACCEPTABLE

71B(CHARGES):

ALL BANKING CHARGES OUTSIDE FRANCE INCLUDING ADVISING CHARGES IF ANY ARE FOR ACCOUNT OF BENEFICIARY

48(PERIOD FOR PRESENTATION):

DOCUMENTS TO BE PRESENTED WITHIN 10 DAYS AFTER THE DATE OF ISSUANCE OF SHIPPING DOCUMENTS BUT WITHIN THE VALTDITY OF THE CREDIT

49(CONFIRMATION INSTRUCTIONS): WITHOUT

78(INSTRUCTION TO THE NEGOTIATING BANK):

ALL DOCUMENTS MUST BE SENT TO US DIRECTLY BY COURIER SERVICES IN TWO LOTS

TRAILER: DEH1238

(一)請完成下述信用狀分析單:

信用狀當事人（請寫出英文抬頭）		
開狀銀行		
通知銀行		☐未註明
申請人		
受益人		
匯票付款人		
限押銀行		☐無
補償銀行		☐無
信用狀種類（請勾選）		
是否為可撤銷信用狀？	☐是	☐否
是否為保兌信用狀？	☐是	☐否
是否為即期信用狀？	☐是	☐否
是否為限押信用狀？	☐是	☐否
是否為可轉讓信用狀？	☐是	☐否
信用狀相關期限（請填 YYYY/MM/DD）		
開狀日期		
信用狀有效期限及地點		☐未註明地點
最後裝運期限		
提示單據期限	裝運日後_____天且不超過信用狀有效期限	
匯票期限	☐即期	☐遠期_____天
運送相關規定		
提單受貨人（英文）		
提單被通知人（英文抬頭）		
起運地		
目的地		
運費預付或到付	☐預付	☐到付
可否分批裝運	☐可	☐否
可否轉運	☐可	☐否

提示單據種類與規定		
提示單據種類（請勾選）	份數	其他規定
□商業發票		
□包裝單		
提單（□海運□空運）	背書方式：	□未註明
□保險單據	保險金額： 保險種類：	
□產地證明書		
□檢驗證明書		
□受益人證明書		
□其他（請依序註明） 1. 2. 3.		
信用狀其他內容		
信用狀號碼		
貿易條件		□未註明
契約／訂單／預期發票號碼		□未註明
信用狀金額		
最高押匯金額		
求償銀行求償方式	寄單次數： 寄單方式：	□未註明

(二)請選擇正確答案：

(　　) 1. 本張信用狀為　①即期、不可撤銷、不可轉讓信用狀　②未限押、不可轉讓、保兌信用狀　③遠期、可轉讓、讓購信用狀　④不可撤銷、保兌、即期信用狀。

(　　) 2. 本張信用狀所要求的匯票，下列敘述何者不正確？　①即期匯票　②銀行匯票　③跟單匯票　④商業匯票。

(　　) 3. 依本張信用狀規定，匯票付款人為　① GENOVATE COMPANY, LIMITED ② CHUNG KUO COMPANY, LIMITED　③ ANY BANK　④ DE CAISSE NATIONALE CREDIT AGRICOLE。

(　　) 4. 本張信用狀所規定提示的提單，其受貨人為　① APPLICANT　② BENE-

FICIARY　③ TO ORDER　④ TO ORDER DE CAISSE NATIONALE CREDIT AGRICOLE。

(　) 5. 本張信用狀有關保險單據之規定，下列敘述何者錯誤？　①投保全險、戰爭險、罷工暴動險　②保險金額為110%商業發票金額　③理賠地點為目的地、理賠幣別同匯票幣別　④ IRRESPECTIVE OF PERCENTAGE為自負額。

(　) 6. 本張信用狀所規定提示單據之期限為　①運送單據簽發日後 10 日內　②運送單據簽發日後 10 日內且必須在信用狀有效期限內　③運送單據簽發日後 21 日內且必須在信用狀有效期限內　④在信用狀有效期限內即可。

(　) 7. 依本張信用狀內容，下列敘述何者錯誤？　①商業發票提示一份正本、兩份副本即可　②數量、押匯金額可增減 3%　③提單以空白背書方式轉讓　④禁止分批裝運及轉運。

(　) 8. 依本張信用狀規定，有關提單之敘述，下列何者正確？　①提單必須為全套、清潔、已裝運　② 1/3 套正本提單直接寄給申請人　③提單上必須註記「運費到付」　④裝運港基隆港。

(　) 9. 依本張信用狀規定，押匯時不需提示的單據為　①包裝單、商業發票　②檢驗證明書　③受益人證明書　④保險證明書。

(　) 10. 依本張信用狀規定，受益人無須負擔哪種費用？　①押匯費用　②瑕疵費用　③開狀費用　④通知費用。

解答：

　　(一)信用狀分析單：

信用狀當事人（請寫出英文抬頭）		
開狀銀行	DE CAISSE NATIONALE CREDIT AGRICOLE	
通知銀行		☒未註明
申請人	GENOVATE COMPANY, LIMITED, FRANCE	
受益人	CHUNG KUO COMPANY, LIMITED, TAIWAN	
匯票付款人	DE CAISSE NATIONALE CREDIT AGRICOLE	
限押銀行		☒無
補償銀行		☒無

信用狀種類（請勾選）		
是否為可撤銷信用狀？	☐是	☒否
是否為保兌信用狀？	☐是	☒否
是否為即期信用狀？	☒是	☐否
是否為限押信用狀？	☐是	☒否
是否為可轉讓信用狀？	☐是	☒否
信用狀相關期限（請填 YYYY/MM/DD）		
開狀日期	2018/01/03	
信用狀有效期限及地點	2018/03/03 臺灣	☐未註明地點
最後裝運期限	2018/02/20	
提示單據期限	裝運日後__10__天且不超過信用狀有效期限	
匯票期限	☒即期	☐遠期_____天
運送相關規定		
提單受貨人（英文）	TO ORDER	
提單被通知人（英文抬頭）	未註明	
起運地	YANTIAN	
目的地	BORDEAUX	
運費預付或到付	☒預付	☐到付
可否分批裝運	☐可	☒否
可否轉運	☐可	☒否

提示單據種類與規定		
提示單據種類（請勾選）	份數	其他規定
☒商業發票	四份	
☒包裝單	四份	
提單（☒海運☐空運）	2/3 套	背書方式：空白背書　☐未註明
☒保險單據	兩份	保險金額：110%商業發票金額 保險種類：全險、戰爭險、罷工暴動險
☐產地證明書		
☐檢驗證明書		
☒受益人證明書		受益人必須在裝運日後立即將商業發票及包裝單各一份副本、1/3 套正本提單以快遞方式寄給申請人
☐其他（請依序註明） *1.* *2.* *3.*		

信用狀其他內容		
信用狀號碼	23-235023-123	
貿易條件	CIF BORDEAUX	☐未註明
契約／訂單／預期發票號碼	ET1233205	☐未註明
信用狀金額	USD23,100.00	
最高押匯金額	USD23,793.00	
求償銀行求償方式	寄單次數：兩次 寄單方式：快遞	☐未註明

(二)正確答案：

1	2	3	4	5
①	②	④	③	④
6	7	8	9	10
②	①	②	②	③

貿易單據製作

第一節　貿易單據製作內容解析

在信用狀作業下，各當事人所處理者為單據（UCP600 第五條），而開狀銀行（或保兌銀行）付款之憑藉亦為單據（UCP600 第七、八條），因此，信用狀受益人在出口押匯時，製作內部單據並審核外來單據，整理及提示符合信用狀之押匯文件，是非常重要的。簡單而言，信用狀的製單，應該要做到正確、完整、及時。

1. 正確

正確製單是對外貿易工作的前提，單據做得不正確，就不能順利押匯。此即所謂嚴格的「單據一致，單單一致」，其次是「單貨一致」三大原則。依 UCP600 第十三條規定，開狀銀行僅以單據為本，審查單據就表面所示是否符合規定；單據間彼此雖無須完全一致，但不得互相牴觸。故從銀行的標準來看，只需達到「單據一致，單單一致」；但對於出口商而言，必須再加上「單貨一致」，如此單據才能真實代表裝運的貨物，確保履約及安全收匯。

2. 完整

所交的單據必須是一套完整的單據，包括單據的格式、貨物、文字、簽署、背書、份數等等。如要求提示一式三份，即必須是一份正本加上兩份副本單據。如要求一式三份正本，則必須在單據上表明三份都是正本，並附有權簽署者的手簽或簽章。信用狀要求提供的單據和條款必須要全部做到，不能有遺漏、差錯和誤期等現象。

3.及時

押匯單據有時間性，必須要在信用狀規定的期限內完成，以保證整套單據的完整。如一些單據需要一定的手續，必須及時辦理，防止誤期。

以下僅就匯票、商業發票、包裝單及裝貨單四種單據之填製注意事項，加以說明：

一、匯票（Bill of Exchange）

國際貿易中，匯票通常作為出口商要求付款的憑證，故屬財務單據（Financial Documents）。茲以所附匯票（表1、表2）說明匯票的填製方法及注意事項。

㈠匯票號碼

由發票人自行編號，通常與商業發票之編號一致。

㈡小寫金額

1. 應填上幣別及阿拉伯數字，必須以信用狀所規定之貨幣表示。
2. 匯票金額必須是一定金額（a certain sum in money），約略金額（如 about USD 15,000.00）的匯票無效。
3. 信用狀項下的匯票，除信用狀另有規定外，須與發票金額一致，且不超過信用狀可使用餘額。若信用狀規定匯票金額為發票金額的百分之幾，則按規定填寫。
4. 託收項下的匯票，其金額應與發票金額一致。
5. 若使用部分託收、部分信用狀方式付款，則兩張匯票金額各按規定填寫，兩者之和等於發票金額。

㈢簽發地點、日期

1. 依 ISBP 規定，信用狀即使未明確規定，匯票、運送單據及保險單據仍必須標示日期，其日期應在信用狀有效期限及提示期間內，不得早於運送單據之裝運日期及相關單據之簽發日期為原則。
2. 我國票據法規定簽發地點、日期為必要記載事項。

㈣匯票期限（Tenor）

1. 匯票付款人履行付款的日期。

2. 即期匯票（Sight Draft），即見票即付（At Sight），在此欄填打 XXX 或畫一橫線。

3. 遠期匯票（Usance Draft），即見票後一段期間付款。如為見票後 30 日付款，則在此欄填上 thirty (30) days after...。如信用狀規定匯票期限為「at XXX days after bill of lading date」時，依 ISBP 須能從匯票本身之資料計算到期日，因此，匯票上亦須記載提單之確實日期，例如：「at XXX days after bill of lading date May 15, 20—.」。

㈤受款人（Payee）

1. 受款人在匯票上是主要債權人。

2. 信用狀方式下，受款人通常為押匯銀行或其代理行，一般出口押匯使用之匯票為押匯銀行印定之格式，皆已印妥，不須另行繕打。

3. 託收方式下，受款人可以是託收銀行，均作成指示式抬頭，也可將出口商寫成受款人，然後由受款人作委託受款背書給託收銀行。

㈥大寫金額

1. 用大寫文字表示，並在文字金額後面加上「ONLY」，以防止塗改，例如：「U.S. DOLLARS TEN THOUSAND ONLY.」。

2. 依信用狀使用的幣別，且小寫數字金額（amount in figures）及大寫文字金額（amount in words）需一致。如兩者相牴觸時，則應以大寫文字所表示之金額作為要求之金額，而予以審查。

㈦發票條款

1. 國際貿易上多以信用狀為支付工具，故匯票上多印有發票條款，表明該匯票係依據某信用狀所簽發，出口商只要填上開狀銀行名稱、信用狀號碼以及開狀日期即可。

2. 其他付款方式，例如 D/P，則於 Drawn under 之後填上「D/P」即可。

㈧付款人（Drawee）

1. 付款人是匯票的主債務人。

2. 信用狀方式下，通常為開狀銀行或其指定的付款銀行為付款人，依據UCP600
第六條規定，信用狀之簽發，不可以開狀申請人為匯票付款人。

3. 其他付款方式，例如託收，匯票一般均以進口商為付款人。

(九)發票人（Drawer）

1. 發票人即簽發匯票的人。

2. 信用狀方式下，匯票須由信用狀受益人簽發並須簽署。

📖表1　空白匯票

BILL OF EXCHANGE

Draft No... (一)匯票號碼⋯⋯ 　　　　　　　　　　　　　　　(三)簽發地點、日期

For 　(二)匯票小寫金額 　　　　　　　　　　　　　　　**Taipei, Taiwan**

At 　(四)匯票期限　**sight of this FIRST of Exchange (Second the same tenor and date being unpaid)**

Pay to the order of HUA NAN COMMERCIAL BANK, LTD. (五)受款人

The sum of 　(六)匯票大寫金額

　　　　　　　　　　　　　　　　　　　　　　　　　　　　value received

Drawn under 　(七)發票條款—開狀銀行

Irrevocable L/C No. (七)發票條款—信用狀號碼 **dated** 　(七)發票條款—開狀日期

To (八)付款人

　　　　　　　　　　　　　　　　　　　　　　　　　　　　(九)發票人

📖表2　匯票實例

BILL OF EXCHANGE

No... 123...

For 　USD150,000.00 　　　　　　　　　Taipei, Taiwan 30-JUNE-2018

At 　×××　sight of this FIRST of Exchange (Second the same tenor and date being unpaid)

Pay to the order of　HUA NAN COMMERCIAL BANK, LTD.

The sum of 　U.S. DOLLARS ONE HUNDRED FIFTY THOUSAND ONLY

　　　　　　　　　　　　　　　　　　　　　　　　　value received

Drawn under　HONGKONG BANK MALAYSIA BERHAD

Irrevocable L/C No.　LC-123456　　　　dated　12-MAY-2018

To　HONG KONG BANK MALAYSIA BERHAD　　　TAIPEI TRADING CO., LTD.

　　　　　　　　　　　　　　　　　　　　　　　　　×××

二、商業發票（Commercial Invoice）

商業發票是出口商簽發的發貨價格清單、裝運貨物的總說明。主要作用有：

1. 便於進、出口商核對已發貨物是否符合契約或信用狀規定。

2. 作為進口商和出口商記帳的依據。

3. 在出口地和進口地作為報關及納稅的憑據。

4. 不用匯票的情況下，可代替匯票作為付款依據。

5. 是整套出口單據的中心及填製和審核的依據。

6. 可作為索賠、理賠的憑據。

商業發票沒有統一的格式，原則上其內容應符合契約規定，在以信用狀方式付款時，還應與信用狀的規定嚴格相符。商業發票也是全套貨運單據的中心，其他單據多參照發票內容繕製，故其製作必須正確無誤。

茲以所附商業發票（表 3、表 4）為例，說明填製方法及注意事項。

1. 出口商名稱或稱箋頭（Letterhead）

為出口商公司行號及地址。

2. 單據名稱

在箋頭下方標明該單據之名稱，依 ISBP 規定：

(1)倘信用狀要求提示「發票」（Invoice）而未有進一步之定義時，則提示任何型態之發票如「Commercial Invoice」（商業發票）、「Customs Invoice」（海關發票）、「Consular Invoice」（領事發票）等即已符合。

(2)除信用狀特別授權外，發票名稱為「provisional」（臨時）、「pro-forma」（預估或預期）或類似者，將不被接受。

(3)當信用狀要求提示「商業發票」（Commercial Invoice），則標示為「Invoice」之單據將被接受。

3. 發票號碼

由發票人以發票製發日期先後，及流水號碼自行編號，注意複查方便與保密考量。

4.發票日期

(1)為製作發票的日期，此日期宜與裝運日期同一天。商業發票的日期不得遲於信用狀有效日期或提示押匯、付款或承兌期限。

(2)依UCP第十八條及ISBP規定，除非信用狀要求，商業發票無須標明簽發日期。

5.貨物名稱及數量

記載交運貨物之貨物名稱與數量，當貨物品名繁多時，則記載「as follows」即可。

6.抬頭人

依 UCP600 第十八條規定，商業發票的抬頭人，除信用狀另有規定外，須以開狀申請人為抬頭人。

7.發貨人

即出口商。

8.船名或其他運送工具名稱

以船舶裝運者，在「Shipped by」之後記入船名航次，如「Shipped by S.S. Hope V.918」。以航空運送者，則填入「Air Freight」、「Airlift」或「Aircraft」等字樣。

9.啟航日期

其日期原則上固然宜與提單「on board date」一致，但因有「on or about」，依據 UCP600 第三條規定：解釋為自特定日期前五曆日訖特定日期後五曆日（含首尾日共十一曆日）之期間，因此，倘運送單據確定裝運日期在此區間內，將不視為瑕疵。

10.裝運地

在貨櫃運輸，裝運地有裝運港（port of loading）及收貨地（place of receipt）之分，在信用狀要求提單時，提單上的裝運港必須與信用狀所規定者相符。因此，商業發票上的裝運地也應與信用狀所規定者相符。

11. 卸貨地

即進口地港埠或目的地，在貨櫃運輸，卸貨地也有卸貨港（port of discharge）與交貨地（place of delivery）之分，在信用狀要求提單時，商業發票上的卸貨地須與提單及信用狀規定一致。

12. 信用狀號碼

填入信用狀號碼，但須與信用狀上所示者一致。

13. 契約號碼

填上契約或訂單號碼，也可免填。

14. 裝運嘜頭

原則上應與運送單據及其他單據記載者相同；但部分單據上嘜頭之內容，通常較信用狀條款規定者多，而包含有諸如：貨物之型號、處理易碎貨物之警告、貨物重量與原產國標示等內容，此並不構成瑕疵；或是整櫃運輸實務之運送單據，有時在其嘜頭標題下僅記載貨櫃之號碼，其餘之單據則記載詳細之裝船標誌，對此並不視為不一致。

15. 貨物敘述

商業發票上有關貨物的記述必須與信用狀上所載者相符（UCP600 第十八條），此為強行規定，所有信用狀當事人均須嚴格遵守。所謂「貨物的敘述」（description of the goods），不僅指貨物的名稱（the name of the goods），而且包括其品質、規格及其他附帶說明。

16. 數量

依照實際交運數量與單位列示，商業發票上所載貨物數量不應與運送單據上所載者有矛盾。除信用狀規定特定貨物之數量不得增加或減少外，5%上下差異應屬容許，但以動支之金額不超逾信用狀之金額為條件。如果信用狀係以包裝單位或個別件數（如 pc、set 等）規定數量條件者，此 5%寬容額度即不適用。如果信用狀內所載之數量條款出現「約」（about）或「大概」（approximately）等用語時，解釋為容許不逾該數量 10%上下之差額（UCP600 第三十條）。

17.單價

依 ISBP 規定，單價及幣別亦須與信用狀規定一致。倘貿易條件（TradeTerm）構成貨物說明之一部分，或與信用狀金額有關，則商業發票須標示該貿易條件；且其敘述亦規定該貿易條件之依據，則該依據須經確認。例如：信用狀之條款為「CIF Singapore Incoterms 2000」，則標示「CIF Singapore」將與信用狀規定不符。

18.商業發票金額（總金額）

商業發票的總金額乃貨物單價與裝運數量的相乘積，表示進口商應付的金額，通稱為發票金額（Invoice Amount 或 Invoice Value）。發票金額須與匯票金額一致，且不超過信用狀可使用餘額。

19.大寫金額

商業發票上大寫文字金額應與小寫數字金額一致。

20.其他事項

信用狀其他規定，如附加條款（Additional Conditions）中規定標示簽發匯票或發票的依據時，則寫明開狀銀行、開狀日期及信用狀號碼。

21.發票人簽署

商業發票的發票人通常為受益人（UCP600 第三十八條規定除外），並由其簽署，但依UCP600 第十八條，可以不簽字。如信用狀有「SIGNED COMMERCIAL IN-VOICE」字樣，則此發票必須簽字；若信用狀中有「MANUALLY SIGNED COM-MERCIAL INVOICE」字樣，則必須要有發票人的手簽。

📖 表3　空白商業發票

1.出口商公司名稱與地址

2.單據名稱

INVOICE

No.　*3.發票號碼*　　　　　　　　　　　　　Date:　*4.發票日期*

INVOICE of　*5.貨物名稱及數量*

For account and risk of Messrs.　*6.抬頭人*

Shipped by　*7.發貨人*　　　　　　per　*8.船名或其他運輸工具名稱*

Sailing on or about　*9.啟航日期*　　From　*10.裝運地*　to　*11.卸貨地*

L/C No.　*12.信用狀號碼*　　　　　Contract No.　*13.契約號碼*

Marks & Nos.	Description of Goods	Quantity	Unit Price	Amount
14.裝運嘜頭	*15.貨物敘述* *19.大寫金額* *20.其他事項*	*16.數量*	*17.單價*	*18.總金額*
			21.發票人簽署	

📖 表4　商業發票實例

TAIPEI TRADING CO., LTD.

INVOICE

No.　123　　　　　　　　　　　　　　Date:　30-JUNE-2018

INVOICE of　10,000 SETS OF TOYS

For account and risk of Messrs.　NEW YORK TRADING CO., LTD.

Shipped by　TAIPEI TRADING CO., LTD.　　per　S.S. HOPE V.918

Sailing on or about　30-JUNE-2018　　From　KEELUNG　to　NEW YORK

L/C No.　LC-123456　　　　Contract No.　AB-654321

Marks & Nos.	Description of Goods	Quantity	Unit Price	Amount
◇ N.Y. ◇ NEW YORK C/NO.:1-500 MADE IN TA-	TOYS	10,000 SETS	**CIF NEW YORK** USD15.00/SET	USD150,000.00
		∨∨∨∨∨∨∨∨∨∨∨∨	∨∨∨∨∨∨∨∨∨∨∨	∨∨∨∨∨∨∨∨∨∨∨
	SAY TOTAL U.S. DOLLARS ONE HUNDRED FIFTY THOUSAND ONLY.			
			TAIPEI TRADING CO., LTD.	
			× × × Sales Manager	

三、包裝單（Packing List）

包裝單又稱裝箱單，為商業發票內容的補充，通常是商品的包裝件數、規格、嘜頭、重量等項目的填製，明確說明商品的包裝情況，便於買方對進口商品包裝及數量、重量的瞭解和掌握，也便於國外買方在貨物到達目的港時，供海關檢查和核對貨物。

包裝單於 UCP600 並未以專屬條文規範，因此，包裝單並無統一固定的格式，製單時可以根據信用狀或契約的要求和貨物的特點自行設計，且不與其他單據發生牴觸即可。

包裝單的作用有：

1. 是出口商繕製商業發票及其他單據時計量計價的基礎資料。

2. 是進口商清點數量或重量，以及銷售貨物的依據。

3. 是海關查驗貨物的憑證。

4. 是公證行或商檢機構查驗貨物的參考資料。

茲以所附包裝單（表5、表6）說明其製作方法及應注意事項。

包裝單的內容可分為兩部分，上半部內容大致與商業發票一致，即第 3 項至第 12 項，讀者可參考商業發票填製說明；下半段內容則以貨物件數、重量、體積為主，即第 13 項至第 21 項。

1. 出口商名稱或稱箋頭

填入出口商公司行號及地址。信用狀如要求「neutral packing list」（中立包裝單），則應依照進口商之特別要求，以第三者名義或無箋頭之白紙製作包裝單。

2. 單據名稱

依 ISBP 規定，信用狀要求「Packing List」（包裝單）時，則只要單據包含包裝之明細，無論該單據冠以「Packing Note」（包裝說明）、「Packing and Weight List」（包裝及重量單）等名稱，或未冠名稱，均符合信用狀之要求。單據之內容必須顯示符合該要求單據之功能。

3. 項至12.項

分別為簽發號碼、簽發日期、貨物名稱及總數量、抬頭人、發貨人、船名或其他運送工具名稱、啟航日期、裝運地、卸貨地、裝運嘜頭，原則上與商業發票相同。

13. 包裝件號

應與提單及商業發票上所載者相同，例如：C/No.：1-500（C/No.為 case number 或 carton number 的縮寫）。

14. 貨物敘述

依照信用狀所示或契約所規定者敘述。

15. 貨物數量

填入貨物包裝單位數量及總數量。

16. 貨物總淨重

填入貨物包裝單位淨重及總淨重。

17. 貨物總毛重

填入貨物包裝單位毛重及總毛重，總毛重應與運送單據上所示者一致。

18. 貨物總體積

填入貨物包裝單位體積及總體積，總體積應與運送單據上所示者一致。

19. 貨物總件數大寫

須與運送單據上所示者一致，例如：Say one hundred cartons only。

20. 其他事項

信用狀所要求的附加條款。

21. 簽署人名稱及簽字

與商業發票相同，應由出口商簽署。

表5　空白包裝單

1. 出口商公司名稱與地址

2. 單據名稱

PACKING LIST

No.　*3. 發票號碼*　　　　　　　　　　　　　Date:　*4. 發票日期*

PACKING LIST of　*5. 貨物名稱及數量*

For account and risk of Messrs.　*6. 抬頭人*

12. 裝運嘜頭

Shipped by　*7. 發貨人*

per　*8. 船名或其他運輸工具名稱*

Sailing on or about　*9. 啟航日期*

From　*10. 裝運地*　to　*11. 卸貨地*

C/ No.	Description	Quantity	Net Weight	Gross Weight	Measurement
13. 包裝件號	*14. 貨物敘述*	*15. 貨物數量*	*16. 貨物總淨重*	*17. 貨物總毛重*	*18. 貨物總體積*
	19. 貨物總件數大寫 *20. 其他事項*				

21. 簽署人名稱及簽字

🏛 表6 包裝單實例

TAIPEI TRADING CO., LTD.
PACKING LIST

No. 123   Date: 30-JUNE-2018

PACKING LIST of 10,000 SETS OF TOYS   MARKS & NOS.

For account and risk of Messrs. NEW YORK TRADING CO., LTD.

◇ N.Y. ◇

Shipped by TAIPEI TRADING CO., LTD.   NEW YORK

per S.S. HOPE   V. 918   C/NO.:1-500

Sailing on or about 30-JUNE-2018   MADE IN TA-

From KEELUNG   to   NEW YORK

C/ No.	Description	Quantity	Net Weight	Gross Weight	Measurement
1-500	TOYS	@20 SETS	@10KGS	@10.2KGS	@1.226CBM
		10,000 SETS	5,000 KGS	5,100 KGS	613 CBM
		vvvvvvvvvvvv	vvvvvvvvvvvv	vvvvvvvvvvvv	vvvvvvvvvvvv

SAY TOTAL FIVE HUNDRED CARTONS ONLY.

TAIPEI TRADING CO., LTD.

×××

Sales Manager

四、裝貨單

　　託運人向船公司洽訂艙位後,應向船公司提交裝貨單(Shipping Order;簡稱 S/O),以作為船公司簽發提單之基本資料。由於船公司係根據託運人所提供之裝貨單內容簽發提單,因此託運人務必完全遵照信用狀規定填製裝貨單,才能使船公司所簽發之提單符合信用狀規定。

　　裝貨單係所有船運文件中最為原始者,為船舶裝貨之憑證。此文件就託運人而言，為船公司同意配予其在某一特定船舶上艙位之憑證；就船舶而言，此為船公司通知船上，准許裝船之通知，並非代表船公司一定要接受託運人之貨物。許多船公司的裝貨單上，大多會於背面註明下列條款：「裝貨單之接受，僅代表接受訂載，運送人得僅裝載貨物之一部或改裝運送人之其他船隻或拒運貨物之一部或全部。」但是，在正常情況下，上述之情況並不多。

裝貨單的格式，內容多大同小異。但值得注意的是，裝貨單之格式與提單的各欄有許多地方雷同，即裝貨單上的許多資料，是作為將來製作提單之參考或依據。茲以所附裝貨單（表7、表8）說明其填製方法。

1. Shipper （託運人）

又稱發貨人。託運人係指委託運送的人，在國際貿易中是契約的賣方。如信用狀無特殊規定，一般都填寫受益人的名稱；除非信用狀另有規定，銀行將接受以信用狀受益人以外的一方作為託運人的提單。

2. Consignee（受貨人）

依信用狀規定填寫，通常可分記名式和指示式，其表示方法為：

(1)記名式

即在受貨人一欄內填寫某人或某公司的名稱。這種提單只能由提單上所指定的受貨人提貨，而不能轉讓他人，故在國際貿易中使用不多。信用狀中的文句一般為：「FULL SET OF B/L CONSIGNED TO ABC COMPANY...」。

(2)指示式

這種提單使用最為普遍。又可分為「記名指示式」和「不記名指示式」兩種。

①記名指示式：

常見的有 TO ORDER OF SHIPPER（託運人指示式）、TO ORDER OF XXX BANK（銀行指示式，一般大多指開狀銀行）、TO ORDER OF ABC COMPANY（受貨人指示式）。信用狀上的辭彙常常是：「FULL SET OF B/L MADE OUT TO ORDER OF XXX BANK」。

②不記名指示式：

又稱空白抬頭、待指示。即在受貨人一欄內填寫「TO ORDER」，然後在提單背面由託運人簽字蓋章，即以空白背書方式轉讓物權。信用狀上用的辭彙常常是：「FULL SET OF B/L MADE OUT TO ORDER」。

3. Notify Party （貨到被通知人）

依信用狀規定填寫。如信用狀無規定時，可填寫開狀申請人或不填寫。

4. Place of Receipt （收貨地點）

託運人實際將貨物交予運送人之地點。

5. Ocean Vessel 及 Voy. No. （船名及航次）

填寫船舶名稱及航次別。

6. Port of Loading （裝運港）

填寫實際裝載貨物之港口。

7. Port of Discharge （卸貨港）

填寫信用狀中的卸貨港名稱。

8. Place of Delivery （交貨地點）

最終目的地名稱。如果貨物的目的地就是目的港，此欄目免填寫。

9. Service Required （標示運送方式）

按實際所需運送方式，在其方格內打「×」或「√」。

10. Marks and Numbers （裝運嘜頭及箱號）

填寫貨物外包裝之嘜頭及箱號，且必須與信用狀項下之單據相符。

11. No. of Containers or Packages （件數）

填寫貨物總櫃數或總箱數。

12. Description of Goods （貨物敘述）

填寫貨物名稱。必須與商業發票、包裝單等單據一致；但裝貨單上貨物名稱的描述可以只寫統稱，而不必如商業發票上描述得那麼詳細。

13. Gross Weight（毛重）

填寫貨物總毛重，應與其他單據一致。如果是裸裝貨物沒有毛重，只有淨重，則在淨重數字前加註「NET WEIGHT」。

14. Measurement （體積）

填寫貨物總體積。

15. Freight to be （付費方式）

除非信用狀有特別要求，一般的提單都不填寫運費金額，而只表明運費是否已付清或什麼時候付清。如貿易條件為 CFR、CIF 時，運費由託運人於出口地領取提單時即應支付，為「Freight Prepaid」（運費預付）。如貿易條件為 FAS、FOB 時，運費由受貨人於進口地換領提貨單（Delivery Order ; D/O）時支付，為「Freight Collect」（運費到付）。

📖 表 7　空白裝箱單

Shipper *1.* 託運人					
統一編號：	發票抬頭：				EVERGREEN
Consignee *2.* 受貨人					EVERGREEN INTERNATIONAL CORPORATION SHIPPING ORDER

Notify Party *3.* 貨到被通知人		*9.* SERVICE REQUIRED：運送方式 □CY/CY □CFS/CY □CY/DRT □CY/CFS □CFS/CFS □CY/DOOR
Pre-carriage by	Place of Receipt *4.* 收貨地點	*15.* FREIGHT TO BE：付費方式 □PREPAID □COLLECT
Ocean Vessel *5.* 船名	Voy. No. 航次	Port of Loading *6.* 裝運港	
Port of Discharge *7.* 卸貨港	Place of Delivery *8.* 交貨地點	Final Destination (for the Merchant's reference only)

Container No. Seal No.: Marks and Numbers. *10.* 裝運嘜頭及箱號	No. of Containers or Packages *11.* 件數	Description of Goods *12.* 貨物敘述	Gross Weight *13.* 毛重	Measurement *14.* 體積

SPECIAL NOTE:

1. 副本＿＿份　*2.* 運費證明＿＿份　*3.* 電報放貨＿＿　*4.* 危險品＿＿　*5.* 其他＿＿

填表請注意：

1. 危險品請註明 UN NO. IMO CLASS 與燃點，並附上 Shipper's Certificate。

2. 嘜頭及品名如超過十行，請以附表繕打，俾便提單製作。

Particulars furnished by the Merchant.

🛎 表 8　裝箱單實例

Shipper			
TAIPEI TRADING CO., LTD.			

統一編號：　　　　發票抬頭：

EVERGREEN
EVERGREEN INTERNATIONAL CORPORATION
SHIPPING ORDER

Consignee			
TO ORDER			

Notify Party			
NEW YORK TRADING CO., LTD.			

⑼ SERVICE REQUIRED

☑ CY/CY　☐ CFS/CY　☐ CY/DRT
☐ CY/CFS　☐ CFS/CFS　☐ CY/DOOR

Pre-carriage by	Place of Receipt	

⑮ FREIGHT TO BE
☑ PREPAID　☐ COLLECT

Ocean Vessel	Voy. No.	Port of Loading	
HOPE	918	KEELUNG	

Port of Discharge.		Place of Delivery		Final Destination (for the Merchant's reference only)
NEW YORK				

Container No. Seal No.: Marks and Numbers	No. of Containers or Packages	Description of Goods	Gross Weight	Measurement
◇ N.Y. ◇ NEW YORK C/NO.:1-500 MADE IN TAIWAN	500 CTNS	TOY	5,100 KGS	613CBM

SPECIAL NOTE:

1.副本＿＿份　2.運費證明＿＿份　3.電報放貨＿＿　4.危險品＿＿　5.其他＿＿

填表請注意：

1.危險品請註明 UN NO. IMO CLASS 與燃點，並附上 Shipper's Certificate。

2.嘜頭及品名如超過十行，請以附表繕打，俾便提單製作。

Particulars furnished by the Merchant.

第二節　勞動部勞動力發展署測驗試題範例解析

一、試題範例

請依加拿大 Bank of Montreal 開來之信用狀摘要及相關工廠出貨明細資料，填製
㈠ Bill of Exchange；㈡ Invoice；㈢ Packing List；㈣ Shipping Order 等單據內容，並請
依照題號①、②、③……欄位依序填入答案紙。

Form of Doc. Credit	*40 A：	IRREVOCABLE
Doc. Credit Number	*20 ：	HKU-8023
Date of Issue	31 C：	080930
Expiry	*31 D：	081215 AT OUR COUNTER
Applicant	*50 ：	LEE INTERNATIONAL CORPORATION
		2527 JOHNSON ROAD, VANCOUVER, B. C. , CANADA
Beneficiary	*59 ：	WANG TRADING CO., LTD.
		NO. 1234, SEC. 1, JHONG SHAN N. RD., TAIPEI, TAIWAN (R.O. C.)
Amount	*32 B：	CURRENCY USD AMOUNT 26,775.00
Available with/by	*41 D：	ANY BANK BY NEGOTIATION
Drafts at...	42 C：	120 DAYS SIGHT
Drawee	42 A：	BANK OF MONTREAL
Partial shipments	43 P：	PROHIBITED
Transhipment	43 T：	ALLOWED
Loading in Charge	44 A：	ANY TAIWANESE PORT
For Transport to...	44 B：	VANCOUVER
Latest Date of Ship	44 C：	081130
Descript. of Goods	45 A：	8,500 DOZENS OF SLIPPERS (MODEL NO. S-238 & S-240) AS PER BUYER'S ORDER NO. L-123, CIFC5 VANCOUVER SHIPPING MARK: LEE238(IN DIA)/VANCOUVER/1-UP
Documents required	46 A：	+ SIGNED COMMERCIAL INVOICE IN TRIPLICATE.

+ PACKING LIST IN QUADRUPLICATE SHOWN Q'TY, G/W, N/W OF EACH CARTON.

+ 2/3 SET CLEAN ON BOARD OCEAN BILLS OF LADING MADE OUT TO ORDER NO-

+ INSURANCE POLICIES OR CERTIFICATES IN DUPLICATE ENDORSED IN BLANK, FOR FULL CIF INVOICE VALUE PLUS 10% COVERING ICC(C) AND INSTITUTE STRIKES CLAUSES(CARGO).

+ BENEFICIARY CERTIFICATE STATING THAT ONE SET OF ORIGINAL DOCUMENTS SENT TO APPLICANT AFTER THE SHIPMENT.

Additional Cond.	47 A :	ALL DOCS. MUST BE SHOWN THE CREDIT NUMBER.
Details of Charges	71 B :	ALL BANKING CHARGES OUTSIDE CANADA ARE FOR ACCOUNT OF BENEFICIARY.
Presentation Period	48 :	15 DAYS AFTER THE DATE OF SHIPMENT BUT WITHIN THE VALIDITY OF THE CREDIT.

工廠出貨明細資料：

型　　號	S-238	S-240
包裝方式	30 DOZ/CTN	20 DOZ/CTN
每箱重量	N.W. 5.35KGS；G.W. 5.85KGS	N.W. 6.35KGS ；G.W. 6.85KGS
出貨數量	6,000 DOZ	2,500 DOZ
每箱尺寸	20"×15"×12"	72×52×52(cm)

備註：

1. S-238 每箱 CBM 計算方式：先求 CFT = (20×15×12)÷1,728 = 2.08；再算 CBM = 2.08÷35.315 = 0.059

2. S-240 每箱 CFT 計算方式：先求 CBM = 0.72×0.52×0.52 = 0.195；再算 CFT = 0.195×35.315 = 6.89

參考題目與答案

BILL OF EXCHANGE

No. __123___

FOR __USD26,775.00___   TAIPEI, TAIWAN __25-NOV.-08___

At ___①___ SIGHT OF THIS FIRST BILL OF EXCHANGE (SECOND UNPAID) PAY TO THE
ORDER OF __**THE FIRST COMM. BANK, LTD.**__

THE SUM OF _____②_____

DRAWN UNDER CREDIT NO. _____③_____ DATE __30-SEP.-08_____

ISSUED BY __BANK OF MONTREAL_____

TO

_____②_____

                                                WANG TRADING CO., LTD.
                                                _____×××_____

INVOICE

No. __123__   Date: __25-NOV.-08__

INVOICE of _____⑤_____

For account and risk of Messrs. _____⑥_____

Shipped by _____×_____

Sailing on or about __25-NOV.-08__   Per __S.S. LINCOLN V.571__

From __KEELUNG__   To __VANCOUVER__

L/C No. __HKU-8023__   Contract No. __L-123__

Marks & Nos.	Description of Goods	Quantity	Unit Price	Amount
	SLIPPERS		⑧	
	AS PER BUYER'S			
⑦	ORDER NO. L-123			
	MODEL NO.S-238	6,000 DOZ.	⑨	USD17,100.00
	MODEL NO.S-240	2,500 DOZ.		USD 9,675.00
		8,500 DOZ.		USD26,775.00
		vvvvvvvvvv		vvvvvvvvvvvv
	SAY TOTAL U.S. DOLLARS ×××× ONLY.			
	DRAWN UNDER BANK OF MONTREAL L/C NO. HKU-8023 DATED 30-SEP.-08			

WANG TRADING CO., LTD.

_____×××_____

PACKING LIST

No.　123

PACKING LIST of _____ ✕ _____

For account and risk of Messrs. _____ ✕ _____

_____

Shipped by _____ ✕ _____

Per S. S.　　LINCOLN V.571 _____

Sailing on or about　25-NOV.-08 _____

Shipment From　　KEELUNG　　to　　VANCOUVER _____

Date:　25-NOV.-08

MARKS & NOS.

Packing No.	Description	Quantity	Net Weight	Gross Weight	Measurement
	SLIPPERS				
1-200	MODEL NO.S-238	@30 DOZ.	@5.35 KGS	@5.85 KGS	
		6,000 DOZ.	1,070.00KGS	1,170.00KGS	⑩ CBM
201-325	MODEL NO.S-240	@20 DOZ.	@6.35 KGS	@6.85 KGS	
		2,500 DOZ.	793.75KGS	856.25KGS	
		8,500 DOZ.	1,863.75 KGS	2,026.25KGS	
		VVVVVVVV	VVVVVVVVVV	VVVVVVVVV	

⑪ SAY TOTAL

L/C NO.HKU-8023

WANG TRADING CO., LTD.

✕ ✕ ✕

Taiwan Marine	SHIPPING ORDER	
Shipper: ⑫	Please receive for shipment the under mentioned goods subject to your published regulations and conditions	S/O NO.
Consignee: ⑬	**Taiwan Marine Transport Corporation** 臺灣海運股份有限公司	
Notify Party: (Full name and address) ⑭		
Also Notify:	洽訂船位之廠商：　　　電話／聯絡人：	
	報關行：　　　　　　　電話／聯絡人：	

Ocean Vessel LINCOLN	Voy. No. 571	Final destination (On Merchant's Account and Risk)				
Place of Receipt KEELUNG	Port of Loading KEELUNG	⑮ Freight to be: ☐Prepaid　　☐Collect				
Port of Discharge VANCOUVER	Place of Delivery VANCOUVER	領提單處：	臺北	臺中	臺中港	高雄

Marks and Numbers/ Container No. and Seal No.	Quantity and Unit	Description of Goods	Gross Weight (KGS)	Measurement (M³)
✕	325 CTNS vvvvvvvv L/C NO. HKU-8023	SLIPPERS	2,026.25KGS 櫃型／櫃數 __✕20'　/ __✕40' SERVICE REQUIRED ☐FCL/FCL　☐LCL/LCL ☐FCL/LCL　☐LCL/ FCL	✕

SPECIAL NOTE:

*1.*副本____份　*2.*運費證明____份　*3.*電報放貨____　*4.*危險品____　*5.*其他____

填表請注意：

*1.*危險品請註明 UN NO. IMO CLASS 與燃點，並附上 Shipper's Certificate。

*2.*嘜頭及品名如超過十行，請以附表繕打，俾便提單製作。

標準答案

題　號	答　案
①	120 DAYS
②	U.S. DOLLARS TWENTY-SIX THOUSAND SEVEN HUNDRED AND SEVEN-TY-FIVE ONLY
③	HKU-8023
④	BANK OF MONTREAL
⑤	8,500 DOZS OF SLIPPERS
⑥	LEE INTERNATIONAL CORPORATION. 2527 JOHNSON ROAD, VANCOUVER, B. C., CANADA
⑦	LEE238 (IN DIA) VANCOUVER C/NO. 1-325 MADE IN TAIWAN
⑧	CIFC5 VANCOUVER
⑨	USD2.85 USD3.87
⑩	@　0.059 CBM 　　11.800 CBM @　0.195 CBM 　　24.375 CBM 　　36.175 CBM 　　vvvvvvvvvv
⑪	THREE HUNDRED TWENTY-FIVE（325）CTNS ONLY.
⑫	WANG TRADING CO., LTD. NO. 1234, SEC. 1, JHONG SHAN N. RD., TAIPEI, TAIWAN (R.O.C.)
⑬	TO ORDER
⑭	LEE INTERNATIONAL CORPORATION 2527 JOHNSON ROAD, VANCOU-VER,B. C. , CANADA
⑮	請勾選：☑ Prepaid　　☐Collect

二、解析

題號	答案	解析
①	120 DAYS	填入匯票期限。
②	U.S. DOLLARS TWENTY-SIX THOUSAND SEVEN HUNDRED AND SEVENTY-FIVE ONLY	填入大寫文字金額，須與小寫數字金額一致。
③	HKU-8023	填入信用狀號碼。
④	BANK OF MONTREAL	填入匯票付款人或付款銀行。
⑤	8,500 DOZS OF SLIPPERS	填入貨物名稱及數量。
⑥	LEE INTERNATIONAL CORPOR-ATION. 2527 JOHNSON ROAD, VANCOU-VER, B. C., CANADA	填入抬頭人名稱及地址，除信用狀另有規定外，須以開狀申請人為抬頭人。
⑦	LEE238 (IN DIAMOND) VANCOUVER C/NO. 1-325 MADE IN TAIWAN	1.填入裝運嘜頭：依序包括主標誌、卸貨港、件數及原產地。 2.包裝方式： (1)S-238 為 30 DOZS/CTN，出貨數量 6,000 DOZS，故可裝 200 箱。 (2)S-240 為 20 DOZ/CTN，出貨數量 2,500 DOZS，故可裝 125 箱。(1)、(2)合計 325 箱。
⑧	CIFC5 VANCOUVER	填入貿易條件。
⑨	USD2.85 USD3.87	1.填入單價。 2.總金額÷總數量： (1) S-238 為 USD17,100÷ 6,000 = USD2.85。 (2) S-240 為 USD9,675÷2,500 = USD3.87。

題號	答案	解析
⑩	@0.059 CBM 11.800 CBM @0.195CBM <u>24.375CBM</u> 36.175CBM vvvvvvv	1. 填入貨物總體積。 2. 1 立方呎 (CFT) = 1,728 立方吋 1 立方公尺 (CBM) = 35.315 立方呎 (1) S-238：20"×15"×12"= 3,600 立方吋 3,600÷1,728 = 2.08 CFT 2.08÷35.315 = 0.059 CBM 0.059×200 箱 = 11.800 CBM (2) S-240：72×52×52÷1,000,000 = 0.195CBM 0.195×125 箱 = 24.375CBM (1)、(2)合計 11.800 + 24.375 = 36.175CBM
⑪	SAY TOTAL THREE HUNDRED TWENTY-FIVE (325) CTNS ONLY.	填入裝運貨物總件數，須以大寫文字填寫。
⑫	WANG TRADING CO., LTD. NO. 1234, SEC. 1, JHONG SHAN N. RD., TAIPEI, TAIWAN (R.O.C.)	1. 填入託運人。 2. 信用狀未規定時，通常以信用狀受益人為託運人。
⑬	TO ORDER	填入受貨人。
⑭	LEE INTERNATIONAL CORPORATION 2527 JOHNSON ROAD, VANCOUVER, B. C. , CANADA	填入貨到被通知人。
⑮	請勾選：☑ Prepaid □Collect	1. 填入付費方式。 2. 貿易條件為 CIF，由出口商預先支付運費，所以勾選 Prepaid。

第三節　練習題

一、請依美國 Manufacturers Hanover Corp.開來之信用狀摘要及相關工廠出貨明細資料，填製㈠ Bill of Exchange；㈡ Invoice；㈢ Packing List；㈣ Shipping Order 等單據內容，並請依題號①、②、③、④……欄位依序填入答案紙。

Manufacturers Hanover Corp.

27	SEQUENCE OF TOTAL：	1/1
40A	FORM OF DOCUMENTARY CREDIT：	IRREVOCABLE
40E	APPLICABLE RULES：	UCP LATEST VERSION
20	DOCUMENTARY CREDIT NUMBER：	MHC220526
31C	DATE OF ISSUE：	180324
31D	DATE AND PLACE OF EXPIRY：	180530 NEGOTIATION BANK'S COUNTER
50	APPLICANT：	

CHANNEL WELL INDUSTRIAL CO., LTD.

1000 S. FREMONT AVE., A1, 1220-21

ALHAMBRA, CA 91803

U.S.A.

59	BENEFICIARY：	

CENDANT CORP.

NO.256 DA AN STREET

TAIPEI, TAIWAN

32B	CURRENCY COOE, AMOUNT：	USD123,750.00
41D	AVAILABLE WITH ...BY... ANY BANK IN TAIWAN BY NEGOTIATION	
42C	DRAFTS AT：	30 DAYS AFTER DATE
42D	DRAWEE：	ISSUING BANK FOR FULL INVOICE VALUE
43P	PARTIAL SHIPMENTS：	PROHIBITED
43T	TRANSHIPMENT：	PERMITTED
44E	PORT OF LOADING：	KEELUNG
44F	PORT OF DISCHARGE：	LOS ANGELES
44C	LATEST DATE OF SHIPMENT：	180518
45A	DESCRIPTION OF GOODS AND/OR SERVICES：	

15,000 SETS RECHARGEABLE HAIR TRIMMER SET MV1900 & MV2000

AS PER SALES CONFIRMATION NO.CL45632 CIF LOS ANGELES INCOTERMS 2010

SHIPPING MARK: CWI (IN DIAMOND) / LOS ANGELES / 1-UP

46A	DOCUMENTS REQUIRED：	

1. SIGNED COMMERCIAL INVOICE 3 COPIES

2. SIGNED PACKING LIST 3 COPIES

3. INSURANCE POLICIES OR CERTIFICATES IN DUPLICATE, ENDORSED IN BLANK,FOR 110 PERCENT OF FULL CIF VALUE, COVERING INSTITUTE CARGO

4. FULL SET OF CLEAN ON BOARD BILLS OF LADING MADE OUT TO ORDER OF MANUFACTURERS HANOVER CORP. MARKED FREIGHT PREPAID AND NOTIFY APPLICANT

5. BENEFICIARY'S CERTIFICATE CERTIFYING THAT ONE SET NON-NEGOTIABLE SHIPPING DOCUMENTS HAVE BEEN SENT TO APPLICANT WITHIN 3 DAYS AFTER SHIPMENT EFFECTED.

71B   CHARGES：

ALL BANKING CHARGES OUTSIDE OPENING BANK ARE FOR A/C OF BENEFICIARY.

48   PERIOD FOR PRESENTATION：

THE DOCUMENTS MUST BE PRESENTED WITHIN 10 DAYS AFTER THE DATE OF SHIPMENT.

49   CONFIRMATION INSTRUCTIONS：   WITHOUT

78   INSTRUCTIONS TO THE PAYING/ACCEPTING/NEGOTIATING BANK：

ALL DOCUMENTS MUST BE SENT TO US IN ONE LOT BY COURIER SERVICE.

***END OF MESSAGE ***

工廠出貨明細資料：

型　　號	MV-1900	MV-2000
包裝方式	30 SETS/CTN	20 SETS/CTN
每箱尺寸	20"×18"×16"	60×45×45(cm)
每箱重量	N.W. 30.25 KGS G.W. 30.75 KGS	N.W. 25.25 KGS G.W. 25.75 KGS
出貨數量	9,000 SETS	6,000 SETS

裝運資料：

1. 承運船名：UNI-CROWN

2. 航次：UN176

(一) Bill of Exchange

BILL OF EXCHANGE

No. AZ-222

FOR USD123,750.00   TAIPEI, TAIWAN   MAY 15, 2018

At ① SIGHT OF THIS FIRST BILL OF EXCHANGE (SECOND UNPAID) PAY TO THE ORDER OF **THE FIRST COMM. BANK, LTD.**

THE SUM OF   ②

DRAWN UNDER CREDIT NO.   MHC220526   DATE   ③

ISSUED BY   MANUFACTURERS HANOVER CORP.

TO

    ④

                                         CENDANT CORP.

                                         × × ×

(二) Invoice

CENDANT CORP.

NO. 256 DA AN STREET

TAIPEI, TAIWAN

INVOICE

No. AZ-222   Date: May 15, 2018

INVOICE of   ⑤

For account and risk of Messrs.   ⑥

Shipped by   ✕

Sailing on or about May 15, 2018   Per   ✕

From   KEELUNG   To   ✕

L/C No.   MHC220526   Contract No.   CL45632

Marks & Nos.	Description of Goods	Quantity	Unit Price	Amount
✕	RECHARGEABLE HAIR TRIMMER SET MV1900 MV2000 (AS PER SALES CONFIRMATION NO.CL45632)	 9,000SETS 6,000SETS 15,000SETS vvvvvvvvvvv	⑦ ⑧	 USD 70,650 USD 53,100 USD123,750 vvvvvvvvvvv
	SAY TOTAL U.S. DOLLARS ✕ ONLY			

L/C NO.: MHC220526

L/C DATE: ✕

NAME OF ISSUING BANK: MANUFACTURERS HANOVER CORP

CENDANT CORP.

✕ ✕ ✕

SALES MANAGER

(三) Packing List

CENDANT CORP.

NO.256 DA AN STREET

TAIPEI, TAIWAN

PACKING LIST

No. AZ-222   Date: May 15, 2018

PACKING LIST of _____×_____   MARKS & NOS.

For account and risk of Messrs. _____×_____

Shipped by _____×_____

Per _____⑨_____   ⑩

Sailing on or about May 15, 2018

Shipment From   KEELUNG   To   ×

Packing No.	Description	Quantity	Net Weight	Gross Weight	Measurement
	RECHARGEABLE HAIR TRIMMER SET				
1-300	MV1900	@30 SETS	@30.25KGS	@30.75KGS	⑪
		9,000 SETS	9,075.00KGS	9,225.00KGS	
301-600	MV2000	@20 SETS	@25.25KGS	@25.75KGS	
		6,000SETS	7,575.00KGS	7,725.00KGS	
		15,000SETS	16,650.00KGS	16,950.00KGS	
		vvvvvvvvv	vvvvvvvvvvv	vvvvvvvvvvv	
		⑫			

L/C NO.: MHC220526

L/C DATE: ×

NAME OF ISSUING BANK: MANUFACTURERS HANOVER CORP

CENDANT CORP.

× × ×

SALES MANAGER

㈣ Shipping Order

Taiwan Marine		SHIPPING ORDER				
Shipper: ⑬		Please receive for shipment the under mentioned goods subject to your published regulations and conditions				S/O NO.
Consignee: ⑭		**Taiwan Marine Transport Corporation** 臺灣海運股份有限公司				
Notify Party: (Full name and address) ╳						
Also Notify:		洽訂船位之廠商： 電話／聯絡人：				
		報關行： 電話／聯絡人：				
Ocean Vessel ╳	Voy. No. ╳	Final destination (On Merchant's Account and Risk)				
Place of Receipt KEELUNG	Port of Loading KEELUNG	Freight to be: ☒Prepaid □Collect				
Port of Discharge ⑮	Place of Delivery ╳	領提單處：	臺北	臺中	臺中港	高雄
Marks and Numbers/ Container No. and Seal No.	Quantity and Unit	Description of Goods	Gross Weight (KGS)		Measurement (M³)	
  ╳	600CTNS	RECHARGEABLE HAIR TRIMMER SET MV1900 & MV2000	16,650.00 KGS 櫃型／櫃數 __╳20' / __╳40' SERVICE REQUIRED □FCL/FCL □LCL/LCL □FCL/LCL □LCL/ FCL		╳	

SPECIAL NOTE:

1. 副本____ 份 *2.* 運費證明____ 份 *3.* 電報放貨____ *4.* 危險品____ *5.* 其他____

填表請注意：

1. 危險品請註明 UN NO. IMO CLASS 與燃點，並附上 Shipper's Certificate。

2. 嘜頭及品名如超過十行，請以附表繕打，俾便提單製作。

答案欄：

題　號	答　案
①	
②	
③	
④	
⑤	
⑥	
⑦	
⑧	
⑨	
⑩	
⑪	
⑫	
⑬	
⑭	
⑮	

解答：

題　號	答　案
①	*1.* 填入匯票期限。 *2.* 30 DAYS AFTER DATE.
②	*1.* 填入大寫文字金額，應與小寫數字金額一致。 *2.* U.S. DOLLARS ONE HUNDRED TWENTY-THREE THOUSAND SEVEN HUNDRED AND FIFTY ONLY.
③	*1.* 填入信用狀開狀日期。 *2.* MAR. 24, 2018
④	*1.* 填入匯票付款人。 *2.* MANUFACTURERS HANOVER CORP.
⑤	*1.* 填入貨物名稱及數量。 *2.* 15,000 SETS RECHARGEABLE HAIR TRIMMER SET.
⑥	*1.* 填入抬頭人名稱，通常為信用狀申請人。 *2.* CHANNEL WELL INDUSTRIAL CO., LTD.1000 S. FREMONT AVE., A1, 1220-21 ALHAMBRA, CA 91803 U.S.A.
⑦	*1.* 填入貿易條件。 *2.* CIF LOS ANGELES INCOTERMS 2010.
⑧	*1.* 填入單價。 *2.* USD7.85 USD8.85 總金額÷數量： (1) MV1900：USD70,650.00÷9,000 ＝ USD7.85 (2) MV2000：USD53,100.00÷6,000 ＝ USD8.85
⑨	*1.* 填入船名及航次。 *2.* S.S. UNI-CROWN V.UN176
⑩	*1.* 填入裝運標誌。 *2.*　　　　　　　　　CWI (IN DIAMOND) LOS ANGELES C/NO. 1-600 MADE IN TAIWAN

題　號	答　案
⑪	*1.* 填入體積。 *2.* @0.094CBM 　　28.200CBM 　@0.122CBM 　　36.600CBM 　　64.800CBM 　　ⅴⅴⅴⅴⅴⅴⅴⅴⅴ (1) MV1900： 　　每箱體積：20"×18"×16" = 5,760CFT，5,760÷1,728 = 3.33CFT 　　　　　　　3.33÷35.315 = 0.094CBM 　　總體積：0.094×300 = 28.200CBM (2) MV2000： 　　每箱體積：60×45×45÷1,000,000 = 0.122CBM 　　總體積：0.122×300 = 36.600CBM
⑫	*1.* 填入大寫文字總件數。 *2.* SAY TOTAL SIX HUNDRED (600) CTNS ONLY.
⑬	*1.* 填入託運人名稱，通常為信用狀受益人。 *2.* CENDANT CORP. 　 NO.256 DA AN STREET 　 TAIPEI, TAIWAN
⑭	*1.* 填入受貨人名稱。 *2.* TO ORDER MANUFACTURERS HANOVER CORP.
⑮	*1.* 填入卸貨港。 *2.* LOS ANGELES

二、請依加拿大 ROYAL BANK OF CANADA 開來之信用狀摘要及相關工廠出貨明細資料，填製㊀ Bill of Exchange；㊁ Invoice；㊂ Packing List；㊃ Shipping Order 等單據內容，並請依題號①、②、③、④……欄位依序填入答案紙。

MT 700 ISSUE OF A DOCUMENTARY CREDIT

SENDER: ROYAL BANK OF CANADA

RECEIVER: MEGA INTERNATIONAL COMMERCIAL BANK

*27：Sequence of Total

　　　1/1

*40：Form of Documentary Credit

　　　IRREVOCABLE

*20：Documentary Credit Number

　　　IBL123745

31C：Date of Issue

　　　180425

*31D：Expiry

　　　Date 180630 Place BENEFICIARY'S COUNTRY

40E：Applicable Rules

　　　UCP LATEST VERSION

*60：Applicant

　　　HOLLYSYS ELECTRIC TECH. CO., LTD.

　　　341 MAIN ST.W. NORTH BAY

　　　TORONTO, CANADA

*59：Beneficiary

　　　TRICON CO., LTD.

　　　NO.125 WU FU ROAD

　　　KAOHSIUNG, TAIWAN

*32B：Amount

　　　Currency USD Amount 15,750.00

*41D：Available with/by

　　　ANY BANK IN THE BENEFICIARY'S COUNTRY BY NEGOTIATION

42C：Drafts at...

　　　SIGHT

42D：Drawee

　　　ROYAL BANK OF CANADA

43 P：Partial Shipments

　　　PROHIBITED

43 T：Transhipment

　　　ALLOWED

44 E：Port of Loading　　　　　　　　　　　：

　　　KAOHSIUNG, TAIWAN

44 F：Port of Discharge

TORONTO, CANADA

44 C：Latest Date of Shipment

180620

45 A：Description of Goods

5,000 PIECES OF COMPUTER ACCESSORIES SB-115 & SB-125,

FOB KAOHSIUNG AS PER PROFORMA INVOICE HU123325 DATE MAR. 31, 2016

SHIPPING MARK：HET152(DIA) / TORONTO / NO.:1-UP

46A：Documents Required　　　　　　　：

1. SIGNED COMMERCIAL INVOICE 2 COPIES.
2. FULL SET OF ORIGINAL CLEAN ON BOARD BILLS OF LADING, ISSUED TO ORDER AND BLANK ENDORSED, MARKED FREIGHT COLLECT, NO-TIFY: APPLICANT WITH FULL NAME AND ADDRESS.

71B：Details of Charges

ALL CHARGES OTHER THAN THOSE OF THE ISSUING BANK ARE FOR THE ACCOUNT OF THE BENEFICIARY.

48：Presentation Period

DOCUMENTS MUST BE PRESENTED WITHIN 21 DAYS AFTER THE SHIPMENT DATE BUT WITHIN THE VALIDITY OF THIS CREDIT.

*49：Confirmation

WITHOUT

78：Instructions

1. WE SHALL REMIT PROCEEDS ON RECEIPT OF CREDIT COMPLIANT DOCUMENTS AT OUR COUNTERS.
2. ALL DOCS MUST BE SENT IN ONE LOT BY COURIER TO : ROYAL BANK OF CANADA. TRADE SUPPORTAERT VAN NESSTRAAT 453012 CA TORO-NTO MPAC CODE GF 3050 CANADA

72：Sender to Receiver Infomation

PLEASE ACKNOWLEDGE RECEIPT OF THIS L/C BY SWIFT STATING YOUR REFERENCE BENE'S ACC. NO 179-97-0001607.

Trailer :　　　　　　MAC:18DE5080

CHK:　　　　　　BD2F842D17F7

SYSMSG>DWS765I Auth OK, key B0051218CE01BF06, HNBKTWTP ABNAN** record

工廠出貨明細資料：

型　　號	SB-115	SB-125
包裝方式	25 PCS/CTN	25 PCS/CTN
每箱尺寸	24"×20"×18"	55×45×45(cm)
每箱重量	N.W. 29.25 KGS ； G.W. 31.75 KGS	N.W. 28.75 KGS ； G.W. 31.25 KGS
出貨數量	2,500 PCS	2,500 PCS

(一) Bill of Exchange

BILL OF EXCHANGE

No.　TH-723

FOR　　①　　　　　　　　　　　　　　　TAIPEI, TAIWAN　JUNE 20, 2018

At　×××　SIGHT OF THIS FIRST BILL OF EXCHANGE (SECOND UNPAID) PAY TO

THE ORDER OF　**HUA NAN COMMERCIAL BANK, LTD.**

THE SUM OF　　　　　　　　　　　　　②

DRAWN UNDER CREDIT NO.　　③　　　　　DATE　　　APR. 25, 2018

ISSUED BY　　　　　　　　　④

TO

　ROYAL BANK OF CANADA

　　　　　　　　　　　　　　　　　　　TRICON CO., LTD.

　　　　　　　　　　　　　　　　　　　×××

(二) Invoice

TRICON CO., LTD.
NO.125 WU FU ROAD
KAOHSIUNG, TAIWAN

INVOICE

No.   TH-723   Date: JUNE 20, 2018

INVOICE of _____⑤_____

For account and risk of Messrs. _____⑥_____

Shipped by _____×_____

Sailing on or about   JUNE 20, 2018   Per   S. S. YM GLORY V. 90N

From   ×   To   TORONTO

L/C No.   ×   Contract No.   HU123325

Marks & Nos.	Description of Goods	Quantity	Unit Price	Amount
⑦	COMPUTER ACCESS-ORIES		⑧	
	SB-115	2,500PCS	USD2.85	USD 7,125.00
	SB-125	2,500PCS	USD3.45	USD 8,625.00
	(AS PER PROFORMA	5,000PCS		USD15,750.00
	INVOICE HU123325)	vvvvvvvvv		vvvvvvv
	SAY TOTAL U.S. DOLLARS ×			

L/C NO.: ×

L/C DATE: APR. 25, 2018

NAME OF ISSUING BANK: ROYAL BANK OF CANADA

TRICON CO., LTD.

× × ×

SALES MANAGER

(三) Packing List

TRICON CO., LTD.

NO.125 WU FU ROAD

KAOHSIUNG, TAIWAN

PACKING LIST

No. TH-723   Date: JUNE 20, 2018

PACKING LIST of   ×   MARKS & NOS.

For account and risk of Messrs.   ×

Shipped by   ⑨

Per   S.S. YM GLORY V. 90N   ×

Sailing on or about   JUNE 20, 2018

Shipment From   ⑩   to   ×

Packing No.	Description	Quantity	Net Weight	Gross Weight	Measurement
	COMPUTER ACCESSORIES				
1-100	SB-115	@25 PCS	@29.25 KGS	@31.75KGS	
		2,500 PCS	2,925.00 KGS	3,175.00KGS	⑪
101-200	SB-125	@25 PCS	@28.75KGS	@31.25KGS	
		2,500 PCS	2,875.00KGS	3,125.00KGS	
		5,000PCS	5,800.00KGS	6,300.00KGS	
		vvvvvvv	vvvvvvvvvvv	vvvvvvvvvvv	
		⑫			

L/C NO.: ×

L/C DATE: APR. 25, 2018

NAME OF ISSUING BANK: ROYAL BANK OF CANADA

TRICON CO., LTD.

× × ×

SALES MANAGER

㈣ Shipping Order

Taiwan Marine	SHIPPING ORDER	
Shipper: ✕	Please receive for shipment the under mentioned goods subject to your published regulations and conditions	S/O NO.
Consignee: ⑬	**Taiwan Marine Transport Corporation** 臺灣海運股份有限公司	
Notify Party: (Full name and address) ⑭		
Also Notify:	洽訂船位之廠商：　　　　電話／聯絡人：	
	報關行：　　　　　　　　電話／聯絡人：	

Ocean Vessel YM GLORY	Voy. No. 90 N	Final destination (On Merchant's Account and Risk)			
Place of Receipt ✕	Port of Loading ✕	Freight to be: ⑮ ☐Prepaid　　☐Collect			
Port of Discharge TORONTO	Place of Delivery ✕	領提單處：	臺北	臺中	臺中港	高雄

Marks and Numbers/ Container No. and Seal No.	Quantity and Unit	Description of Goods	Gross Weight (KGS)	Measurement (M³)
	200CTNS	COMPUTER ACCESSORIES SB-115&SB-125	6,350.00 KGS	✕
✕			櫃型／櫃數 __✕20'　/　__✕40' SERVICE REQUIRED ☐FCL/FCL　☐LCL/LCL ☐FCL/LCL　☐LCL/ FCL	

SPECIAL NOTE:

*1.*副本____份　*2.*運費證明____份　*3.*電報放貨____　*4.*危險品____　*5.*其他____

填表請注意：

*1.*危險品請註明 UN NO. IMO CLASS 與燃點，並附上 Shipper's Certificate。

*2.*嘜頭及品名如超過十行，請以附表繕打，俾便提單製作。

答案欄：

題　號	答　案
①	
②	
③	
④	
⑤	
⑥	
⑦	
⑧	
⑨	
⑩	
⑪	
⑫	
⑬	
⑭	
⑮	

解答：

題　號	答　案
①	*1.* 填入小寫數字金額。 *2.* USD15,750.00
②	*1.* 填入大寫文字金額，應與小寫數字金額一致。 *2.* U.S. DOLLARS FIFTEEN THOUSAND SEVEN HUNDRED AND FIFTY ONLY.
③	*1.* 填入信用狀號碼。 *2.* IBL123745
④	*1.* 填入開狀銀行。 *2.* ROYAL BANK OF CANADA
⑤	*1.* 填入貨物名稱及數量。 *2.* 5,000 PIECES OF COMPUTER ACCESSORIES.
⑥	*1.* 填入抬頭人名稱，通常為信用狀申請人。 *2.* HOLLYSYS ELECTRIC TECH. CO., LTD. 341 MAIN ST.W. NORTH BAY TORONTO, CANADA.

⑦	*1.* 填入裝運嘜頭。
	2.
	    HET 152
	   (IN DIAMOND)
	    TORONTO
	   C/NO. 1-200
	  MADE IN TAIWAN

⑧	*1.* 填入貿易條件。 *2.* FOB KAOHSIUNG
⑨	*1.* 填入發貨人名稱，即出口商。 *2.* TRICON CO., LTD. NO.125 WU FU ROAD, KAOHSIUNG, TAIWAN.
⑩	*1.* 填入裝運港。 *2.* KAOHSIUNG
⑪	*1.* 填入體積。 *2.* @0.142CBM 14.200CBM @0.111CBM 11.100CBM 25.300CBM vvvvvvvvvv

題　號	答　案
⑪	(1) SB-115： 　　每箱體積：24"×20"×18"＝ 8,640，8,640÷1,728 ＝ 5.00 CFT 　　　　　　　　5.00÷35.315 ＝ 0.142CBM 　　總體積：0.142×100 ＝ 14.200CBM (2) SB-125： 　　每箱體積：55×45×45÷1,000,000 ＝ 0.111CBM 　　總體積：0.111×100 ＝ 11.100CBM
⑫	1. 填入大寫文字總件數。 2. SAY TOTAL TWO HUNDRED (200) CTNS ONLY.
⑬	1. 填入受貨人名稱。 2. TO ORDER
⑭	1. 填入貨到通知人，本信用狀為開狀申請人。 2. HOLLYSYS ELECTRIC TECH. CO., LTD 341 MAIN ST.W. NORTH BAY 　　TORONTO, CANADA
⑮	1. 選擇運費預付或後付。 2. □Prepaid　☒Collect

三、請依德國 Westdeutsche Landesbank Girozentrale 開來之信用狀摘要及相關工廠出
　　貨明細資料，填製㈠ Bill of Exchange；㈡ Invoice；㈢ Packing List；㈣ Shipping
　　Order 等單據內容，並請依題號①、②、③、④……欄位依序填入答案紙。

Application Header	0 700 1453 980206 BOANTASA12XXX 4501 854059 1234560 1353
	WESTDEUTSCHE LANDESBANK GIROZENTRALE
Sequence of Total	*27　：1/1
Form of Doc. Credit	*40A：IRREVOCABLE TRANSFERABLE
Applicable Rules	40E：UCP LATEST VERSION
Doc. Credit Number	*20　：100IA127123
Date of Issue	31C：180406
Expiry	*31D：DATE 180625 PLACE AT THE NEGOTIATING BANK
Applicant	*50　：HANNOVER TRADING CO., LTD.
	DURMERSHEIMER STR. 55,76185
	BREMERHAVEN, GERMANY

Beneficiary	*59	：FELLOW TRADING CO., LTD.
		P.O. BOX 911 TAIPEI, TAIWAN
Amount	*32B	：CURRENCY USD AMOUNT 40,728.00
Available with/by	*41D	：ANY BANK BY NEGOTIATION
Drafts at...	42C	：45 DAYS AFTER SIGHT
Drawee	42A	：WESTDEUTSCHE LANDESBANK GIROZENTRALE
Partial Shipments	43P	：PERMITTED
Transhipment	43T	：PERMITTED
Port of Loading	44E	：KEELUNG, TAIWAN
Port of Discharge	44F	：BREMERHAVEN, GERMANY
Latest Date of Ship	44C	：180618
Descript of Goods	45A	：KA-508 ELECTRONIC GUITA 1,200 PIECES
		CIF BREMERHAVEN
		AS PER PURCHASE ORDER NO.KA-50811
		DATED JAN. 28, 2018
Documents Required	46A	：＋SIGNED COMMERCIAL INVOICE IN 4 FOLDS
		＋FULL SET OF CLEAN ON BOARD BILLS OF LADING MARKED "FREIGHT PREPAID" MADE OUT TO OR-DER OF WESTDEUTSCHE LANDESBANK GIROZENTRALE AND NOTIFY APPLICANT.
		＋PACKING LIST IN 2 FOLDS.
		＋INSURANCE POLICIES IN DUPLICATE FOR 110% IN-VOICE VALUE COVERING INSTITUTE CARGO CLAUSE（A）.
Details of Charges	71B	：ALL BANKING CHARGES OUTSIDE THE GERMANY ARE FOR ACCOUNT OF BENEFICIARY.
Presentation Period	48	：DOCUMENTS TO BE PRESENTED WITHIN 14 DAYS AFTER THE DATE OF SHIPMENT BUT WITHIN THE VALIDITY OF THE CREDIT.
Confirmation	*49	：WITHOUT

工廠出貨明細資料：

型　　號	KA-508
包裝方式	2PCS/CTN
每箱尺寸	70×30×40(cm)
每箱重量	N.W. 5.4KGS；G.W. 6.4KGS
出貨數量	600PCS

裝運資料：

1. 承運船名：WESTERDAM

2. 航次：102S

(一) Bill of Exchange

BILL OF EXCHANGE

No.　KA-888

FOR　　×　　　　　　　　　　　　　TAIPEI, TAIWAN　JUNE 18, 2018

At　①　　SIGHT OF THIS FIRST BILL OF EXCHANGE (SECOND UNPAID) PAY TO THE

ORDER OF　**HUA NAN COMMERCIAL BANK, LTD.**

THE SUM OF　　　　　　　　　　　②

DRAWN UNDER CREDIT NO.　　100IA127123　　DATE　　APR. 6, 2018

ISSUED BY　　　　　　　　　×

TO

　　　③

FELLOW TRADING CO., LTD.

×××

SALES MANAGER

(二) Invoice

FELLOW TRADING CO., LTD.
P.O. BOX 911 TAIPEI, TAIWAN
INVOICE

No.   KA-888   Date: JUNE 18, 2018

INVOICE of _____④_____

For account and risk of Messrs. _____⑤_____

_____

Shipped by _____✕_____

Sailing on or about   JUNE 18, 2018   Per _____✕_____

From   KEELUNG   To   BREMERHAVEN

L/C No.   ✕   Contract No.   KA-50811

Marks & Nos.	Description of Goods	Quantity	Unit Price	Amount
⑥	KA-508 ELECTRONIC GUITA (AS PER PURCHASE ORDER KA-50811)	600 PIECES	⑦ ⑧	✕✕✕✕

L/C NO.: 100IA127123

L/C DATE: APR. 6, 2018

NAME OF ISSUING BANK: ✕

FELLOW TRADING CO., LTD.

✕✕✕

SALES MANAGER

(三) Packing List

FELLOW TRADING CO., LTD.

P.O. BOX 911 TAIPEI, TAIWAN

PACKING LIST

No. __KA-888__   Date: __JUNE 18, 2018__

PACKING LIST of _____×_____   MARKS & NOS.

For account and risk of Messrs. _____×_____

Shipped by _____×_____

per _____⑨_____   ×

Sailing on or about __JUNE 18, 2018__

Shipment From __KEELUNG__ to __BREMERHAVEN__

Packing No.	Description	Quantity	Net Weight	Gross Weight	Measurement
1-300	KA-508 ELECTRONIC GUITA	@2 PCS 600 PCS	@5.4 KGS 1,620.00 KGS	@6.4 KGS 1,920.00KGS	×××
		⑩			

L/C NO.: 100IA127123

L/C DATE: APR. 6, 2018

NAME OF ISSUING BANK: ×

FELLOW TRADING CO., LTD.

×××

_____

SALES MANAGER

(四) Shipping Order

Taiwan Marine		SHIPPING ORDER					
Shipper: ⑪		Please receive for shipment the under mentioned goods subject to your published regulations and conditions					S/O NO.
Consignee: ⑫		Taiwan Marine Transport Corporation 臺灣海運股份有限公司					
Notify Party: (Full name and address) ⑬							
Also Notify:		洽訂船位之廠商： 電話／聯絡人：					
		報關行： 電話／聯絡人：					
Ocean Vessel ✕	Voy. No. ✕	Final destination (On Merchant's Account and Risk)					
Place of Receipt ✕	Port of Loading KEELUNG	⑭ Freight to be: ☐Prepaid ☐Collect					
Port of Discharge BREMERHAVEN	Place of Delivery ✕	領提單處：	臺北	臺中		臺中港	高雄
Marks and Numbers/ Container No. and Seal No.	Quantity and Unit	Description of Goods	Gross Weight (KGS)			Measurement (M³)	
✕	300CTNS	KA-508 ELECTRONIC GUITA	1,920.00KGS			✕	
			櫃型／櫃數 __✕20' / __✕40' ⑮ SERVICE REQUIRED ☐FCL/FCL ☐LCL/LCL ☐FCL/LCL ☐LCL/ FCL				
SPECIAL NOTE: 1.副本___份 2.運費證明___份 3.電報放貨___ 4.危險品___ 5.其他___							

填表請注意：

1.危險品請註明 UN NO. IMO CLASS 與燃點，並附上 Shipper's Certificate。

2.嘜頭及品名如超過十行，請以附表繕打，俾便提單製作。

答案欄：

題　號	答　案
①	
②	
③	
④	
⑤	
⑥	
⑦	
⑧	
⑨	
⑩	
⑪	
⑫	
⑬	
⑭	☐Prepaid　☐Collect
⑮	☐FCL/FCL　☐LCL/LCL ☐FCL/LCL　☐LCL/FCL

解答：

題　號	答　案
①	1. 填入匯票期限。 2. 45 DAYS AFTER SIGHT.
②	1. 填入大寫文字金額，應與小寫數字金額一致。 2. U.S. DOLLARS TWENTY THOUSAND THREE HUNDRED AND SIXTY-FOUR ONLY.
③	1. 填入匯票付款人。 2. WESTDEUTSCHE LANDESBANK GIROZENTRALE.
④	1. 填入貨物名稱及數量。 2. 600 PIECES OF ELECTRONIC GUITA.
⑤	1. 填入抬頭人名稱，通常為信用狀申請人。 2. HANNOVER TRADING CO., LTD. DURMERSHEIMER STR. 55,76185 BRE-MERHAVEN, GERMANY.
⑥	1. 填入裝運嘜頭。 2. <div align="center">HT BREMERHAVEN C/NO. 1-300 MADE IN TAIWAN</div>
⑦	1. 填入貿易條件。 2. CIF BREMERHAVEN
⑧	1. 填入單價。 2. USD33.94 　 總金額÷數量＝USD40,728÷1,200＝USD33.94
⑨	1. 填入船名及航次。 2. S.S. WESTERDAM V.102S
⑩	1. 填入大寫文字總件數。 2. SAY TOTAL THREE HUNDRED（300）CTNS ONLY.
⑪	1. 填入託運人名稱，通常為信用狀受益人。 2. FELLOW TRADING CO., LTD.P.O. BOX 911 TAIPEI, TAIWAN.
⑫	1. 填入受貨人名稱。 2. TO ORDER OF WESTDEUTSCHE LANDESBANK GIROZENTRALE.
⑬	1. 填入貨到通知人，本信用狀為開狀申請人。 2. HANNOVER TRADING CO., LTD. DURMERSHEIMER STR. 55,76185 BR.MER-HAVEN, GERMANY.
⑭	1. 選擇付費方式，貿易條件為CIF，則由出口商預先支付運費，所以勾選Prepaid。 2. ☑ Prepaid　□Collect

題　號	答　案
⑮	1. 選擇運送方式。 　每箱體積：0.70×0.30×0.40 ＝ 0.084 CBM 　總體積：0.084 CBM×300 ＝ 25.200 CBM 約可裝滿一只 20 呎貨櫃，所以勾選 FCL/ FCL。 2. ☑ FCL/FCL　　□LCL/LCL 　　□FCL/LCL　　□LCL/FCL

四、請依美國BANKERS TRUST NEW YORK CORP.開來之信用狀摘要及相關工廠出貨明細資料，填製㈠ Bill of Exchange；㈡ Invoice；㈢ Packing List；㈣ Shipping Order 等單據內容，並請依題號①、②、③、④……欄位依序填入答案紙。

40A (FORM OF DOCUMENTARY CREDIT)：	IRREVOCABLE
20 (DOCUMENTARY CREDIT NUMBER)　：	01-13242312-45
31C (DATE OF ISSUE)：	180105
40E (APPLICABLE RULES)：	UCP LATEST VERSION
3ID (DATE AND PLACE OF EXPIRY)：	180320 TAIWAN
50 (APPLICANT)：	ZEBRA TECHNOLOGIES CORP. 12121 CENTRALIA AVE, #305, LA KEWOOD, OREGON, U.S.A.
59 (BENEFICIARY)：	SAN STAR INDUSTRIAL CO., LTD. 8RD FL, NO.16, ALLEY 26, LANE102, SECTION 4, KWANGFU S. RD., TAIPEI,TAIWAN
32B (CURRENCY CODE, AMOUNT)：	USD15,470.00
41D (AVAILABLE WITH...BY...)：	ANY BANK BY NEGOTIATION
42C (DRAFTS AT...)：	SIGHT
42A (DRAWEE)：	BANKERS TRUST NEW YORK CORP.
43P (PARTIAL SHIPMINTS)：	PROHIBITED
43T (TRANSHIPMENT)：	PROHIBITED
44E (PORT OF LOADING.)：	KEELUNG
44F (PORT OF DISCHARGE)：	PORTLAND
44C (LATEST DATE OF SHIPMENT)：	180311
45A (SHIPMENT OF GOODS)：	

TENDER BRAND BABY BLANKET BS007 & BS009 AS PER S/C NO.TU-1258

QUANTITY: 3,500 PIECES

USD 4.42/PC CIF PORTLAND INCOTERMS 2010

SHIPPING MARK：ZT124（IN DIA）/ PORTLAND /1 — UP

46B (DOCUMENTS REQUIRED)：

+ SIGNED COMMERCIAL INVOICE 3 COPIES

+ PACKING LIST 3 COPIES SHOWING GROSS WEIGHT , NET WEIGHT AND ME-
ASUREMENT.

+ FULL SET OF CLEAN ON BOARD BILLS OF LADING MADE OUT TO ORDER
AND BLANK ENDORSED, MARKED "FREIGHT PREPAID" AND THIS L.C. NUM-
BER NOTIFY APPLICANT.

+ INSURANCE POLICIES/ CERTIFICATES IN DUPLICATE, ENDORSED IN BLANK
FOR 110PCT OF INVOICE VALUE COVERING INSTITUTE CARGO CLAUSES (A)
AND INSTITUTE WAR CLAUSES WITH CLAIMS PAYABLE AT DESTINATION IN
THE CURRENCY OF THE DRAFTS.

+ BENEFICIARY'S CERTIFICATE CERTIFYING THAT ONE COPY OF INVOICE,
PACKING LIST AND B/L HAVE BEEN SENT TO APPLICANT BY COURIER SER-
VICES IMMEDIATELY AFTER SHIPMENT.

71B (CHARGES)：   ALL BANKING CHARGES OUTSIDE
                                              U.S.A. ARE FOR ACCOUNT
                                              OF BENEFICIARY.

48(PERIOD FOR PRESENTATION)：   DOCUMENTS TO BE PRESENTED
                                              WITHIN 10 DAYS AFTER THE
                                              DATE OF ISSUANCE OF SHIPPING
                                              DOCUMENTS BUT WITHIN THE
                                              VALIDITY OF THE CREDIT.

49(CONFIRMATION INSTRUCTIONS)：   WITHOUT

工廠出貨明細資料：

型　　　號	BS007	BS009
包裝方式	20 PCS/CTN	20 PCS/CTN
每箱尺寸	38"×18"×13"	100×45×40(cm)
每箱重量	N.W. 37.5KGS；G.W.40.5KGS	N.W. 37.8KGS；G.W.40.8KGS
出貨數量	2,500 PCS	1,000 PCS

裝運資料：

　1. 承運船名：YM HAWK

　2. 航次：T777

(一) Bill of Exchange

BILL OF EXCHANGE

No.　AO-159

FOR　　①　　　　　　　　　　　　　　TAIPEI, TAIWAN　MAR. 11, 2018

At　②　　SIGHT OF THIS FIRST BILL OF EXCHANGE (SECOND UNPAID) PAY TO THE

ORDER OF　**HUA NAN COMMERCIAL BANK, LTD.**

THE SUM OF　　　　　　　　　　　　　③

DRAWN UNDER CREDIT NO.　　　④　　　　　DATE　　　　　⑤

ISSUED BY　　　　　　　　　　　　　⑥

TO

　　　⑦

　　　　　　　　　　　　　　　SAN STAR INDUSTRIAL CO., LTD.

　　　　　　　　　　　　　　　×××

　　　　　　　　　　　　　　　SALES MANAGER

　　答案欄：

題　號	答　案
①	
②	
③	
④	
⑤	
⑥	
⑦	

(二) Invoice

SAN STAR INDUSTRIAL CO., LTD.

8RD FL, NO.16, ALLEY 26, LANE102, SECTION 4,

KWANGFU S. RD., TAIPEI, TAIWAN

INVOICE

No.   AO-159   Date: MAR. 11, 2018

INVOICE of _____ ⑧ _____

For account and risk of Messrs. _____ ⑨ _____

_____

Shipped by _____ ⑩ _____

Sailing on or about _____ MAR. 11, 2018 _____ Per _____ ⑪ _____

From _____ ⑫ _____ To _____ ⑬ _____

L/C No. _____ ⑭ _____ Contract No. _____ ⑮ _____

Marks & Nos.	Description of Goods	Quantity	Unit Price	Amount
			⑲	
⑯	⑰	⑱	⑳	㉑
		㉒		

L/C NO.: ✕

L/C DATE: ✕

NAME OF ISSUING BANK: ✕

SAN STAR INDUSTRIAL CO., LTD.

✕ ✕ ✕

SALES MANAGER

答案欄：

題　號	答　案
⑧	
⑨	
⑩	
⑪	
⑫	
⑬	
⑭	
⑮	
⑯	
⑰	
⑱	
⑲	
⑳	
㉑	
㉒	

(三) Packing List

SAN STAR INDUSTRIAL CO., LTD.

8RD FL, NO.16, ALLEY 26, LANE102, SECTION 4,

KWANGFU S. RD., TAIPEI, TAIWAN

PACKING LIST

No.　AO-159　　　　　　　　　　　　　　　　　　　　Date:　MAR. 11, 2018

PACKING LIST of ㉓　　　　　　　　　　　　　　　MARKS & NOS.

For account and risk of Messrs.　㉔

Shipped by　㉕

per　　　　㉖　　　　　　　　　　　　　　　　　　　　　㉙

Sailing on or about　MAR. 11, 2018

Shipment From　㉗　　to　㉘

Packing No.	Description	Quantity	Net Weight	Gross Weight	Measurement
㉚	㉛	㉜	㉝	㉞	㉟
		㊱			

L/C NO.: ✕

L/C DATE: ✕

NAME OF ISSUING BANK: ✕

SAN STAR INDUSTRIAL CO., LTD.

✕ ✕ ✕

SALES MANAGER

答案欄：

題　號	答　案
㉓	
㉔	
㉕	
㉖	
㉗	
㉘	
㉙	
㉚	
㉛	
㉜	
㉝	
㉞	
㉟	
㊱	

㈣ Shipping Order

Taiwan Marine		SHIPPING ORDER			
Shipper: ㊲		Please receive for shipment the under mentioned goods subject to your published regulations and conditions		S/O NO.	
Consignee: ㊳		**Taiwan Marine Transport Corporation** 臺灣海運股份有限公司			
Notify Party: (Full name and address) ㊴					
Also Notify:		洽訂船位之廠商： 電話／聯絡人： 報關行： 電話／聯絡人：			
Ocean Vessel ㊵	Voy. No. ㊶	Final destination (On Merchant's Account and Risk)			
Place of Receipt	Port of Loading ㊷	㊾ Freight to be: ☐Prepaid ☐Collect			
Port of Discharge ㊸	Place of Delivery	領提單處：	臺北	臺中	臺中港	高雄
Marks and Numbers/ Container No. and Seal No.	Quantity and Unit	Description of Goods	Gross Weight (KGS)	Measurement (M³)
㊹	㊺	㊻	㊼	㊽
			櫃型／櫃數 __×20' / __×40' ㊿ SERVICE REQUIRED ☐FCL/FCL ☐LCL/LCL ☐FCL/LCL ☐LCL/ FCL	
SPECIAL NOTE: 1.副本___份 2.運費證明___份 3.電報放貨___ 4.危險品___ 5.其他___					

填表請注意：

1. 危險品請註明 UN NO. IMO CLASS 與燃點，並附上 Shipper's Certificate。

2. 嘜頭及品名如超過十行，請以附表繕打，俾便提單製作。

答案欄：

題 號	答 案
㊲	
㊳	
㊴	
㊵	
㊶	
㊷	
㊸	
㊹	
㊺	
㊻	
㊼	
㊽	
㊾	☐Prepaid　☐Collect
㊿	☐FCL/FCL　☐LCL/LCL ☐FCL/LCL　☐LCL/FCL

解答：

(一) Bill of Exchange

題　號	答　案
①	1.填入小寫數字金額。 2. USD15,470.00
②	1.填入匯票期限。 2.×××
③	1.填入大寫文字金額，應與小寫數字金額一致。 2. U.S. DOLLARS FIFTEEN THOUSAND FOUR HUNDRED AND SEVENTY
④	1.填入信用狀號碼。 2. 01-13242312-45
⑤	1.填入開狀日期。 2. JAN. 5, 2018
⑥	1.填入開狀銀行。 2. BANKERS TRUST NEW YORK CORP.
⑦	1.填入匯票付款人。 2. BANKERS TRUST NEW YORK CORP.

(二) Invoice

題　號	答　案
⑧	1.填入貨物名稱及數量。 2. 3,500 PIECES OF TENDER BRAND BABY BLANKET
⑨	1.填入抬頭人名稱，通常為信用狀申請人。 2. ZEBRA TECHNOLOGIES CORP. 12121 CENTRALIA AVE, #305, LAKEWOOD, OREGON, U.S.A.
⑩	1.填入發貨人名稱，通常為出口商。 2. SAN STAR INDUSTRIAL CO., LTD.
⑪	1.填入船名及航次。 2. S.S. YM HAWK V.T777
⑫	1.填入裝運港。 2. KEELUNG

題　號	答　案
⑬	1. 填入卸貨港。 2. PORTLAND
⑭	1. 填入信用狀號碼。 2. 01-13242312-45
⑮	1. 填入契約號碼。 2. TU-1258
⑯	1. 填入裝運標誌。 2.　　　ZT124 　　(IN DIAMOND) 　　　PORTLAND 　　C/NO.:1-175 　MADE IN TAIWAN
⑰	1. 填入貨物敘述。 2. TENDER BRAND BABY BLANKET 　　　　BS007 　　　　BS009 　(AS PER S/C NO.TU-1258)
⑱	1. 填入數量。 2. 2,500 PIECES 　1,000 PIECES 　3,500PIECES 　vvvvvvv
⑲	1. 填入貿易條件。 2. CIF PORTLAND INCOTERMS 2010
⑳	1. 填入單價。 2. USD4.42 　USD4.42
㉑	1. 填入總金額。 2. USD11,050.00 　USD 4,420.00 　USD15,470.00 　vvvvvvvvvvv
㉒	1. 填入大寫文字金額。 2. U.S. DOLLARS FIFTY THOUSAND FOUR HUNDRED AND SEVENTY ONLY

(三) Packing List

題　號	答　案
㉓	1. 填入貨物名稱及數量。 2. 3,500 PIECES OF TENDER BRAND BABY BLANKET
㉔	1. 填入抬頭人名稱，通常為信用狀申請人。 2. ZEBRA TECHNOLOGIES CORP. 12121 CENTRALIA AVE, #305, LAKEWOOD, OREGON, U.S.A.
㉕	1. 填入發貨人名稱，通常為出口商。 2. SAN STAR INDUSTRIAL CO., LTD.
㉖	1. 填入船名及航次。 2. S.S. YM HAWK V.T777
㉗	1. 填入裝運港。 2. KEELUNG
㉘	1. 填入卸貨港。 2. PORTLAND
㉙	1. 填入裝運標誌。 2.　　　ZT124 　　(IN DIAMOND) 　　PORTLAND 　　C/NO.:1-175 MADE IN TAIWAN
㉚	1. 填入包裝件數。 2. 1-125 　126-175
㉛	1. 填入貨物敘述。 2. TENDER BRAND BABY BLANKET BS007 (AS PER S/C NO.TU-1258)
㉜	1. 填入貨物數量。 2. @20 PIECES 　2,500 PIECES 　@20 PIECES 　1,000 PIECES 　3,500 PIECES 　vvvvvvvvvvv

題 號	答 案
㉝	1. 填入貨物總淨重。 2. @ 37.5 KGS 　　4,687.5 KGS 　@ 37.8 KGS 　　1,890.0 KGS 　　6,577.5 KGS 　　ⅴⅴⅴⅴⅴⅴⅴⅴ
㉞	1. 填入貨物總毛重。 2. @ 40.5 KGS 　　5,062.5 KGS 　@ 40.8 KGS 　　2,040.0 KGS 　　7,102.5 KGS 　　ⅴⅴⅴⅴⅴⅴⅴⅴⅴ
㉟	1. 填入貨物總體積。 2. @ 0.146CBM 　　　18.250CBM 　@ 0.180CBM 　　　9.000CBM 　　　27.250CBM 　　　ⅴⅴⅴⅴⅴⅴⅴⅴⅴ (1) BS007： 　　每箱體積：38"×18"×13" = 8,892，8,892÷1,728 = 5.15CFT 　　　　　　　　5.15÷35.315 = 0.146CBM 　　總體積：0.146×125 = 18.250CBM (2) BS009： 　　每箱體積：100×45×40÷1,000,000 = 0.180CBM 　　總體積：0.180×50 = 9.000CBM
㊱	1. 填入大寫文字總件數 2. SAY TOTAL ONE HUNDRED SEVENTY-FIVE（175）CTNS ONLY.

㈣ Shipping Order

題　號	答　案
㊲	1. 填入託運人名稱，通常為信用狀受益人。 2. SAN STAR INDUSTRIAL CO., LTD. 8RD FL, NO.16, ALLEY 26, LANE102, SECTION 4, KWANGFU S. RD., TAIPEI, TAIWAN.
㊳	1. 填入受貨人名稱。 2. TO ORDER
㊴	1. 填入貨到被通知人。 2. ZEBRA TECHNOLOGIES CORP. 　12121 CENTRALIA AVE, #305, LAKEWOOD, 　OREGON, U.S.A.
㊵	1. 填入船名。 2. YM HAWK
㊶	1. 填入航次。 2. T777
㊷	1. 填入裝運港。 2. KEELUNG
㊸	1. 填入卸貨港。 2. PORTLAND
㊹	1. 填入裝運嘜頭。 2.　　　　　　　　　　　ZT 124 　　　　　　　　　　(IN DIAMOND) 　　　　　　　　　　PORTLAND 　　　　　　　　　　C/NO. 1-175 　　　　　　　　MADE IN TAIWAN
㊺	1. 填入貨物件數。 2. 175 CTNS
㊻	1. 填入貨物敘述。 2. TENDER BRAND BABY BLANKET BS007
㊼	1. 填入總毛重。 2. 7,102.5 KGS
㊽	1. 填入總體積。 2. 27.250CBM
㊾	1. 選擇付費方式。貿易條件為CIF，則由出口商預先支付運費，所以勾選Prepaid。 2. ☑Prepaid ☐Collect
㊿	1. 選擇運送方式。總體積為25.55CBM，約可裝滿一只20呎貨櫃，所以勾選FCL/FCL。 2. ☑FCL/FCL　☐LCL/LCL 　　☐FCL/LCL　☐LCL/FCL

五、請依日本 DAI-ICHI KANGYO BANK 開來之信用狀摘要及相關工廠出貨明細資
料，填製㈠ Bill of Exchange；㈡ Invoice；㈢ Packing List；㈣ Shipping Order 等單
據內容，並請依題號①、②、③、④……欄位依序填入答案紙。

MT700		
RECEIVED FROM: ***	=NG: 1812 04 EDLOC;XXX27907	
*DAI-ICHI KANGYO BANK	=Orn: 1258930BFHVNIWDJVKX4261538	
*TOKYO		
Sequence of Total	*27	：1/1
Form of Doc. Credit	*40A	：IRREVOCABLE
Doc. Credit Number	*20	：LC23562154
Date of Issue	31C	：180109
Applicable Rules	*40E	：UCP LATEST VERSION
Date and Place of Expiry	*31D	：DATE 180403 AT YOUR COUNTER
Applicant	*50	：FENRIR & CO.
		5-5-3 NAKANO, KIMITSU-SHI,
		TOKYO 229-1151 JAPAN
Beneficiary	*59	：BIOPHARM COMPANY LIMITED
		NO.125, SEC. 2, NANJING W. RD.,
		TAIPEI, TAIWAN
Currency Code, Amount	*32B	：USD 24,600.00
Available with / by	*41D	：ANY BANK BY NEGOTIATION
Drafts at…	42C	：90 DAYS AFTER SIGHT
Drawee	42A	：DAI-ICHI KANGYO BANK
Partial Shipments	43P	：PERMITTED
Latest Date of Shipment	44C	：180325
Transhipment	43T	：PROHIBITED
Port of Loading	*44E	：KEELUNG
Port of Discharge	*44F	：TOKYO
Shipment of Goods	*45A	：2,400 DOZENS OF BOA SLIPPERS SH27
		AS PER ORDER NO. BO-0983 FOB KEELUNG
		SHIPPING MARK：FEN123(IN DIA)/ TOKYO/1-UP
Documents Required	*46A	：

+ SIGNED COMMERCIAL INVOICE IN 6 COPIES INDICATING THIS CREDIT NUMBER.

+ FULL SET CLEAN ON BOARD BILLS OF LADING MADE OUT TO ORDER AND
  BLANK ENDORSED MARKED "FREIGHT COLLECT" NOTIFY APPLICANT

+ PACKING LIST IN 6 COPIES

Additional Conditions   *47A：

+ ONE SET OF NON-NEGOTIABLE SHIPPING DOCUMENTS SHOULD BE SENT TO
  THE APPLICANT WITHIN 3 DAYS AFTER THE SHIPMENT EFFECTED

+ INSURANCE TO BE EFFECTED BY APPLICANT

Details of Charges   *71B：ALL BANKING CHARGES OUTSIDE JAPAN ARE
                                FOR ACCOUNT OF BENEFICIARY.

Presentation of Period   *48 ：DOCUMENTS TO BE PRESENTED WITHIN 7 DAYS
                                AFTER THE DATE OF SHIPMENT BUT WITHIN THE
                                VALIDITY OF CREDIT

Confirmation Instruction   49 ：WITHOUT

Trailer   ：AUT/7A32

工廠出貨明細資料：

型　　號	SH277
包裝方式	4 DOZENS/CTN
每箱尺寸	22"×16"×18"(inch)
每箱重量	N.W. 8.2KGS；G.W. 10.2KGS
出貨數量	2,000 DOZENS

裝運資料：

1. 承運船名：HANJIN IRENE

2. 航次：V-0086W

(一) Bill of Exchange

BILL OF EXCHANGE

No. YM-043

FOR ___①___   TAIPEI, TAIWAN   MAR. 25, 2018

At __②__ SIGHT OF THIS FIRST BILL OF EXCHANGE (SECOND UNPAID) PAY TO THE

ORDER OF __HUA NAN COMMERCIAL BANK, LTD.__

THE SUM OF _____③_____

DRAWN UNDER CREDIT NO. _____④_____ DATE _____⑤_____

ISSUED BY _____⑥_____

TO

_____⑦_____

BIOPHARM COMPANY LIMITED

×××

SALES MANAGER

答案欄：

題　號	答　案
①	
②	
③	
④	
⑤	
⑥	
⑦	

(二) Invoice

BIOPHARM COMPANY LIMITED

NO.125, SEC. 2, NANJING W. RD.,

TAIPEI, TAIWAN

INVOICE

No. __YM-043__   Date: __MAR. 25, 2018__

INVOICE of _____⑧_____

For account and risk of Messrs. _____⑨_____

Shipped by _____⑩_____

Sailing on or about __MAR. 25, 2018__   Per _____⑪_____

From _____⑫_____   To _____⑬_____

L/C No. _____⑭_____   Contract No. _____⑮_____

Marks & Nos.	Description of Goods	Quantity	Unit Price	Amount
			⑲	
⑯	⑰	⑱	⑳	㉑
		㉒		

L/C NO.: ✕

L/C DATE: ✕

NAME OF ISSUING BANK: ✕

BIOPHARM COMPANY LIMITED

✕ ✕ ✕

SALES MANAGER

答案欄：

題　號	答　案
⑧	
⑨	
⑩	
⑪	
⑫	
⑬	
⑭	
⑮	
⑯	
⑰	
⑱	
⑲	
⑳	
㉑	
㉒	

(三) Packing List

BIOPHARM COMPANY LIMITED
NO.125, SEC. 2, NANJING W. RD.,
TAIPEI, TAIWAN

PACKING LIST

No.   YM-043   Date: MAR. 25, 2018

PACKING LIST of _____㉓_____   MARKS & NOS.

For account and risk of Messrs. _____㉔_____

Shipped by _____㉕_____

per _____㉖_____   ㉙

Sailing on or about   MAR. 25, 2018

Shipment From _____㉗_____ to _____㉘_____

Packing No.	Description	Quantity	Net Weight	Gross Weight	Measurement
㉚	㉛	㉜	㉝	㉞	㉟
		㊱			

L/C NO.: ✕

L/C DATE: ✕

NAME OF ISSUING BANK: ✕

BIOPHARM COMPANY LIMITED

✕✕✕

SALES MANAGER

答案欄：

題　號	答　案
㉓	
㉔	
㉕	
㉖	
㉗	
㉘	
㉙	
㉚	
㉛	
㉜	
㉝	
㉞	
㉟	
㊱	

㈣ Shipping Order

Taiwan Marine		SHIPPING ORDER			
Shipper: ㉧		Please receive for shipment the under mentioned goods subject to your published regulations and conditions			S/O NO.
Consignee: ㊳		**Taiwan Marine Transport Corporation** 臺灣海運股份有限公司			
Notify Party: (Full name and address) ㊴					
Also Notify:		洽訂船位之廠商：　　電話／聯絡人：			
		報關行：　　　　　　電話／聯絡人：			
Ocean Vessel ㊵	Voy. No. ㊶	Final destination (On Merchant's Account and Risk)			
Place of Receipt	Port of Loading ㊷	㊾ Freight to be: ☐Prepaid　　☐Collect			
Port of Discharge ㊸	Place of Delivery	領提單處：　臺北　｜　臺中　｜　臺中港　｜　高雄			
Marks and Numbers/ Container No. and Seal No.	Quantity and Unit	Description of Goods	Gross Weight (KGS)	Measurement (M^3)	
㊹	㊺	㊻	㊼	㊽	
			櫃型／櫃數 ＿×20'　/　＿×40' ㊿ SERVICE REQUIRED ☐FCL/FCL　☐LCL/LCL ☐FCL/LCL　☐LCL/ FCL		
SPECIAL NOTE: *1.*副本＿＿份　*2.*運費證明＿＿份　*3.*電報放貨＿＿　*4.*危險品＿＿　*5.*其他＿＿					

填表請注意：

1. 危險品請註明 UN NO. IMO CLASS 與燃點，並附上 Shipper's Certificate。

2. 嘜頭及品名如超過十行，請以附表繕打，俾便提單製作。

答案欄：

題　號	答　案
㊲	
㊳	
㊴	
㊵	
㊶	
㊷	
㊸	
㊹	
㊺	
㊻	
㊼	
㊽	
㊾	☐Prepaid　☐Collect
㊿	☐FCL/FCL　☐LCL/LCL ☐FCL/LCL　☐LCL/FCL

解答：

(一) Bill of Exchange

題 號	答 案
①	*1.* 填入小寫數字金額。 *2.* USD 20,500.00
②	*1.* 填入匯票期限。 *2.* 90 DAYS AFTER
③	*1.* 填入大寫文字金額，應與小寫數字金額一致。 *2.* U.S. DOLLARS TWENTY THOUSAND AND FIVE HUNDRED ONLY.
④	*1.* 填入信用狀號碼。 *2.* LC23562154
⑤	*1.* 填入開狀日期。 *2.* JAN. 9, 2018
⑥	*1.* 填入開狀銀行。 2. DAI-ICHI KANGYO BANK
⑦	*1.* 填入匯票付款人。 *2.* DAI-ICHI KANGYO BANK

(二) Invoice

題 號	答 案
⑧	*1.* 填入商品數量及商品名稱。 *2.* 2,000 DOZENS OF BOA SLIPPERS
⑨	*1.* 填入抬頭人名稱，通常為信用狀申請人。 *2.* FENRIR & CO.5-5-3 NAKANO, KIMITSU-SHI, TOKYO, JAPAN.
⑩	*1.* 填入發貨人名稱，通常為出口商。 *2.* BIOPHARM COMPANY LIMITED
⑪	*1.* 填入船名及航次。 *2.* S.S. HANJIN IRENE V-0086W
⑫	*1.* 填入裝運港。 *2.* KEELUNG
⑬	*1.* 填入卸貨港。 *2.* TOKYO
⑭	*1.* 填入信用狀號碼。 *2.* LC23562154

題 號	答 案
⑮	*1.* 填入契約號碼。 *2.* BO-0983
⑯	*1.* 填入裝運嘜頭。 *2.*　　　　　　　　　FEN 123 　　　　　　　　　(IN DIAMOND) 　　　　　　　　　TOKYO 　　　　　　　　　C/NO. 1-500 　　　　　　　　　MADE IN TAIWAN
⑰	*1.* 填入貨物敘述。 *2.* BOA SLIPPERS SH277(AS PER ORDER NO. BO-0983)
⑱	*1.* 填入數量。 *2.* 2,000 DOZENS
⑲	*1.* 填入貿易條件。 *2.* FOB KEELUNG
⑳	*1.* 填入單價。 *2.* USD10.25
㉑	*1.* 填入總金額。 *2.* USD20,500.00
㉒	*1.* 填入大寫文字金額。 *2.* U.S. DOLLARS TWENTY THOUSAND AND FIVE HUNDRED ONLY.

㈢ Packing List

題 號	答 案
㉓	*1.* 填入貨物名稱及數量。 *2.* 2,000 DOZENS OF BOA SLIPPERS
㉔	*1.* 填入抬頭人名稱，通常為信用狀申請人。 *2.* FENRIR & CO.5-5-3 NAKANO, KIMITSU-SHI, TOKYO, JAPAN.
㉕	*1.* 填入發貨人名稱，通常為出口商。 *2.* BIOPHARM COMPANY LIMITED
㉖	*1.* 填入船名及航次。 *2.* S.S. HANJIN IRENE V-0086W
㉗	*1.* 填入裝運港。 *2.* KEELUNG
㉘	*1.* 填入卸貨港。 *2.* TOKYO

題 號	答 案
㉙	*1.* 填入裝運嘜頭。 *2.* <div align="center">FEN 123 (IN DIAMOND) TOKYO C/NO. 1-500 MADE IN TAIWAN</div>
㉚	*1.* 填入包裝件數。 *2.* 1-500
㉛	*1.* 填入貨物敘述。 *2.* BOA SLIPPERS SH277
㉜	*1.* 填入貨物數量。 *2.* @4 PIECES 2,000 PIECES
㉝	*1.* 填入貨物總淨重。 *2.* @8.2 KGS 4,100.0 KGS
㉞	*1.* 填入貨物總毛重。 *2.* @10.2 KGS 5,100.0KGS

㉟	*1.* 填入貨物總體積。
	2. @0.104 CBM
	   52.0 CBM
	每箱體積：$22'' \times 16'' \times 18'' = 6,336$，$6,336 \div 1,728 = 3.67$ CFT，
	       $3.67 \div 35.315 = 0.104$ CBM
	總體積：$0.104 \times 500 = 52.0$ CBM

㊱	*1.* 填入大寫文字總件數。 *2.* SAY TOTAL FIVE HUNDRED (500) CTNS ONLY.

㈣ Shipping Order

題 號	答 案
㊲	*1.* 填入託運人名稱，通常為信用狀受益人。 *2.* BIOPHARM COMPANY LIMITED NO.125, SEC. 2, NANJING W. RD., TAIPEI, TAIWAN.
㊳	*1.* 填入受貨人名稱。 *2.* TO ORDER

題　號	答　案
㊴	1. 填入貨到被通知人。 2. FENRIR & CO. 　 5-5-3 NAKANO, KIMITSU-SHI 　 TOKYO, JAPAN
㊵	1. 填入船名。 2. HANJIN IRENE
㊶	1. 填入航次。 2. V-0086W
㊷	1. 填入裝運港。 2. KEELUNG
㊸	1. 填入卸貨港。 2. TOKYO
㊹	1. 填入裝運嘜頭。 2.　　　　　　　　　 FEN 123 　　　　　　　　　 (IN DIAMOND) 　　　　　　　　　 TOKYO 　　　　　　　　　 C/NO. 1-500 　　　　　　　　　 MADE IN TAIWAN
㊺	1. 填入貨物件數。 2. 500 CTNS
㊻	1. 填入貨物敘述。 2. BOA SLIPPERS SH277
㊼	1. 填入總毛重。 2. 5,100.0KGS
㊽	1. 填入總體積。 2. 52.0CBM
㊾	1. 選擇付費方式，貿易條件為 FOB，則由進口商支付運費，所以勾選 Collect。 2. □Prepaid　☑Collect
㊿	1. 選擇運送方式。總體積為 52CBM，約可裝滿一只 40 呎貨櫃，所以勾選 FCL/FCL。 2. ☑FCL/FCL　□LCL/LCL 　 □FCL/LCL　□LCL/FCL

1072 丙級術科測試試題及解答

附錄一

一、基礎貿易英文（本大題合計 20 分）

㈠請於下列答案語群中，選出最適當之答案，並將答案代號填入答案紙，完成
　函電之內容。（本題語群選項不可重覆，共 5 小格，每小格 2 分，合計 10 分）

答案代號	答案語群
A	delay
B	regular
C	as
D	but
E	shipment advice
F	shipping instructions
G	of
H	for
I	prompt
J	postpone

Dear Mr. Campbell:

On April 25 we placed our order No. AR311 ___①___ scarves and handkerchiefs. In your ac-

knowledgement of our order you stated that the goods would be shipped within two weeks,

and we are therefore much surprised that we have had no ___②___ yet.

When we sent you our order, we pointed out that ___③___ delivery was most essential.

This ___④___ places us in an awkward position as we assured our own customers that the ar-

ticles would be available in mid-June.

We must ask you to fulfill the order immediately; otherwise, we will have no choice ⑤
o cancel it and obtain the accessories elsewhere.

Regards,

Robert Chen

(二)請填入適當的語詞以完成下列翻譯。（本題為填空題，共 10 小格，每小格 1 分，合計 10 分）

1. 本公司為提供優質辦公室設備的製造商。

   We are ① of high quality office ② .

2. 隨函附上 1,530.75 美元的支票，支付編號 A531 發票帳款。

   We ③ our check ④ $1,530.75 in payment of your invoice number A531.

3. 請退回受損的貨品，我們將免費替換。

   Please return the ⑤ goods. We will ⑥ them free of charge.

4. 若您能寄一些材料的樣品過來，我們將感激不盡。

   It would be ⑦ if you could send some samples of the ⑧ .

5. 這些餐盤的包裝表面看起來完好無缺。

   The ⑨ ⑩ the dinner plates appeared to be in good condition.

解答

(一)

①	②	③	④	⑤
H	E	I	A	D

(二)

①	manufacturers/producers/makers	②	equipment
③	enclose	④	for
⑤	damaged	⑥	replace
⑦	appreciated	⑧	material(s)
⑨	package(s)	⑩	containing

二、貿易流程圖（本題共 5 小題，每小題 2 分，合計 10 分）

請依下列之貿易流程圖，依序將①②③④⑤之步驟名稱填入答案紙之答案欄內。（本測試項目評分依公佈範例為準）

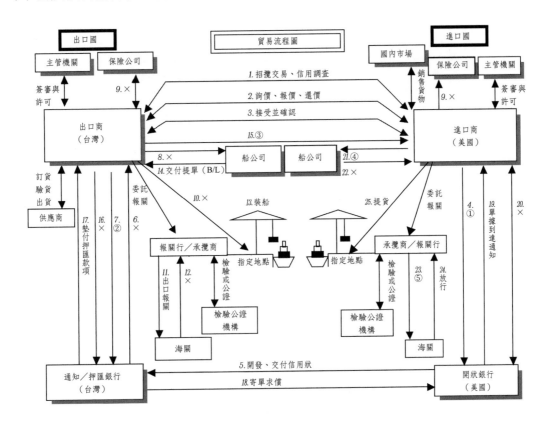

解答

題號	答案
①	申請開狀
②	預售外匯（避險操作）
③	裝船通知
④	提示提單（B/L）
⑤	進口報關

三、出口價格核算（本題共 10 小題，每小題 2 分，合計 20 分）

根據以下資料，對貨號 A 與貨號 B 兩種以體積噸計算海運運費的貨物，分別以併櫃與整櫃運量，核算相關運費與報價。

產品資料：

貨號	KB001	KB002
包裝方式	6 SETS/CTN	12 PCS/CTN
包裝尺寸	18"×20"×26"	56 CM×48 CM×42 CM
採購成本	TWD480/SET	TWD120/PC

運費資料：

運費	併櫃（CFS）	20 呎整櫃	40 呎整櫃
	USD80	USD1,100	USD1,800
最低裝運量	1 CBM	25 CBM	50 CBM

其他報價資料：

匯率：USD1＝TWD29.80	利潤率：15％
保險費率：ICC(A) 0.10%、罷工險 0.02%	業務費率：6％

注意事項：

1. 核算要求：計算過程無法整除者，CBM 計算至小數點第 4 位，四捨五入後取 3 位；其餘請計算至小數點第 3 位，四捨五入後取 2 位。

2. 傭金計算方式：以所求報價條件本身為傭金計算基礎，如 CFRC, CIFC 以 CFR, CIF 為基礎之含傭價。

3. 計算過程不需列出，直接填入數字答案。

解答及解析

貨號 A：併櫃方式報價

題目	答案	單位
1. 每箱 CFT 數	$(18" \times 20" \times 26") \div 1728 = 5.42$	CFT
2. 每箱 CBM 數	$5.42 \div 35.315 = 0.153$	CBM
3. 每 SET 運費	$USD80 \times 0.153 \div 6 = 2.04$	USD/SET
4. FOB 報價	$(TWD480 \div 29.80) + (1 - 15\%) \div (1 - 6\%) = 20.16$	USD/SET
5. CIFC5 報價	$(TWD480 \div 29.80 + 2.04) \div [1 - 1.1 \times (0.10\% + 0.02\%)] \div (1 - 15\%) \div (1 - 6\%) \div (1 - 5\%) = 23.94$	USD/SET

貨號 B：40 呎整櫃（FEU）方式報價

題目	答案	單位
6. 每箱 CBM 數	$0.56 \times 0.48 \times 0.42 = 0.113$	CBM
7. FEU 報價箱數	$50 \div 0.113 = 442.48$，無條件進位取整數 443	CTNS
8. 每 PC 運費	$USD180 \div (443 \times 20) = 0.20$	USD/PC
9. CFRC5 報價	$(TWD120 \div 29.80 + 0.20) \div (1 - 15\%) \div (1 - 6\%) \div (1 - 5\%) = 5.75$	USD/PC
10. CIF 報價	$(TWD120 \div 29.80 + 0.20) \div [1 - 1.1 \times (0.10\% + 0.02\%)] \div (1 - 15\%) \div (1 - 6\%) = 5.30$	USD/PC

四、商業信用狀分析（本題為填空題，合計 20 分）

請依下列信用狀之內容，回答答案紙所列問題，並將正確答案填入。

------------------------------------Message Header------------------------------------

Priority　　　　　　　　：Normal

Swift Output　　　　　　：FIN710 ADV OF THIRD BANK'S DOC CREDIT

Sender　：HONG KONG AND SHANGHAI BANKING CORP. LTD., HONG KONG
　　　　　（HSBC, HONG KONG）(HSBCHKXXXXX)

Receiver　：SHANGHAI COMMERCIAL BANK LTD., HK (SCBKHKXXXXX)

------------------------------------Message Text------------------------------------

27：Sequence of Total

1/1

40A：Form of Documentary Credit

IRREVOCABLE TRANSFERABLE

20：Documentary Credit Number

DCBHKH-805111

31C：Date of Issue

180309

40E：Applicable Rules

UCP LATEST VERSION

31D：Date and Place of Expiry

180601 IN COUNTRY OF BENEFICIARY

52D：Issuing Bank

HSBC BANK USA N.A., NEW YORK, USA

50：Applicant

EINSTEIN CO., LTD.

250 COCHITUATE RD., FRAMINGHAM, MA 01701, USA

59：Beneficiary

FREEDMAN CO., LTD.

RM.305, 3 FL.,18 CANTON RD., TSIM SHA TSUI KOWLOON, HONG KONG

32B：Currency Code, Amount

USD30,000.00

39A：Positive/Negative Tolerance

02/00

41D：Available with.....by.....

ANY BANK BY NEGOTIATION

42C：Drafts at

30 DAYS AFTER SIGHT FOR FULL INVOICE VALUE

42D：Drawee

HSBC, HONG KONG

43P：Partial Shipments

NOT ALLOWED

43T：Transshipment

ALLOWED

44A：PLACE OF TAKING IN CHARGE/DISPATCH FROM/PLACE OF RECEIPT

CHINA

44B：PLACE OF FINAL DESTINATION/ FOR TRANSPORTATION TO/PLACE

OF DELIVERY

UNITED STATES OF AMERICA

44C　Latest Date of Shipment

180522

45A：Description of Goods and/or Services

2,000 PAIRS OF LADIES FOOTWEAR

AS PER P/O NUMBER E123

FCA CHINA

46A：Documents Required

1. SIGNED COMMERCIAL INVOICE IN TRIPLICATE INDICATING THE CREDIT NUMBER AND P/O NUMBER

2. DAMCO (FORWARDER) ORIGINAL OR PHOTOCOPY OF THE ORIGINAL FORWARDER(S CARGO RECEIPT(FCR) MARKED FREIGHT COLLECT CONSIGNED TO APPLICANT EVIDENCING RECEIPT OF MERCHANDISE AND THE FORWARDER(S CARGO RECEIPT NOTIFY PARTY IS: EXPEDITOR(S INTERNATIONAL (1234 WEST CENTURY BLVD., SUITE 200, LOS ANGELES, CA 90045, USA)

3. PACKING LIST IN TRIPLICATE

47A：Additional Conditions

1. THE CREDIT IS TRANSFERABLE WITH SCBKHKXXXXX. HOWEVER, THIS CREDIT MAY NOT BE TRANSFERRED TO ANY FOREIGN ENTITY WHICH HAS BEEN IN VIOLATION OF THE U.S. LAWS (U.S.C. 1592 OR 1592A)

2. DATE CARGO RECEIVED ON FREIGHT FORWARDER(S CARGO RECEIPT WILL BE CONSIDERED THE SHIPMENT DATE

3. ALL DOCUMENTS SHOULD BE ISSUED IN ENGLISH

4. THIRD PARTY DOCUMENTS ARE PERMITTED, BUT NOT INCLU-

DING THE DRAFT

5.A DISCREPANCY FEE FOR USD75.00 WILL BE DEDUCTED FROM THE PAYMENT FOR EACH SET OF DOCUMENTS CONTAINING DIS-CREPANCIES

71B：Charges

ALL BANKING CHARGES OUTSIDE THE UNITED STATES OF AMERICA ARE FOR ACCOUNT OF BENEFICIARY

48：Period for Presentation

DOCUMENTS MUST BE PRESENTED WITHIN 14 DAYS AFTER THE DATE OF SHIPMENT BUT WITHIN THE VALIDITY OF THE CREDIT

49：Confirmation Instructions

WITHOUT

78：Instructions to Paying/Accepting/Negotiating Bank

+DOCUMENTS MUST BE SENT TO PAYING BANK (HSBC, HONG KONG) BY COURIER SERVICE IN ONE COVER

+THIS CREDIT IS PAYABLE AT MATURITY AFTER RECEIPT OF DOCU-MENTS　COMPLYING WITH THE TERMS OF THIS CREDIT AT THE COUNTER OF PAYING BANK

--Message Trailer--

解答

題目	答案
匯票之付款人？（寫出英文名稱）（2分）	HSBC, HONG KONG
轉讓銀行？（寫出英文全名）（2分）	SHANGHAI COMMERCIAL BANK LTD., HK
裝運單據上之受貨人？ （寫出公司名稱）（2分）	EINSTEIN CO., LTD.
銀行如何從裝運單據判斷 shipment date？ （中文作答）（2分）	貨運承攬收據上的收貨日期
信用狀有效期限？ （地點請寫出地名）	日期：2018 年＿6＿月＿1＿日（1分） 地點：HONG KONG（或香港）（1分）
依本信用狀內容，請選出（單選）下列各小題之正確答案	
信用狀使用方式？（1分）	□即期付款　□延期付款　□承兌　■讓購
是否可分批裝運？（1分）	□是　■否
信用狀使用金額之增減彈性？（1分）	□不可增減　■可增加　□可減少

貿易條件？（1分）	☐FCA USA ■FCA CHINA ☐CIP CHINA ☐CIP USA
要求提示之裝運單據？（1分）	☐B/L ☐AWB ■FCR
可接受之 THIRD PARTY DOCUMENTS 不包括？（1分）	☐裝運單據 ■匯票 ☐裝箱單
提示之單據應如何寄送？（1分）	☐一批郵寄 ☐分兩批郵寄 ■一批快遞 ☐分兩批快遞
提示銀行應將單據寄給誰？（1分）	☐開狀銀行 ■付款銀行
第二受益人有何限制？（1分）	☐限香港當地廠商 ■不得為違反美國法律的廠商
單據瑕疵費由何方負擔？（1分）	☐EINSTEIN CO., LTD. ■FREEDMAN CO., LTD.

五、貿易單據製作（本題共 15 小題，每小題 2 分，合計 30 分）

請依所附信用狀部分內容及相關工廠出貨明細資料，填製㈠ Bill of Exchange、㈡ Invoice、㈢ Packing List、㈣ Shipping Order 等單據所要求之內容，並請依照題號①、②、③…依序將正確答案填入答案紙之答案欄內。下列為信用狀部分內容：

20：Documentary Credit Number
　　NE-173456

31C：Date of Issue
　　171124

31D：Date and Place of Expiry
　　180122 IN THE BENEFICIARY(S COUNTRY

52D　Issuing Bank
　　NEDBANK LTD.

50：Applicant
　　BEAUTY INTERNATIONAL (PTY) LTD.
　　50 JOHNSTONE RD., MAYDON WHARF, DURBAN SOUTH AFRICA 4052,
　　SOUTH AFRICA

59：Beneficiary
　　LUCKY ENTERPRISE CO., LTD.
　　10 FL., NO. 100, SEC. 3, TAIWAN BLVD., TAICHUNG CITY

TAIWAN, R.O.C.

32B：Currency Code, Amount

USD26,100.00

41D：Available with...by...

ANY BANK BY NEGOTIATION

42C：Drafts at

60 DAYS AFTER BILL OF LADING DATE FOR 100 PCT OF INVOICE VALUE

42A：Drawee

ISSUING BANK

44E：Port of Loading/Airport of Departure

ANY TAIWANESE PORT

44F：Port of Discharge/Airport of Destination

DURBAN

44C：LATEST DATE OF SHIPMENT

180115

45A：Description of Goods and/or Services

GOLF BAGS

GB-N1 240 PCS USD60.00/PC

GB-G2 180 PCS USD65.00/PC

CFR DURBAN INCOTERMS 2010

46A：Documents Required

1. SIGNED COMMERCIAL INVOICE IN TRIPLICATE STATING THE GOODS ARE OF TAIWAN ORIGIN

2. FULL SET CLEAN ON BOARD BILLS OF LADING MARKED FREIGHT PREPAID CONSIGNED TO ORDER OF SHIPPER AND BLANK ENDORSED NOTIFY APPLICANT

3. PACKING LIST IN DUPLICATE SHOWING NET WEIGHT, GROSS WEIGHT AND MEASUREMENT

47A：Additional Conditions

1. COMMERCIAL INVOICE AND PACKING LIST MUST SHOW ORDER

NO. BI-171103

2. SHIPPING MARK: BI (IN REC) C/NO.:1-UP

工廠出貨明細資料：

貨　號	GB-N1	GB-G2
包裝方式	3 PCS/CTN	3 PCS/CTN
每箱重量	NW: 9.00 KGS；GW: 12.00 KGS	NW: 10.50 KGS；GW:14.00 KGS
每箱尺寸	40 cm×40 cm×100 cm	40 cm×45 cm×100 cm
出貨數量	240 PCS	180 PCS

BILL OF EXCHANGE

DRAFT NO.　LE-170095

FOR　　　×××　　　　　　　　DATED:　　　×××

AT 60 DAYS AFTER B/L DATE ~~SIGHT~~ OF THIS FIRST OF EXCHANGE (SECOND OF THE SAME TENOR AND DATE BEING UNPAID) PAY TO THE ORDER OF

BANK OF TAIWAN

THE SUM OF　　　　　　　　　①　　　　　　　　　VALUE RECEIVED

DRAWN UNDER LETTER OF CREDIT NO.　NE-173456　DATED:　NOV. 24, 2017

ISSUED BY　　　　　　　　　×××

B/L DATE:　　　　　②　　　　　　LUCKY ENTERPRISE CO., LTD.

TO　　　　　③　　　　　　　　*Vanessa Chou*

LUCKY ENTERPRISE COMPANY LIMITED

10 FL., NO. 100, SEC. 3, TAIWAN BLVD.

TAICHUNG CITY

TAIWAN, R.O.C.

INVOICE

No.   LE-170095   Date: JAN. 12, 2018

Invoice of   420 PCS OF GOLF BAGS

For account and risk of Messrs   ④

Shipped Per S.S.   EVER GAREND V.1862-085W

Sailing on or about   JAN. 12, 2018

Shipment From   ⑤   To   XXX

Marks & Nos.	Description of Merchandise	Quantity	Unit Price	Amount
			⑦	
	GOLF BAGS			
		240 PCS	× × ×	× × ×
	GB-N1	180 PCS		
⑥	GB-G2	420 PCS		
		vvvvvvvvv		
	ORDER NO. BI-171103			
	SAY × × ×			
	THE GOODS ARE OF TAIWAN ORIGIN			
		LUCKY ENTERPRISE CO., LTD.		
		Vanessa Chou		

LUCKY ENTERPRISE COMPANY LIMITED

10 FL., NO. 100, SEC. 3, TAIWAN BLVD.

TAICHUNG CITY

TAIWAN, R.O.C.

PACKING LIST

No. _____LE-170095_____ Date: _____JAN. 12, 2018_____

Packing List of _420 PCS OF GOLF BAGS_ MARKS & NOS.

For account and risk of Messrs ____×××____

_____ ×××

Shipped Per S.S. _EVER GAREND V.1862-085W_

Sailing on or about _____JAN. 12, 2018_____

Shipment From ____×××____ To ____×××____

Packing No.	Description of Goods	Quantity	Net Weight	Gross Weight	Measurement
⑧	GOLF BAGS GB-N1 GB-G2	@3 PCS 240 PCS @3 PCS 180 PCS	@9.00 KGS 720.00 KGS @10.50 KGS 630.00 KGS	⑨	×××
××× vvvvvv	ORDER NO. BI-171103 SAY TOTAL	××× vvvvvv ⑩	××× vvvvvv	××× vvvvvv	××× vvvvvv

LUCKY ENTERPRISE CO., LTD.

Vanessa Chou

長榮國際股份有限公司 EVERGREEN INTERNATIONAL CORPORATION		SHIPPING ORDER (B/L INSTRUCTION)	
Shipper：（發票如需另列抬頭人請註明） 　　××× 發票抬頭： 統一編號：　　提單傳真號碼：		Please receive for shipment the under mentioned goods subject to your published regulations and conditions(including those as to liability)	S/O NO.
Consignee: ⑪ Notify Party:(Full name and address) ⑫		SPECIAL NOTE： *1.*副本＿＿＿份　*2.*運費證明＿＿＿份 *3.*電報放貨＿＿＿ *4.*危險品＿＿＿　*5.*其他＿＿＿ 填表請注意： *1.*危險品請註明 UN NO. IMO CLASS 與燃點，並附上 Shipper's Certificate。（吉達地區請另附 Packing list 兩份）。 *2.* S/O 上之內容若有變更，請圈劃出，並於結關當天前傳真或送底至本公司。 *3.*傳真專線：遠洋航線請傳(02)25063878，近洋航線請傳(02)25006658。	
		洽訂船位之廠商： 電話／聯絡人：	
		報關行： 電話／聯絡人：	
		Final destination (On Merchant's Account And Risk)	
Ocean Vessel 船名 EVER GAREND	Voy. No. 航次 ⑬		
Place of Receipt 收貨地	Port of Loading 裝貨港 TAICHUNG	Freight to be： 付費方式：■Prepaid 預付 □Collect 到付	

Port of Discharge 卸貨港 ⑭	Place of Delivery 交貨地（美國線請註明州別）	領提單處	□台北	■台中	□台中港	□高雄

Marks and Numbers/ Container No. and Seal No.	Quantity and Unit	Description of Goods （請詳實註明，如僅為 "GENERAL MERCHAN- DISE"恕無法接受）	Gross Weight (KGS)	Measu- rement (CBM)
×××	×××	GOLF BAGS	×××	

		SAY TOTAL XXX	櫃型／櫃數 ___X20'/___X40' SERVICE REQUIRED ☐FCL/FCL ☐LCL/LCL ☐FCL/LCL ☐LCL/FCL

解答

題號	答案
①	U.S. DOLLARS TWENTY SIX THOUSAND AND ONE HUNDRED ONLY.
②	JAN. 12, 2018
③	NEDBANK LTD.
④	BEAUTY INTERNATIONAL (PTY) LTD. 50 JOHNSTONE RD., MAYDON WHARF, DURBAN SOUTH AFRICA 4052, SOUTH AFRICA
⑤	TAICHUNG
⑥	BI (IN REC) DURBAN C/NO:1-140 MADE IN TAIWAN
⑦	CFR DURBAN INCOTERMS 2010
⑧	1-80 81-140
⑨	@12.00KGS 960.00KGS @14.00KGS 840.00KGS
⑩	ONE HUNDRED AND FORTY (140) CARTONS ONLY
⑪	TO ORDER OF SHIPPER
⑫	BEAUTY INTERNATIONAL (PTY) LTD. 50 JOHNSTONE RD., MAYDON WHARF, DURBAN SOUTH AFRICA 4052, SOUTH AFRICA

⑬	1862-085W
⑭	DURBAN
⑮	23.6

（備註：1072 丙級術科測試 P289 第三行之重覆應為重複；P291 第三行之公佈應為公布，基於尊重原考題不予修改。）

1071 國貿業務丙檢試題解答

一、基礎貿易英文（本大題合計 20 分）

（一）請填入適當的語詞以完成下列函電。（本題語群選項不可重覆，共 5 小格，每小格 2 分，合計 10 分）

答案代號	答案語群
A	affordable
B	manufacturer
C	provide
D	trading company
E	expand
F	procure
G	advise
H	transit
I	regular
J	transact

Dear Sirs,

We have obtained your name from Exportpages. We are an established ___①___ in Taiwan, specializing in high-end kitchenware. As we are looking to ___②___ our business across China, we are searching for a reliable supplier and a long-time business partner.

Could you send us your latest catalogue and price list? Also, would you kindly ___③___ us of your payment terms, lead time, and discounts for ___④___ purchases? In view of China's booming economy, we would expect to ___⑤___ a substantial volume of business provided your prices are competitive and your terms favorable.

We look forward to hearing from you soon.

Sincerely,

Bill Kuo

㈡請填入適當的語詞以完成下列翻譯。（本題為填空題，共十小格，每小格 1 分，合計 10 分）

1. 我們想進口瑞士乳酪，希望收到您目前的目錄及外銷價目表。

    We are interested in ___①___ Swiss cheese and would appreciate receiving your ___②___ catalog and export price list.

2. 貨到時少了三箱。

    Three cases in the consignment were ___③___ on ___④___ .

3. 請盡快開立相關信用狀，以便我方可以安排裝運，不致耽擱。

    Please open the relative L/C as soon as ___⑤___ so we can arrange shipment without ___⑥___ .

4. 為了成交，我方願意在價格上有一點彈性。

    In order to ___⑦___ the sale, we are willing to be a little ___⑧___ on the price.

5. 除了上述的同業折扣外，我們還會給初次訂購九七折特別優待。

    In ___⑨___ to the trade discount stated, we would allow you a special first-order discount of ___⑩___ .

解答

㈠

①	②	③	④	⑤
D	E	G	I	J

㈡

①	importing	②	current/latest
③	missing/short-shipped	④	arrival
⑤	possible	⑥	delay
⑦	make	⑧	flexible
⑨	addition	⑩	3%

二、貿易流程圖（本題共 5 小題，每小題 2 分，合計 10 分）

　　請依下列之貿易流程圖，依序將①②③④⑤之步驟名稱填入答案紙之答案欄內。（本測試項目評分依公佈範例為準）

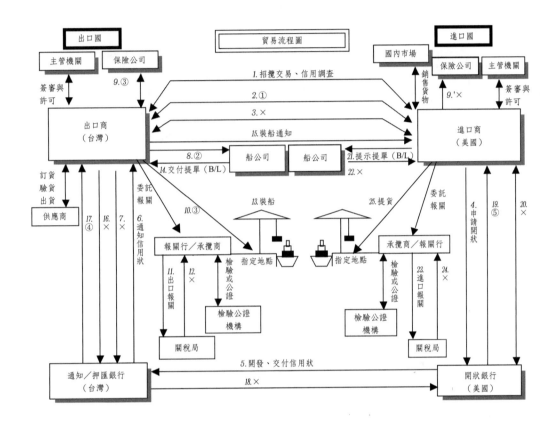

解答

題號	答案
①	詢價、報價、還價
②	洽訂艙位
③	投保並取得保險單據（CIF）
④	墊付押匯款項
⑤	單據到達通知

三、出口價格核算（本題共 10 小題，每小題 2 分，合計 20 分）

　　根據以下資料，對貨號 A 與貨號 B 兩種以體積噸計算海運運費的貨物，分別以併櫃與整櫃運量，核算相關運費與報價。

　　產品資料：

貨號	A	B
包裝方式	12 PCS/CTN	15 SETS/CTN
包裝尺寸	25"×18"×16"	48×40×40(cm)
採購成本	TWD320/PC	TWD250/SET

　　運費資料：

運費	併櫃（CFS）	20 呎整櫃	40 呎整櫃
	USD90	USD1,500	USD2,400
最低裝運量	1 CBM	25 CBM	50 CBM

　　其他報價資料：

匯率：USD1＝NTD30.37	利潤率：12%
保險費率：0.35%，投保120%	業務費率：8%

　　注意事項：

1. 核算要求：計算過程無法整除者，CBM計算至小數點第 4 位，四捨五入後取 3 位；其餘請計算至小數點第 3 位，四捨五入後取 2 位。

2. 佣金計算方式：以所求報價條件本身為佣金計算基礎，如CIFC以CIF為基礎之含佣價。

3. 計算過程不需列出，直接填入數字答案。

解答及解析

貨號 A：整櫃方式報價

題目	答案	單位
1. 每箱才數	$(25" \times 18" \times 16") \div 1728 = 4.17$	CFT
2. 每箱 CBM 數	$4.17 \div 35.315 = 0.118$	CBM
3. 20 呎櫃報價數量	$25 \div 0.118 = 211.86$ 無條件進位 212　$212 \times 12 = 2544$	PCS
4. CFR 報價	$(320 \div 30.37 + 0.59) \div (1 - 12\%) \div (1 - 8\%) = 13.74$	USD/PC
5. CIFC3 報價	$(320 \div 30.37 + 0.59) \div (1 - 1.2 \times 0.35\%) \div (1 - 12\%)$ $\div (1 - 8\%) \div (1 - 3\%) = 14.23$	USD/PC

貨號 B：20 呎整櫃方式報價

題目	答案	單位
6. 每箱 CBM 數	$0.48 \times 0.40 \times 0.40 = 0.077$	CBM
7. 每箱運費	$USD90 \times 0.077 = 6.93$	USD/CTN
8. FOB 報價	$(250 \div 30.37) \div (1-12\%) \div (1 - 8\%) = 10.17$	USD/SET
9. CFRC4 報價	$(250 \div 30.37 + 0.46) \div (1 - 12\%) \div (1 - 8\%) \div (1 - 4\%) = 11.18$	USD/SET
10. CIFC6 報價	$(250 \div 30.37 + 0.46) \div (1 - 1.2 \times 0.35\%) \div (1 - 12\%)$ $\div (1 - 8\%) \div (1 - 6\%) = 11.47$	USD/SET

四、商業信用狀分析（本題為填空題，合計 20 分）

請依下列信用狀之內容，回答答案紙所列問題，並將正確答案填入。

---Message Header---

Swift Output：FIN 700 ISSUE OF A DOCUMENTARY CREDIT

Sender ：BANK OF TAIWAN CHUNGLUN BRANCH

Receiver ：BANK OF TAIWAN GUANGZHOU BRANCH

---Message Text ---

：40A：Form of Documentary Credit

IRREVOCABLE AND TRANSFERABLE

：20：Documentary Credit Number

DC00045127

：31C： Date of Issue

171223

：40E： Applicable Rules

UCP LATEST VERSION

：31D： Date and Place of Expiry

180323 IN THE COUNTRY OF BENEFICIARY

：50： Applicant

MAYFULL CO., LTD..

8F., NO.52, SEC. 1, BADE RD., ZHONGZHENG DIST.,

TAIPEI CITY 100, TAIWAN (R.O.C.)

：59： Beneficiary

GENERAL LIGHT ELECTRICAL APPLANCES CO., LTD.

3F., NO.11, DEZHENG ROAD SOUTH, GUANGZHOU, CHINA

：32B： Currency Code, Amount

USD 38,400.00

：41D： Available with . . . by . . .

ANY BANK BY NEGOTIATION

：42C： Drafts at

AT 60 DAYS AFTER SIGHT FOR 100% INVOICE VALUE

：42A： Drawee

ISSUING BANK

：43P： Partial Shipments

ALLOWED

：43T： Transshipment

PROHIBITED

：44E： Port of Loading

GUANGZHOU PORT, CHINA

：44F： Port of Discharge

KEELUNG PORT, TAIWAN

：44C： Latest Date of Shipment

180310

：45A： Description of Goods and/or Services

12,000 PCS TUNGSTEN HALOGEN LAMPS W600

AS PER SALES CONFIRMATION NO. HF1456 DATE NOV. 22, 2017

PRICE：USD 3.20 /PC CFR KEELUNG PORT, TAIWAN

CCC CODE：8539.21.00.00-9

：46A：Documents Required

1. SIGNED INVOICE IN 2 ORIGINALS AND 3 COPIES INDICATING THIS CREDIT NUMBER.

2. PACKING LIST IN 2 ORIGINALS AND 3 COPIES SHOWING ITEM CODE AS PER HARMONIZED SYSTEM.

3. 2/3 SET OF ORIGINAL CLEAN ON BOARD BILL OF LADING MADE OUT TO THE ORDER OF SHIPPER AND BLANK ENDORSED MARKED FREIGHT PREPAID, NOTIFY APPLICANT.

4. BENEFICIARY'S CERTIFICATE STATING THAT ONE ORIGINAL B/L AND ONE SET OF NON-NEGOTIABLE SHIPPING DOCUMENTS HAVE BEEN SENT DIRECTLY TO THE APPLICANT WITHIN 24 HOURS AFTER SHIPMENT BY AIR COURIER.

5. PRE-SHIPMENT INSPECTION CERTIFICATE TO BE ISSUED BY SGS-CSTC STANDARDS TECHNICAL SERVICES CO., LTD.GUANGZHOU BRANCH REGARDING THE GOODS OF QUANTITY, QUALITY, SPECIFICATION AND MANUFACTURING YEAR.

：47A：Additional Conditions

1. SHORT FORM BILL OF LADING/ BLANK BACK BILL OF LADING, CHARTER PARTY BILL OF LADING ARE NOT ACCEPTABLE.

2. INSURANCE ARRANGED BY APPLICANT.

3. THIS L/C IS TRANSFERABLE BY THE ADVISING BANK.

4. NEGOTIATION AGAINST DISCREPANT DOCUMENTS MUST NOT BE MADE UNDER RESERVE WITHOUT OUR PRIOR APPROVAL.

5. ADDITIONS, CORRECTIONS, ERASURES, AMENDMENTS MUST BE DULY STAMPED BY THE PARTY/AUTHORITY ISSUING THE DOCUMENT IN QUESTION.

6. USD90.00 (OR EQUIVALENT) WILL BE DEDUCTED AT PAYMENT FOR EACH PRESENTATION OF DISCREPANT DOCUMENTS UNDER THIS

CREDIT.

：71B： Charges

ALL BANKING CHARGES OUTSIDE TAIWAN ARE FOR ACCOUNT OF BENEFICIARY.

：49： CONFIRMATION INSTRUCTIONS

MAY ADD

：78： Instructions to Pay/Acc/Neg Bank

ALL DOCUMENTS MUST BE FORWARDED TO US (ADDRESS: NO.184 AND 2F.-8&2F.-9,NO.188, SEC. 5, NANJING E. RD., SONGSHAN DIST., TA-IPEI CITY 105, TAIWAN (R.O.C.)) BY COURIER SERVICE IN ONE LOT.

解答

題目	答案
PAYING BANK？（英文作答）（2分）	BANK OF TAIWAN CHUNGLUN BRANCH
TRANSFERRING BANK？（英文作答）（2分）	BANK OF TAIWAN GUANGZHOU BRANCH
如提單簽發日為 2018 年 2 月 25 日，最遲單據提示日期為何？(2分)	2018 年　3　月　19　日 （3 月 18 日是週日）
信用狀種類（2分）	■賣方遠期信用狀　□買方遠期信用狀 ■可轉讓信用狀　□不可轉讓信用狀
售貨確認書號碼（1分）	HF1456
在何種情況下允許受益人辦理保結押匯？（中文作答）（2分）	開狀銀行事先批准
根據本信用狀 46A 第 2 項規定，裝箱單上記載的 ITEM CODE 號碼？（2分）	8539.21
根據本信用狀 46A 第 5 項規定，請回答有關 PRE-SHIPMENT INSPECTION CERTIFICATE 相關問題。（中文回答）（3分）	1. 單據名稱（1分） 　　裝運前檢驗證明書 2. 應記載內容除商品品質及數量外，尚包括 (1)　　規格　　（1分） (2)　製造年分　（1分）
根據本信用狀 46A 第 3 項規定，受益人僅需提示 2/3 SET B/L，請問剩下 1/3 SET B/L：（中文作答）（4分）	1. 寄送給誰（1分） 　申請人 2. 寄送方式（1分） 　航空快遞 3. 通常可用於何種提貨方式（2分） 　副提單背書

五、貿易單據製作（本題共 15 小題，每小題 2 分，合計 30 分）

請依所附信用狀部分內容及相關工廠出貨明細資料，填製㈠ Bill of Exchange、㈡ Invoice、㈢ Packing List、㈣ Shipping Order 等單據所要求之內容，並請依照題號 ①、②、③⋯依序將正確答案填入答案紙之答案欄內。下列為信用狀部分內容：

---Message Header---

Swift Output：FIN 700 Issue of a Documentary Credit

Sender　　　：KCB BRUSSELS ORBAN

　　　　　　　RUE DE LA SCIENCE 25, 1040 BRUSSEL, BELGIUM

Receiver　　：HUA NAN BANK NORTH NANGANG BRANCH.

　　　　　　　2F.-10 NO.3, PARK ST., NANGANG DIST., TAIPEI CITY115, TAIWAN

　　　　　　　(R.O.C.)

---Message Text ---

50：　　Applicant

　　　　BRUSSELS LACES AND GIFTS SERV. SA.

　　　　RUE DE LUSAMBO 21/28, 1190 BRUSSEL, BELGIUM

59：　　Beneficiary

　　　　PLUSTEX CO., LTD.

　　　　NO.145, PARK ST., NANGANG DIST., TAIPEI CITY 115, TAIWAN (R.O.C.)

32B：　Currency Code, Amount

　　　　USD 21,200.00

39A：　Percentage Credit Amount Tolerance

　　　　05/05

42C：　Drafts at......

　　　　AT 60 DAYS AFTER B/L DATE FOR FULL INVOICE VALUE

42A：　Drawee

　　　　ISSUING BANK

43P：　Partial Shipments

　　　　ALLOWED

43T：　Transshipment

　　　　ALLOWED

44E： Port of Loading

ANY PORT IN CHINA

44F： Port of Discharge

ANY PORT IN BELGIUM

44C： Latest Date of Shipment

180329

45A： Descript.of Goods

HUCK BOBTAIL

BOM-T20-12GA　4,000PCS　@USD2.80

BOM-A20-12GA　4,000PCS　@USD2.50

AS PER ORDER NO.4529 CIF ANY PORT IN BELGIUM INCOTERMS 2010

SHIPPING MARK： PUE (IN DIA) /C/NO:1-UP

46A： Documents Required

1. MANUALLY SIGNED COMMERCIAL INVOICE IN TRIPLICATE.

2. PACKING LIST IN TRIPLICATE.

3. FULL SET CLEAN SHIPPED ON BOARD MULTIMODAL TRANSPORT BIL-LS OF LADING MADE OUT TO OUR ORDER INDICATING SANYEI CO. LTD. AS SHIPPER AND NOTIFYING APPLICANT AND US GIVING FULL NAME AND ADDRESS..

4. INSURANCE POLICY/CERTIFICATE IN NEGOTIABLE FORM AND BLANK ENDORSED COVERING ICC(B) FOR 110PCT INVOICE VALUE SHOWING CLAIM PAYABLE AT BRUSSEL, BELGIUM.

47A： Additional Conditions

1. ALL SHIPPING DOCUMENTS MUST BE STATED L/C NO. AND DATE AND ISSUING BANK NAME.

2. COMMERCIAL INVOICE AND PACKING LIST MUST INDICATE COUNTRY OF ORIGIN

3. FIVE PERCENT MORE OR LESS IN QUANTITY ALLOWED

工廠出貨明細資料：

型號	BOM-T20-12GA	BOM-A20-12GA
包裝方式	50PCS/CTN	18 CANS/CTN
每箱重量	NW: 4KGS；GW: 5KGS	NW: 8.5KGS；GW: 10KGS
出貨數量	4,200PCS	4,200PCS
每箱尺寸	48×30×30(cm)	20"×16"×16"

BILL OF EXCHANGE

Draft No.　HB-4256　　　　　　　　　　　TAIWAN,　MARCH 20, 2018

For　　　　×

At　　　①　　　　sight of this **FIRST** of Exchange (Second of the same tenor and date be-ing unpaid)

Pay to the order of　　**HUA NAN BANK**

The sum of　　　　　　　　　　②

Drawn under　　　　　　　　×

Credit No.　KCB-4265389　　　Dated　　　DEC. 20, 2017

To　　　③　　　　　　　　　　　**PLUSTEX CO., LTD.**

　　　　　　　　　　　　　　　　　　× × ×

PLUSTEX CO., LTD.

NO.145, PARK ST., NANGANG DIST.,

TAIPEI CITY 115, TAIWAN (R.O.C.)

INVOICE

No.   HB-4256   Date: MARCH 20, 2018

INVOICE of   AS FOLLOWS

For account and risk of Messrs.   BRUSSELS LACES AND GIFTS SERV. SA.., RUE DE

LUSAMBO 21/28, 1190 BRUSSEL, BELGIUM

Sailing on   MARCH 20, 2018   Per S.S.   ④

From   SHANGHAI   To   ⑤

Marks & Nos.	Description of Goods	Quantity	Unit Price	Amount
			⑦	
✕	⑥	✕	✕	✕

SAY TOTAL   ✕

DRAWN UNDER   ✕

COUNTRY OF ORIGIN: CHINA

PLUSTEX CO., LTD.

✕ ✕ ✕

SALES MANAGER

PLUSTEX CO., LTD.

NO.145, PARK ST., NANGANG DIST.,

TAIPEI CITY 115, TAIWAN (R.O.C.)

PACKING LIST

No.   HB-4256   Date: MARCH 20, 2018

PACKING LIST of   **AS FOLLOWS**   MARKS & NOS.

For account and risk of Messrs.   ╳

Sailing on or about   MARCH 20, 2018   Per   S.S.   ╳   ⑧

From   ╳   To   OSAKA

Packing No.	Descriptionof Goods	Quantity	Net Weight (KGS)	Gross Weight (KGS)	Measurement (CBM)
⑨	╳	╳	@4.0 336.0 @8.5 714.0	@5.0 420.0 @10.0 840.0	⑩
╳ ⅴⅴⅴⅴⅴⅴⅴⅴⅴ		╳ ⅴⅴⅴⅴⅴ	╳ ⅴⅴⅴⅴⅴⅴⅴⅴⅴ	╳ ⅴⅴⅴⅴⅴⅴⅴⅴ	

SAY TOTAL   ⑪

DRAWN UNDER   ╳

COUNTRY OF ORIGIN   ╳

PLUSTEX CO., LTD.

╳ ╳ ╳

SALES MANAGER

Eco Transport Corporation	SHIPPING ORDER		
Shipper: × B/L Shipper ⑫	Please receive for shipment the under men-tioned goods subject to your published regu-lations and conditions		S/O NO.
Consignee: ⑬	ECO TRANSPORT CORPORATION		
Notify Party: (Full name and address) ⑭			
Also Notify: ×	洽訂船位之廠商： 電話／聯絡人： 報關行： 電話／聯絡人：		

Ocean Vessel COSOT	Voy. No. 0023C	Final destination (On Merchant's Account And Risk)				
Place of Receipt	Port of Loading ×	Freight to be: ⑮☐ Prepaid ☐ Collect				
Port of Discharge ANTWERP	Place of Delivery	領提單處：	台北	台中	台中港	高雄

Marks and Numbers	No. of P'kgs or Units	Description of Goods	Gross Weight (KGS)	Measurement (M³)
			×	×
× TOTAL × DRAWN UNDER ×	× 	×	櫃型／櫃數 ____×20'/ ____×40' SERVICE REQUIRED ☐FCL/FCL ☐LCL/LCL ☐FCL/LCL ☐LCL/FCL	

SPECIAL NOTE:

1. 副本_____ 份 *2.* 運費證明_____ 份 *3.* 電報放貨_____ *4.* 危險品_____ *5.* 其他____

填表請注意：

1. 危險品請註明 UN NO. IMO CLASS 與燃點，並附上 Shipper's Certificate。

2. 嘜頭及品名如超過十行，請以附表繕打，俾便提單製作。

解答

題號	答案
①	60 DAYS AFTER B/L DATE MARCH 20, 2018 或 60 DAYS AFTER MARCH 20, 2018 或 MAY 19, 2018
②	U.S. DOLLARS TWENTY TWO THOUSAND TWO HUNDRED (AND) SIXTY ONLY.
③	KCB BRUSSELS ORBAN
④	COSOT V.00237
⑤	ANTWERP
⑥	HUCK BOBTAIL AS PER ORDER NO. 4529 BOM-T20-12GA BOM-A20-12GA
⑦	CIF ANTWERP INCOTERMS 2010
⑧	PUE (IN DIA) ANTWERP C/NO:1-189 MADE IN CHINA
⑨	1-84 85-189
⑩	@0.043 　3.612 @0.084 　8.820 　12.432 vvvvvvvvv
⑪	ONE HUNDRED EIGHTY NINE (189) CARTONS ONLY
⑫	SANYEI CO. LTD.
⑬	TO ORDER OF KCB BRUSSELS ORBAN
⑭	BRUSSELS LACES AND GIFTS SERV. SA. RUE DE LUSAMBO 21/28, 1190 BRUSSEL, BELGIUM KCB BRUSSELS ORBAN RUE DE LA SCIENCE 25, 1040 BRUSSEL, BELGIUM
⑮	■ Prepaid　□ Collect

1062 國貿業務丙檢試題解答

一、基礎貿易英文（本大題合計 20 分）

　　㊀請於下列答案語群中，選出最適當之答案，並將答案代號填入答案紙，完成
　　函電之內容。（本題語群選項不可重覆，共 5 小格，每小格 2 分，合計 10 分）

答案代號	答案語群
A	shipment
B	following
C	quantity
D	kitchenware
E	follows
F	stocks
G	offering
H	supply
I	furniture
J	quoted

Dear Mr. Hathaway,

Thank you for your e-mail of May 18. We appreciate the interest you have shown in our new
range of are pleased to ___①___ quote as: ___②___

Extendable Dining Table　　　　　　$2,500

Coffee Table with Double Drawers　　$250

3-Drawer Mobile File Cabinet $145

The prices   ③   are CIF Kaohsiung, and we are prepared to grant you a special discount of 15% if your order value is over $10,000 for one   ④   .

As our   ⑤   of these goods are limited, we suggest you place an order as soon as possible.

Sincerely,

Lisa Wu

(二)請填入適當的語詞以完成下列翻譯。（本題為填空題，共 10 小格，每小格 1 分，合計 10 分）

1. 請立刻結清逾期的貨款。

   Please   ①   the   ②   payments immediately.

2. 我們已經報上最優惠的價格。

   We have   ③   our most   ④   prices.

3. 貨物一裝運，我們就會以電郵告知。

   As   ⑤   as shipment has been effected, we will   ⑥   you by email.

4. 本公司專門生產時尚和負擔得起的鞋。

   We   ⑦   in fashionable and   ⑧   footwear.

5. 就類似品質的貨品而言，我們的價格遠比競爭對手的價格低得多。

   Our prices are considerably lower than those of our   ⑨   for goods of   ⑩   quality.

解答

(一)

①	②	③	④	⑤
I	E	J	A	F

（二）

①	settle	②	overdue
③	quoted/offered	④	favorable
⑤	soon	⑥	advise/inform/notify
⑦	specialize	⑧	affordable
⑨	competitors	⑩	similar

二、貿易流程圖（本題共 5 小題，每小題 2 分，合計 10 分）

　　請依下列之貿易流程圖，依序將①②③④⑤之步驟名稱填入答案紙之答案欄內。（本測試項目評分依公佈範例為準）

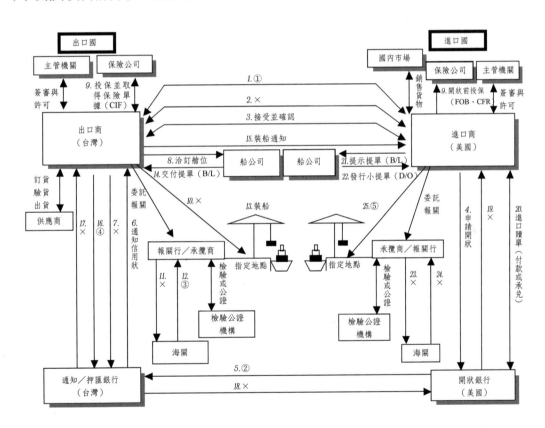

解答

題號	答案
①	招攬交易、信用調查
②	開發、交付信用狀
③	放行
④	辦理押匯
⑤	提貨

三、出口價格核算（本題共 10 小題，每小題 2 分，合計 20 分）

根據以下資料，對貨號 TH-796 與貨號 TH-850 兩種以體積噸計算海運運費的貨物，分別以併櫃與整櫃運量，核算相關運費與報價。

產品資料：

貨號	TH-796	TH-850
包裝方式	16 DOZ/CTN	8 BUNDLES/W/CASE
包裝尺寸	17"×16"×14"	128cm×119cm×95cm
採購成本	NTD250/DOZ	NTD580/BUNDLE

運費資料：

運費	併櫃（CFS）	20 呎（TEU）整櫃	40 呎（FEU）整櫃
	USD60	USD830	USD1,100
最低裝運量	1 CBM	25 CBM	50 CBM

其他報價資料：

匯率：USD1 = EUR0.919 EUR1 = NTD33.90	利潤率：15％
保險費率：ICC(A)0.08%、罷工險 0.015%	業務費率：3.5%

注意事項：

1. 計算過程不需列出，直接填入數字答案。

2. 核算要求：CBM計算至小數點第 4 位，四捨五入後取 3 位；其餘請計算至小數點第 3 位，四捨五入後取 2 位。

3. 含佣價計算方式：以所求報價條件本身為佣金計算基礎，如 FOBC, CFRC 與 CIFC 分別為 FOB, CFR 與 CIF 基礎之含佣價。

解答

貨號 TH-796：併櫃方式報價

題目	答案	單位
1. 每箱 CFT 數	$(17" \times 16" \times 14") \div 1728 = 2.20$	CFT
2. 每箱 CBM 數	$2.20 \div 35.315 = 0.062$	CBM
3. 每 DOZ（打）運費	$USD60 \times 0.919 \times 0.062 \div 16 = 0.21$	EUR/DOZ
4. FOBC5 報價	$(250 \div 33.90) \div (1 - 15\%) \div (1 - 3.5\%) \div (1 - 5\%) = 9.46$	EUR/DOZ
5. CFR 報價	$(250 \div 33.90 + 0.21) \div (1 - 15\%) \div (1 - 3.5\%) = 9.25$	EUR/DOZ

貨號 TH-850：TEU 方式報價

題目	答案	單位
6. 每箱 CBM 數	$1.28 \times 1.19 \times 0.95 = 1.447$	CBM
7. TEU 報價箱數	$25 \div 1.447 = 17.27$，無條件進位取整數 18	CTNS（註）
8. 每 BUNDLE（梱）運費	$18 \times 8 = 144BUNDLES$ $USD830 \times 0.919 \div 144 = 5.30$	EUR/BUNDLE
9. CFRC6 報價	$(580 \div 33.90 + 5.30) \div (1 - 15\%)$ $\div (1 - 3.5\%) \div (1 - 6\%) = 29.06$	EUR/BUNDLE
10. CIFC8 報價	$(580 \div 33.90 + 5.30) \div [1 - 1.1 \times (0.08\% + 0.015\%)] \div (1 - 15\%) \div (1 - 3.5\%)$ $\div (1 - 8\%) = 29.73$	EUR/BUNDLE

註：單位錯誤，應是 W/CASE

四、商業信用狀分析（本題為填空題，合計 20 分）

請依下列信用狀之內容，回答答案紙所列問題，並將正確答案填入。

Authentication Result: Correct with current key

Instance Type and Transmission

Original received from SWIFT

Priority:	Normal
Swift Output:	700 ISSUE OF A DOCUMENTARY CREDIT
Sender:	HNBKTWTPA 00
	HUA NAN COMMERCIAL BANK LTD.
Receiver:	DEUTDEFFXXX
	DEUTSCHE BANK AG

---Message Text ---

27:     Sequence of Total
        1/1

40A: Form of Documentary Credit
        IRREVOCABLE

20:     Documentary Credit Number
        6PH2-789356-201

31C: Date of Issue
        170512

40E: Applicable Rules
        UCP LATEST VERSION

31D: Date and Place of Expiry
        170720 IN THEBENEFICIARY(S COUNTRY

50:     Applicant
        NICE VILLAGEINDUSTRIAL CO., LTD.
        NO.789 SEC.5, CHUNG SHAN ROAD, LINKOU DIST.,NEW TAIPEI CITY 244
        TAIWAN, R.O.C.

59:     Beneficiary
        GERMANSTARLING VALVE GMBH

FRIEDRICHPLATZ 999A,47495 RHEINBERG, GERMANY

32B: Currency Code, Amount

EUR104,250.00

39B: Maximum Credit Amount

NOT EXCEEDING

41A: Available with.....by.....

ISSUING BANK BY DEFERRED PAYMENT AT 30 DAYS AFTER B/L DATE

43P: Partial Shipments

PROHIBITED

43T: Transshipment

PROHIBITED

44E: Port of Loading/Airport of Departure

HAMBURG, GERMANY

44F: Port of Discharge/Airport of Destination

KEELUNG, TAIWAN

44C LATEST DATE OF SHIPMENT

170705

45A: Description of Goods and/or Services

150 PCS. OFSTARTING VALVE

46A: Documents Required

1. MANUALLY SIGNED COMMERCIAL INVOICE IN TRIPLICATE INDICATING L/C NUMBER AND P/I NO.NV-170410

2. FULL SET(3/3) OF CLEAN ON BOARD BILLS OF LADING MADE OUT TO THEORDER OF HUA NAN COMMERCIAL BANK LTD. MARKED FREIGHT PREPAID AND THIS CREDIT NUMBER NOTIFYING APPLICANT, INDICATING EURO NICE GLOBAL GMBHD AS SHIPPER

3. INSURANCE POLICY OR CERTIFICATE IN DUPLICATE IN NEGOTIABLE FORM FOR 110PCT OF INVOICE VALUE BLANK ENDORSED AND WITH CLAIMS PAYABLE IN TAIWAN COVERING INSTITUTE CARGO CLAUSES (A) AND INSTITUTE STRIKES CLAUSES (CARGO) ALL IRRESPECTIVE OF PERCENTAGE FROM SELLER'S WAREHOUSE TO

BUYER'S WAREHOUSE NEW TAIPEI CITY

4. NETURAL PACKING LIST IN TRIPLICATE

5. BENEFICIARY'S CERTIFICATE STATING THAT ONE COMPLETE SET OF NON-NEGOTIABLE STIPULATED DOCUMENTS HAVE BEEN FOR-WARDED BY COURIER TO APPLICANT WITHIN 5 DAYS AFTER SHIPMENT

47A: Additional Conditions

1. ALL DOCUMENTS MUST BEAR OUR CREDIT NUMBER

2. A DISCREPANCY FEE FOR EUR60.00 WILL BE DEDUCTED FROM THE PAYMENT FOR EACH SET OF DOCUMENTS CONTAINING DISCREP-ANCY(IES)

3. ALL DOCUMENTS SHOULD BE ISSUED IN ENGLISH

4. TRANSPORT DOCUMENTS DATED PRIOR TO THE DATE OF ISSUANCE OF THIS CREDIT ARE NOT ACCEPTABLE

5. SHORT FORM B/L NOT ACCEPTABLE

71B: Charges

ALL BANKING CHARGES OUTSIDE TAIWAN ARE FOR ACCOUNT OF BENEFICIARY

48:     Period for Presentation

DOCUMENTS MUST BE PRESENTED WITHIN 15 DAYS AFTER THE DATE OF SHIPMENT BUT WITHIN L/C EXPIRY DATE

49:     Confirmation Instructions

WITHOUT

78:     Instructions to Paying/Accepting/Negotiating Bank

+ALL DOCUMENTS MUST BE SENT TO US BY COURIER SERVICE IN ONE COVER ADDRESSED TO HUA NAN COMMERCIAL BANK LTD. NO.331, WENHUA 3RD RD., LINKOU DIST., NEW TAIPEI CITY 244, TAIWAN (R.O.C.)

+UPON RECEIPT OF DOCUMENTS AT OUR COUNTERS AND PROVIDED ALL TERMS AND CONDITIONS HAVE BEEN COMPLIED WITH , WE WILL PAY AS PER INSTRUCTIONS

--Message Trailer--

解答

題目	答案
受益人？（英文作答）（2分）	GERMANSTARLING VALVE GMBH
ADVISING BANK？（英文作答）（2分）	DEUTSCHE BANK AG
提單之託運人？（英文作答）（2分）	EURO NICE GLOBAL GMBHD
信用狀有效期限及地點？（2分）	西元 2017 年 7 月 20 日 地點：GERMANY（請寫出英文國名）
裝船港？（2分）（英文作答）	HAMBURG, GERMANY
依本信用狀內容，請選出（單選）下列各小題之正確答案。	
保險金額幣別？（1分）	☐USD ■EUR ☐TWD
有效期限與裝船期限之順延，若遇地震？（1分）	☐僅有效期限　☐僅裝船期限 ☐兩者皆可　■兩者皆不可
貿易條件？（1分）	☐FOB KEELUNG　☐FOB HAMBURG ■CIF KEELUNG　☐CIF HAMBURG
通知手續費由何方負擔？（1分）	☐通知銀行　☐開狀申請人　■受益人
運送單據日期不可早於何日？（1分）	☐有效日期　☐裝船日期　■開狀日期
使用方式？（1分）	☐讓購　■延期付款　☐即期付款　☐承兌
投保時是否須加保內陸險？（1分）	■是　☐否
瑕疵費由何方負擔？（1分）	☐買方　■賣方
包裝單之簽署？（1分）	☐開狀申請人　☐受益人　■不需要
信用狀種類？（1分）	■跟單 L/C　☐無跟單 L/C

五、貿易單據製作（本題共 15 小題，每小題 2 分，合計 30 分）

　　請依所附信用狀部分內容及相關工廠出貨明細資料，填製㈠ Bill of Exchange、㈡ Invoice、㈢ Packing List、㈣ Shipping Order 等單據所要求之內容，並請依照題號①、②、③…依序將正確答案填入答案紙之答案欄內。下列為信用狀部分內容：

31C:　　Date of Issue

　　　　170425

31D:　　Date and Place of Expiry

　　　　170710 IN THEBENEFICIARY'S COUNTRY

52D　　DC Issuing Bank

ALLIANCE BANK MALAYSIA BERHAD

50:     Applicant

ASIA ENTERPRISES SDN BHD

NO.6862, JALAN DATO LIM HOE LEK, PAHANG, 25200 KUANTANG,MA-LAYSIA

59:     Beneficiary

NOVELTY INDUSTRIAL COMPANY LIMITED

NO. 7986, SEC. 2, DENG LIN ROAD WUGU DISTRICT, NEW TAIPEI CITY

TAIWAN (R.O.C.)

32B: Currency Code, Amount

USD53,325.00

42C: Drafts at

90 DAYS FROM DATEFOR 100 PCT OF INVOICE VALUE

42A: Drawee

OPENING BANK

44E: Port of Loading/Airport of Departure

ANY PORT IN TAIWAN

44F: Port of Discharge/Airport of Destination

PORT KLANG

45A: Description of Goods and/or Services

CHILDREN TRICYCLE

BT-12 1,500 PCS. AT USD18.75/PC

BT-15 2,000 PCS. AT USD12.60/PC

TRADE TERMS: FOB ANY PORT IN TAIWAN INCOTERMS 2010

46A: Documents Required

    1. MANUALLY SIGNED COMMERICAL INVOICE INQUADRUPLICATE

    2. FULL SET OF CLEAN ON BOARD BILLS OF LADING MADE OUT TO OR-DER AND ENDORSED IN BLANK MARKED FREIGHT PAYABLE AT DES-TINATION AND NOTIFYAPPLICANT

    3. MANUALLY SIGNED PACKINGLIST IN TRIPLICATE SHOWINGNET WEIGHT, GROSS WEIGHT AND MEASUREMENT

47A:　　Additional Conditions

　　　　1. INVOICE AND PACKINGLIST MUST SHOW P/O NO.NI-170220

　　　　2. SHIPPING MARK: AE (IN REC)

　　　　3. DRAFTS AND INVOICE MUST SHOW DRAWN UNDER ROYAL BANK

　　　　OF CANADA L/C NO.RB-86493 DATED JAN. 25, 2015

　　工廠出貨明細資料：

貨　　號	BT-12	BT-15
包裝方式	1 PC/CTN	6PCS/CTN
每箱重量	N.W.: 4.20 KGS；G.W.: 5.20 KGS	N.W.: 12.50 KGS；G.W.:14.25 KGS
每箱尺寸	34cm×59cm×54cm	24"×18"×16"
出貨數量	600 PCS	1,000 PCS

BILL OF EXCHANGE

DRAFT NO.　　　1968

FOR 　　　　　①　　　　　　　　　　　DATED　JUNE 10, 2017

AT　90 DAYS FROM DATE　SIGHT OF THIS FIRST OF EXCHANGE (SECOND OF THE

SAME TENOR AND DATE BEING UNPAID) PAY TO THE ORDER OF

FIRST COMMERCIAL BANK

THE SUM OF 　　　　　×××　　　　　　VALUE RECEIVED

DRAWN UNDER LETTER OF CREDIT NO.　ABMB-7988　DATED　　②

ISSUED BY 　　　　　　　　　③

TO　　×××　　　　　　　　　×××

NOVELTY INDUSTRIAL COMPANY LIMITED

No. 7986, Sec.2, Deng Lin Road

Wugu Dist., New Taipei City

Taiwan, R.O.C.

INVOICE

No.　AE-170608 　　　　　　　　　　　　　　Date:　JUNE 10, 2017

Invoice of 　　　　　④

For account and risk of Messrs 　　　× × ×

Shipped Per S.S.　 EVER LIBRA V.1492-025W

Sailing on or about 　JUNE 10, 2017

Shipment From: 　　× × ×　　　　　　To: 　　　　　⑤

Marks & Nos.	Quantity	Description of Merchandise	Unit Price	Amount
× × ×	× × × × × ×PCS vvvvvvvvvv	CHILDREN TRICYCLE BT-12Plastic Tricycle Size: 70cm×45cm×50cm BT-15Plastic Tricycle Size: 53cm×49cm×45cm	× × × ⑥	× × × × × × USD × × × vvvvvvvvvv

SAY 　　　　　⑦

DRAWN UNDER 　× × ×

　　　　× × ×

　　　　　　　　　　　　　　　　　　　　　⑧

NOVELTY INDUSTRIAL COMPANY LIMITED

No. 7986, Sec.2, Deng Lin Road

Wugu Dist., New Taipei City

Taiwan, R.O.C.

PACKING LIST

No.　AE-170608

Packing List of 　　　　× × ×

For account and risk of Messrs 　　　⑨

Shipped Per S.S.　EVER LIBRA V.1492-025W

Sailing on or about　JUNE 10, 2017

Shipment From　　KEELUNG

To 　　× × ×

Date:　JUNE 10, 2017

MARKS & NOS.

× × ×

Packing No.	Descriptionof Goods	Quantity	Net Weight	Gross Weight	Measurement
⑩	CHILDREN TRICYCLE BT-12Plastic Tricycle Size: 　70cm×45cm×50cm BT-15Plastic Tricycle Size: 　53cm×49 cm×45cm —DO—	@1 PC. 600 PCS @6 PCS 996 PCS 4 PCS	× × ×	× × ×	× × ×
		× × × PCS vvvvv	KGS vvvvvvvvvv	KGS vvvvvvvvvv	CBM vvvvvvvvvv

TOTAL: × × × CTNS

　　　vvvvvvvvvvv

SAY TOTAL　× × ×

　　　⑪

× × ×

長榮國際股份有限公司 EVERGREEN INTERNATIONAL CORPORATION		SHIPPING ORDER (B/L INSTRUCTION)			
Shipper:（發票如需另列抬頭人請註明） 　　××× 發票抬頭： 統一編號：　　提單傳真號碼：		Please receive for shipment the under mentioned goods subject to your published regulations and conditions (including those as to liability)		S/O NO.	
Consignee: 　TO ORDER		SPECIAL NOTE: *1.*副本＿＿份*2.*運費證明＿＿份*3.*電報放貨＿＿ *4.*危險品＿＿　*5.*其他＿＿＿＿ 填表請注意： *1.*危險品請註明 UN NO. IMO CLASS 與燃點，並附上 Shipper's Certificate。（吉達地區請另附 Packing list 兩份）。			
Notify Party: (Full name and address) 　ASIA ENTERPRISES SDN BHD 　NO.6862, JALAN DATO LIM HOE LEK, PAHANG 25200 KUANTANG, MALAYSIA		*2.* S/O 上之內容若有變更，請圈劃出，並於結關當天前傳真或送底至本公司。 *3.* 嘜頭及品名如超過十行，請以附表繕打，俾便提單製作。 *4.* 傳真專線：遠洋航線請傳(02)25063878，近洋航線請傳(02)25006658。			
		洽訂船位之廠商：　　電話／聯絡人：			
		報關行：　　　　電話／聯絡人：			
Ocean Vessel 船名 　⑫	Voy. No. 航次 　×××	Final destination (On Merchant's Account And Risk)			
Place of Receipt 收貨地	Port of Loading 裝貨地 ⑬	⑭ Freight to be：付費方式：□Prepaid 預付　□Collect 到付			
Port of Discharge 卸貨港 ×××	Place of Delivery 交貨地 （美國線請註明州別）	領提單處：　■台北	□台中	□台中港	□高雄
Marks and Numbers/ Container No. and Seal No.	Quantity and Unit	Description of Goods （請詳實註明，如僅為" GENERAL MERCHAN- DISE"恕無法接受）	Gross Weight (KGS)	Measurement (M³)	
EISU80429xx/ 45'/10175xx ⑮ 　　SAY TOTAL　×××	××× 	CHILDREN TRI- CYCLE	××× 櫃型／櫃數 普通櫃：＿＿×20'/＿＿×40' 冷凍櫃：＿＿×20'/＿＿×40' HQ：＿＿×40' 超重櫃：＿＿×20' 貨主自有櫃：＿＿＿＿ 其他特殊櫃：＿＿＿＿ SERVICE REQUIRED 1. FCL/FCL 整櫃／整櫃 2. LCL/LCL 併裝／併裝 3. FCL/LCL 整櫃／併裝 4. LCL/FCL 併裝／整櫃	××× 	

解答

題號	答案
①	USD23,850.00
②	APR 25, 2017
③	ALLIANCE BANK MALAYSIA BERHAD
④	*1.* AS FOLLOWS *2.* 1600 PCS CHILDREN TRICYCLE
⑤	PORT KLANG
⑥	USD 18.75/PC USD12.60/PC
⑦	US DOLLARS TWENTY THREE THOUSAND EIGHT HUNDRED AND FIFTY ONLY
⑧	NOVELTY INDUSTRIAL COMPANY LIMITED
⑨	ASIA ENTERPRISES SDN BHD NO.6862, JALAN DATO LIM HOE LEK, PA-HANG, 25200 KUANTANG, MALAYSIA
⑩	1-600 601-766 767
⑪	P/O NO.NI-170220
⑫	EVER LIBRA
⑬	KEELUNG
⑭	FREIGHT TO BE: ☐ PREPAID ■ COLLECT
⑮	AE (IN REC) PORT KLANG C/NO. 1-767 MADE IN TAIWAN

1061 國貿業務丙檢試題解答

一、基礎貿易英文（本大題合計 20 分）

㈠請於下列答案語群中，選出最適當之答案，並將答案代號填入答案紙，完成
函電之內容。（本題語群選項不可重覆，共 5 小格，每小格 2 分，合計 10 分）

答案代號	答案語群
A	account
B	advice
C	amount
D	doing
E	enclosed
F	overcharged
G	is attached
H	making
I	overlooked
J	reminder

Dear Mr. Graham,

May I draw your attention to our invoice of September 3 in the ___①___ of $1,175.00, which is now more than a month overdue.

I am sure that the seasonal rush has kept you busy and that the invoice was ___②___. Your prompt remittance would be appreciated.

A copy of Invoice No. A115 ___③___ in case you have misplaced your copy. If payment has already been made, please disregard this ___④___.

Let me take this opportunity to thank you for placing orders with us, and I look forward to

_____⑤_____ business with you again in the near future.

Best regards,

Julia Chang

(二)適當的語詞以完成下列翻譯。（本題為填空題，共 10 小格，每小格 1 分，合
計 10 分）

1. 謝謝您 10 月 12 日來函詢問數位影音光碟機。

   Thank you for your _____①_____ of October 12 conerning DVD _____②_____ .

2. 我們從波士頓的商會得知，貴公司為台灣首屈一指的防水錶製造商。

   We have _____③_____ from the Chamber of Commerce in Boston that you are a _____④_____
   manufacturer of waterproof watches in Taiwan.

3. 本公司為紡織品進口商，想與同行供應商取得聯繫。

   We are importers in the _____⑤_____ trade and would like to get in _____⑥_____ with suppliers
   of this line.

4. 我們可以直接從庫存供貨，如期交貨絕對沒有問題。

   We can _____⑦_____ from stock and will have no trouble meeting your _____⑧_____ date.

5. 因裝船時間即將來臨，我們必須請您立即將信用狀及裝運指示傳真過來。

   As the time of shipment is fast _____⑨_____ , we must ask you to fax the L/C and shipping
   _____⑩_____ immediately.

解答

(一)

①	②	③	④	⑤
C	I	G	J	D

(二)

①	inquiry/enquiry	②	players
③	learned	④	leading
⑤	textile	⑥	touch/contact
⑦	supply	⑧	delivery
⑨	approaching	⑩	instructions

二、貿易流程圖（本題共 5 小題，每小題 2 分，合計 10 分）

請依下列之貿易流程圖，依序將①②③④⑤之步驟名稱填入答案紙之答案欄內。
（本測試項目評分依公佈範例為準）

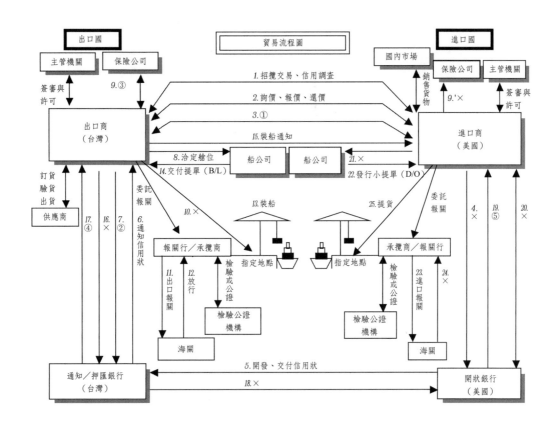

解答

題號	答案
①	接受並確認
②	預售外匯（避險操作）
③	投保並取得保險單據（CIF）
④	墊付押匯款項
⑤	單據到達通知

三、出口價格核算（本題共 10 小題，每小題 2 分，合計 20 分）

根據以下資料，對貨號 A01 與貨號 A02 兩種以體積噸計算海運運費的貨物，分別以整櫃與併櫃運量，核算相關運費與報價。

產品資料：

貨號	A01	A02
包裝方式	15 SETS/CTN	18 SETS/CTN
包裝尺寸	4'5"×3'5"×2'5"	80cm×50cm×70cm
採購成本	TWD280/SET	TWD320/SET

運費資料：

運費	併櫃（CFS）	20 呎整櫃	40 呎整櫃
	USD75	USD1,500	USD2,500
最低裝運量	1 CBM	25 CBM	50 CBM

其他報價資料：

匯率：USD1 = TWD31.45	利潤率：15%
保險費率：投保 ICC(A)條款 0.18%　　　　ICC(WAR)條款 0.02%	業務費率：10%

注意事項：

1. 計算過程不需列出，直接填入數字答案。
2. 核算要求：CBM 計算至小數點第 4 位，四捨五入後取 3 位；其餘請計算至小數點第 3 位，四捨五入後取 2 位。
3. 含佣價計算方式：以所求報價條件本身為佣金計算基礎，如 FOBC 與 CIFC 分別為 FOB 與 CIF 為基礎之含佣價。

解答

貨號 A01：併櫃方式報價

題目	答案	單位
1. 每箱才數	$(4'5'' \times 3'5'' \times 2'5'') \div 1728 = 36.47$	才（CFT）
2. 每箱 CBM 數	$36.47 \div 35.315 = 1.033$	CBM
3. 每 SET 運費	$USD75 \times 1.033 \div 15 = 5.17$	USD/SET
4. FOBC8 報價	$(280 \div 31.45) \div (1 - 15\%) \div (1 - 10\%) \div (1 - 8\%) = 12.65$	USD/SET
5. CIF 報價	$(280 \div 31.45 + 5.17) \div [1 - 1.1 \times (0.18\% + 0.02\%)]$ $\div (1 - 15\%) \div (1 - 10\%) = 18.44$	USD/SET

貨號 A02：40 呎整櫃方式報價

題目	答案	單位
6. 每箱 CBM 數	$0.8 \times 0.5 \times 0.7 = 0.280$	CBM
7. 每箱才數	$0.0.280 \times 35.316 = 9.89$	才（CFT）
8. 40 呎櫃報價箱數	$50 \div 0.280 = 178.57$，無條件進位取整數 179。	CTNS
9. 每 SET 運費	$179 \times 18 = 3,222$ SETS $USD2500 \div 3,222 = 0.78$	USD/SET
10. CFR 報價	$(320 \div 31.45 + 0.78) \div (1 - 15\%) \div (1 - 10\%) = 14.32$	USD/SET

四、商業信用狀分析（本題為填空題，合計 20 分）

請依下列信用狀之內容，回答答案紙所列問題，並將正確答案填入。

-- Message Header--

Message Type：MT700 ISSUE OF A DOCUMENTARY CREDIT

Sender ：TAI SHIN INTERNATIONAL BANK KAOHSIUNG BRANCH

Receiver ：KEB HANA BANK HAEUNDAE SINDOSHI BRANCH

--Message Text --

27： SEQUENCE OF TOTAL

1/1

40A： FORM OF DOCUMENTARY CREDIT

IRREVOCABLE

20： DOCUMENTARY CREDIT NUMBER

NHAF16S00

31C： DATE OF ISSUE

160803

40E： APPLICABLE RULES

UCP LATEST VERSION

31D： DATE AND PLACE OF EXPIRY

161209 IN THE COUNTRY OF BENEFICIARY

50： APPLICANT

WEN MING CO., LTD.

NO.135, CHUNG HWA 3RD RD., KAOHSIUNG, TAIWAN

59： BENEFICIARY

WART MARINE SYSTEMS CO., LTD.

8F SAESAM BUILDING, 39 SESIL-RO, BUSAN, KOREA

32B： CURRENCY CODE, AMOUNT

USD1,028,000

41D： AVAILABLE WITH ... BY ...

ADVISING BANK BY NEGOTIATION

42C： DRAFTS AT ...

AT SIGHT

42D： DRAWEE

ISSUING BANK

43P： PARTIAL SHIPMENTS

ALLOWED

43T： TRANSSHIPMENT

PROHIBITED

44E： PORT OF LOADING/AIRPORT OF DEPARTURE

ANY KOREAN PORT

44F： PORT OF DISCHARGE/AIRPORT OF DESTINATION

KAOHSIUNG, TAIWAN

44C： LATEST DATE OF SHIPMENT

161110

45A： DESCRIPTION OF GOODS AND/OR SERVICES

2 SHIPSETS OF INTEGRATED BRIDGE SYSTEM

AS PER CONTRACT NO. S2465 AND INVITATION NO. R5468

FOB KOREA

46A： DOCUMENTS REQUIRED

1. MANUALLY SIGEND COMMERCIAL INVOICE IN 1 ORIGINAL.

2. MANUALLY SIGEND PACKING LIST IN 1 ORIGINAL.

3. 2/3 SET OF CLEAN ON BOARD OCEAN BILLS OF LADING MADE OUT TO ORDER AND BLANK ENDORSED MARKED "FREIGHT COLLECT" AND NOTIFY APPLICANT AS INDICATED ABOVE.

4. BENEFICIARY'S CERTIFICATE STATING THAT 1/3 SET OF ORIGINAL B/L AND ONE COMPLETE SET OF NON-NEGOTIABLE DOCUMENTS INCLUDING 6 COPIES OF INVOICE AND PACKING LIST HAVE BEEN FORWARDED BY REGISTERED AIRMAIL DIRECTLY TO THE BUYER BY BENEFICIARY WITHIN 3 DAYS AFTER THE SHIPMENT EFFECTED.

5. TEST REPORT ISSUED BY INDEPENDENT SURVEYOR IN DUPLICATE.

6. CLASSIFICATION CERTIFICATE ISSUED BY DNV IN DUPLICATE

7. LETTER OF BANK GUARANTEE ADVISED THROUGH MEGA INTERNATIONAL COMMERCIAL BANK CO., LTD., KAOHSIUNG BRANCH.

47A： ADDITIONAL CONDITIONS

1. ALL DOCUMENTS MUST BEAR THE CREDIT NUMBER.

2. PARTIAL SHIPMENTS ARE ALLOWED BUT NOT MORE THAN 2 SHIPMENTS.

3. THE BILL OF LADING DATED WITHIN 30 DAYS AFTER THE LATEST SHIPMENT DATE IS ACCEPTABLE. BUT BENEFICIARY HAS TO PAY A DELAY PENALTY ON THE BASIS OF 0.1 PCT OF THE INVOICE VALUE FOR EACH DAY DELAYED. SUCH PENALTY SHOULD BE DEDUCTED FROM THE NEGOTIATING AMOUNT BY THE NEGOTIATING BANK.

4. THE DRAFT(S) MUST BEAR "DRAWN UNDER DOCUMENTARY CREDIT NO."

5. CLASSIFICATION CERTIFICATE SHALL BEAR INVOICE. NUMBER, CONTRACT. NUMBER AND INVITATION NUMBER.

6. ON DECK B/L IS NOT ACCEPTABLE.

7. OCEAN BILLS OF LADING MUST BE ISSUED BY KANA SHIPPING CO., LTD.

TEL:82-2-752-2145 FAX:82-2-756-3245

71B： CHARGES

ALL BANKING CHARGES OUTSIDE TAIWAN INCLUDING REIMBURSEMENT COMMISSION ARE FOR ACCOUNT OF BENEFICIARY.

49： CONFIRMATION INSTRUCTIONS

WITHOUT

78： INSTRUCTIONS TO THE PAYING/ACCEPTING/NEGOTIATING BANK

1. TO NEGOTIATING BANK ONLY：PLEASE FORWARD ALL DOCUMENTS TO US BY COURIER/EXPRESS IN ONE LOT.

2. UPON RECEIPT OF DOCUMENTS IN COMPLIANCE WITH THE TERMS OF THE CREDIT, WE WILL REMIT THE PROCEEDS TO PRESENTING BANK AS INSTRUCTED.

解答

題目	答案
RESTRICTED NEGOTIATING BANK？（英文作答）（2分）	KEB HANA BANK (HAEUNDAE SINDOSHI BRANCH)
PAYING BANK？（英文作答）（2分）	TAI SHIN INTERNATIONAL BANK (KAOHSIUNG BRANCH)
本信用狀規定須由哪一家運輸公司簽發提單？（英文作答）（2分）	KANA SHIPPING CO., LTD.
根據 46A，除了商業發票、包裝單、提單及受益人證明書外，押匯單據還有哪些？（英文作答）（2分／小題）	(1) TEST REPORT (2) CLASSIFICATION CERTIFICATE (3) LETTER OF BANK GUARANTEE

題目	答案
FORM OF CREDIT？（1 分／小題）	(1)☐GENERAL L/C　■SPECIAL L/C (2)☐CONFIRMED L/C　■UNCONFIRMED L/C
押匯時，提示下列提單銀行會接受嗎？ (1) STRAIGHT B/L (2) SHORT FORM B/L (3) ON DECK B/L (4) THIRD PARTY B/L	(1)☐YES　■NO　（1 分） (2)■YES　☐NO　（1 分） (3)☐YES　■NO　（1 分） (4)■YES　☐NO　（1 分）
分批裝運最多限幾次？（1 分）	■2 次　☐3 次　☐4 次
若提單的簽發日為 11/月 15 日，則出口商會被扣幾天的遲延罰款？（1 分）	☐1 天　☐3 天　■5 天

五、貿易單據製作（本題共 15 小題，每小題 2 分，合計 30 分）

　　請依下列信用狀部分內容及相關工廠出貨明細資料，填製㈠ Bill of Exchange、㈡ Invoice、㈢ Packing List、㈣ Shipping Order 等單據所要求之內容，並請依照題號①、②、③…依序將正確答案填入答案紙之答案欄內。

--Message Header--

Swift Output : FIN 700 Issue of a Documentary Credit

Sender　　　: BANK OF AMERICA

Receiver　　: MEGA INTERNATIONAL COMMERCIAL BANK CO., LTD. KAOHSI-UNG BRANCH

--Message--

50：　　　APPLICANT

　　　　　HANA TRADING CO., LTD.

　　　　　2324 WEST BLEVEN MILE ROAD, SOUTHFIELD, MT 484123, USA

59：　　　BENEFICIARY

　　　　　MINGO TRADING CO., LTD.

　　　　　12F-3, NO.297, CHUNG SHAN 2ND ROAD, CHIEN CHEN DIST., KAOHSI-UNG, TAIWAN

32B：　　CURRENCY CODE,AMOUNT

　　　　　USD162,000.00

41D： AVAILABLE WITH...BY...

ANY BANK BY NEGOTIATION

42C： DRAFTS AT

AT 180 DAYS AFTER SIGHT FOR 100% INVOICE VALUE

42A： DRAWEE

ISSUING BANK

44E： PORT OF LOADING

VERACRUZ, MEXICO

44F： PORT OF DISCHARGE

HOUSTON, TX, USA

44C： LATEST DATE OF SHIPMENT

161016

45A： SHIPMENT OF GOODS

5,000 PCS OF SWEATER AS PER P/I NO.25146.

TRADE TERMS: CFR HOUSTON (INCOTERMS 2010)

46A： DOCUMENTS REQUIRED

1. SIGNED COMMERCIAL INVOICE IN ONE ORIGINAL MARKED P/I NO.

2. PACKING LIST IN ONE ORIGINAL.

3. FULL SETOF CLEAN ON BOARD OCEAN BILLS OF LADING ISSUED TO OUR ORDER MARKED "FREIGHT PREPAID" AND NOTIFY APPLICANT WITH ADDRESS.

47A： ADDITIONAL CONDITIONS

1. ALL DOCUMENTS MUST INDICATE THIS CREDIT NUMBER

2. SHIPPING MARK：HT（IN DIA）/C/NO.：1-UP

3. COMMERCIAL INVOICE AND PACKING LIST MUST INDICATE THE COUNTRY OF ORIGIN：MEXICO.

工廠出貨明細資料：

型號	A-200	A-134	A-224
包裝方式	20 PCS/CTN	20 PCS/CTN	25 PCS/CTN
每箱重量	NW: 25KGS GW: 26KGS	NW: 25KGS GW: 26KGS	NW: 24.5KGS GW: 25.5KGS
出貨數量	1,000 PCS	1,000 PCS	500 PCS
價格	USD320/PC	USD340/PC	USD300/PC
每箱尺寸	45×65×78(cm)	45×65×78(cm)	18"×26"×30"

BILL OF EXCHANGE

Draft No. ___HJ16538___   TAIWAN, ___SEPT. 20, 2016___

Exchange for _____×_____

At _____①_____ sight of this FIRST of Exchange (Second of the same tenor and date being unpaid)

Pay to the order of **TAIWAN SHIN KONG COMMERCIAL BANK.**

The sum of _____×_____

Drawn under _____②_____

Credit No. ___HF-007628753___   Dated ___AUG. 11, 2016___

To _____×_____   ③

_____×××_____

MINGO TRADING CO., LTD.

12F-3, NO.297, CHUNG SHAN 2ND ROAD

CHIEN CHEN DIST., KAOHSIUNG

TAIWAN

INVOICE

No.　CD543　　　　　　　　　　　　　　Date:　SEPT. 20, 2016

INVOICE of 　　　AS FOLLOWS

For account and risk of Messrs.　　　　　　　④

Sailing on or about　　SEPT. 20, 2016　　Per S.S. YU HENG V. 6214

From　VERACRUZ. MEXICO　　　　　To　　　HOUSTON, TX, USA

Marks & Nos.	Description of Merchandise	Quantity	Unit Price	Amount
	SWEATER		⑤	
	AS PER P/I NO. 25146.			
×	A-200	×	USD32.00/PC	×
	A-134		USD34.00/PC	
	A-224	×	USD30.00/PC	×
		vvvvvvvvv	×	vvvvvvvvv

SAY TOTAL　　　　⑥

Credit No.HF-007628753

　　　　⑦

MINGO TRADING CO., LTD.

×××

SALES MANAGER

MINGO TRADING CO., LTD.

2F-3, NO.297, CHUNG SHAN 2ND ROAD

CHIEN CHEN DIST., KAOHSIUNG

TAIWAN

PACKING LIST

No. CD543　　　　　　　　　　　　　　　　　Date: SEPT. 20, 2016

PACKING LIST of AS FOLLOWS　　　　　　　　　　MARKS & NOS.

For account and risk of Messrs. 　　　　　✕

　　　　　　　　　　　　　　　　　　　　　　　　　　⑧

about SEPT. 20, 2016　　　　Per S.S. YU HENG V. 6214

From VERACRUZ. MEXICO　　　To HOUSTON, TX, USA

Packing No.	Description	Quantity	Net Weight (KGS)	Gross Weight (KGS)	Measurement (CBM)
✕	SWEATER A-200 A-134 A-224	⑨	@25.0 1250.0 @25.0 1250.0 @24.5 490.0	✕	✕
✕ vvvvvvvvvv		✕ vvvvvvvvvv	✕ vvvvvvvvvv	⑩ vvvvvvvvvv	✕ vvvvvvvvvv

SAYTOTAL　　　　　⑪　　　　　　　　

　　　　　　　　✕

MINGO TRADING CO., LTD.

✕ ✕ ✕

SALES MANAGER

Taiwan Marine		SHIPPING ORDER				
Shipper: ✕		Please receive for shipment the undermentioned goods subject to your published regulations and conditions			S/O NO.	
Consignee: ⑫		Taiwan Marine Transport Corporation 台灣海運股份有限公司				
Notify Party: (Full name and address) ⑬						
Also Notify: ✕		洽訂船位之廠商： 電話／聯絡人：				
		報關行： 電話／聯絡人：				
Ocean Vessel YU HENG	Voy. No. 6214	Final destination (On Merchant's Account And Risk)				
Place of Receipt	Port of Loading ✕	Freight to be: ☐ Prepaid ☐ Collect				
Port of Discharge ⑭	Place of Delivery	領提單處：	台北	台中	台中港	高雄
Marks and Numbers	No. of P'kgs or Units	Description of Goods	Gross Weight (KGS)		Measurement (M³)	
			✕		⑮	
  ✕ SAY TOTAL _____✕_____ CREDIT NO.HF-007628753	✕	SWEATERS	櫃型／櫃數 ____✕20'/____✕40' SERVICE REQUIRED ☐FCL/FCL ☐LCL/LCL ☐FCL/LCL ☐LCL/FCL			

SPECIAL NOTE:

1.副本_____份 2.運費證明_____份 3.電報放貨_____ 4.危險品_____ 5.其他_____

填表請注意：

1.危險品請註明 UN NO. IMO CLASS 與燃點，並附上 Shipper's Certificate。

2.嘜頭及品名如超過十行，請以附表繕打，俾便提單製作。

解答

題號	答案
①	180 DAYS AFTER
②	BANK OF AMERICA
③	MINGO TRADING CO., LTD.
④	HANA TRADING CO., LTD. 2324 WEST BLEVEN MILE ROAD, SOUTHFIELD, MT 484123, USA
⑤	CFR HOUSTON (INCOTERMS 2010)
⑥	U.S. DOLLARS EIGHT HUNDRED (AND) TEN THOUSAND ONLY
⑦	THE COUNTRY OF ORIGIN：MEXICO
⑧	HT (IN DIA) HOUSTON, TX, USA C/NO:1-120 MADE IN MEXICO
⑨	@20 PCS 1000 PCS @20 PCS 1000 PCS @25 PCS 500 PCS
⑩	3110 (KGS)
⑪	ONE HUNDRED (AND) TWENTY (120) CARTONS ONLY
⑫	TO ORDER OF BANK OF AMERICA
⑬	HANA TRADING CO., LTD. 2324 WEST BLEVEN MILE ROAD, SOUTHFIELD, MT 484123, USA
⑭	HOUSTON, TX, USA
⑮	27.400 (CBM)

國貿業務技術士（丙級）技能檢定規範

級　　別：丙級
工作範圍：從事各行業之進出口貿易業務
應具知能：應具備下列各項技能及相關知識

工作項目	技能種類	技能標準	相關知識
一、貿易概論與流程	(一)國際貿易基本概念 (二)進出口業務流程	能瞭解國際貿易之種類與特性，具體敘述進出口相關當事人的業務操作流程： 1.進出口基本流程 2.貿易結算（匯付、託收及信用狀等）流程	1.瞭解經貿常識及從事國貿業務應具備之商業道德 2.瞭解進出口簽證、檢驗、報關等相關知識 3.瞭解託收、匯付等交易方式 4.瞭解國際貿易相關法規
二、基礎貿易英文	(一)貿易基本交易條件 (二)貿易書信格式與內容	能熟悉國貿英文字彙與句型，理解下列進出口交易過程中各類英語函電的內容： 1.推銷（Promotion）函 2.詢價（Inquiry）函 3.報價（Offer）函 4.催款（Collection）函 5.索賠（Claim）函	1.瞭解國際貿易的基本交易條件 2.瞭解貿易英文基本概念 3.瞭解報價、接受與貿易契約的成立 4.瞭解貿易索賠與仲裁
三、出口價格核算	(一)貿易條件 (二)運保費計算 (三)出口報價計算	能熟練掌握不同貿易條件之價格組成要素，準確、迅速地完成下列出口價格核算：	1.瞭解國貿條規（Incoterms 2000）的規定 2.瞭解國際貨物運輸的作業

工作項目	技能種類	技能標準	相關知識
		*1.*公制、英制材積計算 *2.*整櫃、併櫃海運運費計算 *3.*保險、佣金等相關費用計算 *4.*出口報價	方式 *3.*瞭解運輸保險與輸出保險
四、商業信用 狀分析	㈠信用狀的種類 ㈡各類信用狀的 格式與內容	能瞭解各類信用狀的格式，並 正確解釋信用狀內容中下列條 款： *1.*信用狀相關當事人 *2.*信用狀對所提示單據的種類 與要求 *3.*裝運、提示等各種期限的要 求 *4.*其他重要條款	*1.*瞭解信用狀與其他結算方 式的差異 *2.*瞭解信用狀統一慣例與實 務的相關規定
五、貿易單據 製作	㈠出口相關單據 填製 ㈡出口押匯	能根據信用狀和出貨明細熟練 填製下列單據： *1.*商業發票（Commercial In- voice） *2.*裝箱單（Packing List） *3.*匯票（Bill of Exchange） *4.*裝貨單（Shipping Order）	*1.*瞭解貿易單據的種類、內 容、格式規範 *2.*瞭解進出口結匯的作業方 式

國家圖書館出版品預行編目資料

國貿實務：國貿業務技術士丙級術科／國貿研
究小組著. －－ 七版. －－臺北市：五南，
2018.09
　　面；　公分.
ISBN: 978-957-11-9946-7（平裝）

1.國際貿易實務

558.7　　　　　　　　　　　　107015738

1O60

國貿實務：國貿業務技術士丙級術科

作　　　者 －	國貿研究小組
發 行 人 －	楊榮川
總 經 理 －	楊士清
主　　　編 －	侯家嵐
責任編輯 －	黃梓雯
文字校對 －	許宸瑞　黃志誠
封面完稿 －	姚孝慈
出 版 者 －	五南圖書出版股份有限公司
地　　　址：	106 台北市大安區和平東路二段 339 號 4 樓
電　　　話：	(02)2705-5066　傳　　真：(02)2706-6100
網　　　址：	http://www.wunan.com.tw
電子郵件：	wunan@wunan.com.tw
劃撥帳號：	01068953
戶　　　名：	五南圖書出版股份有限公司

法律顧問　林勝安律師事務所　林勝安律師

出版日期　2007 年 8 月初版一刷
　　　　　2009 年 7 月二版一刷
　　　　　2010 年 7 月三版一刷
　　　　　2011 年 9 月四版一刷
　　　　　2013 年 7 月五版一刷
　　　　　2016 年 8 月六版一刷
　　　　　2018 年 9 月七版一刷

定　　　價　新臺幣 380 元